WORLDVIEW **STUDENT MANUAL** TRAINING

LIGHTBEARERS

A Summit Ministries Curriculum

W9-AUA-495

Lightbearers Worldview Curriculum
3rd Edition, Revised 2008

Editors
Dr. David Noebel President, Summit Ministries
Pat Maloy Curriculum Author (Original 1997 Version)
Kevin Bywater *A World of Ideas* Author (2003 Version)
Chuck Edwards *A World of Ideas* Author (2008 Version)

Assistant Editors
Todd Cothran, Administrator Resources
Jason Graham, Assistant Resources
Amanda Lewis, Assistant Resources

Video and Graphics
Kevin Carlson, Video and DVD Production
Joel Putnam, Graphics Designer

The Lightbearers Curriculum is based on Dr. David A. Noebel's book *Understanding the Times* and has been re-written for a younger audience by Kevin Bywater (2003) and Chuck Edwards (2008).

Special thanks to the many teachers and students who have provided ideas and suggestions to make this program a success. We're also grateful for the many contributions of the following individuals:

Charissa Imken	Christopher Norfleet
John Albert	Chris White
Blake Roeber	Micah Wierenga
Sonnie Wierenga	Angela Bywater
Ron and Norma Fields	Elizabeth Ringwood
Sarah Lang	Brian Genda

The following have contributed their time and ideas, or allowed their image and written materials to be used in the *Lightbearers* Curriculum:

Jobe Martin, Reel Productions, Scott Klusendorf, Focus on the Family, John Stonestreet, John Sutherland Films, Coral Ridge Ministries, Dr. Bill Brown and Cedarville University, Michael Koerbel and re: Films.

Scripture quotations marked (HCSB) have been taken from the Holman Christian Standard Bible®, Copyright © 1999, 2000, 2002, 2003 by Holman Bible Publishers. Used by permission. Holman Christian Standard Bible®, Holman CSB®, and HCSB® are federally registered trademarks of Holman Bible Publishers.

Scripture quotations marked (NIV) are taken from the HOLY BIBLE, NEW INTERNATIONAL VERSION ®. NIV®. Copyright © 1973, 1978, 1984 by International Bible Society. Used by permission. All rights reserved worldwide.

Scripture quotations marked (NKJV) are taken from the New King James Version. Copyright © 1982 by Thomas Nelson, Inc. Used by permission. All rights reserved.

Printed in April 2010 at Courier Corporations, 22 Town Farm Road, Westford, MA 01886, USA

Copyright © 1997, 2004, 2008 Summit Ministries.
All Rights Reserved.
Unauthorized Duplication Prohibited.

Table of Contents

LIGHTBEARERS

Preparation

A Summit Ministries Curriculum

The Purpose of This Curriculum

Have you ever put together a 1,000 piece puzzle? At first all the pieces spread out on the table look like a mass of confusion. So you begin looking for the straight-edge ones that go around the edge to frame the picture. Then, with lots of patience, you slowly begin to find where the other pieces go until finally you have the completed picture. But what guides you through the process? It's the picture on the box top. Without that picture, it would be almost impossible to make any sense out of all the individual pieces.

Your life can be like a puzzle without the box top. Often, the different parts of your life don't seem to fit together. You go to school but seldom think about how the things you are learning relate to what you do when you're with your friends. You watch a movie but never reflect on what it might be saying about how to live a better life. What you learn in church stays in church. You pray before a meal but don't think about God while you talk with your family over dinner. Everything seems disconnected. It's all a jumble of scattered pieces lying on the table.

The idea that life is like a puzzle was developed by the late Christian author, Francis Schaeffer. He had a lot of insight when he wrote that most Christians in America "have seen things in bits and pieces instead of totals."[1] What he means is that we have failed to step back to take a look at the total picture. We miss out on how the various parts fit into God's overall plan for our life. As a result, we are not experiencing all that God has in mind for us individually—a life full of meaning and purpose. And we fail to have a positive influence on those living around us in society.

This Lightbearers curriculum is designed, first, to help you see the big picture. In these pages you will discover how every person on the planet tries to make sense out of life. That's because life comes at you fast and is often confusing. *Where did everything come from? Who am I? Why are we here? What's right and wrong, and who decides? What happens when we die?*

What you rely on to answer these and other questions are the ideas that give your life direction. And the answers fit together into a larger picture—what we call a "worldview," a way of understanding and making sense of our world. Your worldview determines (consciously or unconsciously) how you interpret and respond to everything in life. This is why it is so important to begin thinking about your worldview and the ideas you believe to be true.

A second purpose of this course is to show you how the Bible provides answers to all of life's most important questions. You will discover that God not only has communicated how to have a relationship with Him through Christ, but also has provided guidelines for shaping society for everyone's benefit. By understanding God's total plan, you will develop a worldview that influences everything you do.

A third goal of this curriculum is to open your eyes to the fact that ideas have consequences. Good ideas have positive consequences, and bad ideas have negative consequences. You will begin to see that there is an ongoing battle in our society over which ideas will dominate. As it turns out, there are other worldviews that do not start with biblical ideas and therefore arrive at different answers to the key questions of life. Throughout this course, you will have the opportunity to discover how and why the Bible has better answers for all life's important issues.

The main point is this: those who understand how to think well about life will have the opportunity to influence the ideas that rule the world. In fact, in the Bible we are told the story of one small tribe in Israel that was chosen to lead the nation because they "understood the times, and knew what Israel ought to do" (1 Chronicles 12:32, NIV). It is our hope that through this course you will also gain a better understanding of the times in which we live, so that you will know what God would have you do.

The Need for This Curriculum

The goals for this curriculum are twofold. The first goal is defensive: to keep you from being deceived by anti-Christian worldviews. The second goal is offensive: to train you to actively live out the truth of Christianity in a culture of relativism and confusion.

These two goals are summed up in a statement by James Dobson and Gary Bauer: "Nothing short of a great Civil War of Values rages today throughout North America. Two sides with vastly differing and incompatible worldviews are locked in a bitter conflict that permeates every level of society…the struggle

---

[1] Francis A. Schaeffer, *A Christian Manifesto* (Westchester, IL: Crossway Books, 1981), 17.

now is for the hearts and minds of the people. It is a war over ideas. And someday soon, I believe, a winner will emerge and the loser will fade from memory. For now, the outcome is very much in doubt."[2]

What Dobson and Bauer describe is the current struggle among the worldviews vying for the hearts and minds of every person in our society. You are not immune to false ideas simply because you have been raised in a Christian environment. Because secular ideas permeate every part of our culture, from TV to movies to music to advertising, even students who have been raised in Christian homes, attend church regularly, and are enrolled in Christian schools are vulnerable to non-Christian ways of thinking.

A number of surveys indicate that large numbers of Christian youth are rejecting certain biblical truths or even turning away from Christianity altogether. Without proper worldview training, the trends outlined below will likely continue to increase:

CHRISTIAN TEENS REJECT TRUTH: A study conducted by well-known Christian speaker and author Josh McDowell found that 29% of Christian teens agreed with the following statement: "There is no such thing as absolute truth; people may define truth in contradictory ways and still be correct." Another 28% were not sure, and less than half could say they disagreed.[3] The problem with this is that a biblical worldview says that truth is not contradictory!

CHRISTIAN TEENS REJECT MORAL ABSOLUTES: The Bible teaches that morals are objective and absolute. Yet, according to the well-known Christian statistician George Barna, a mere 9% of Christian teenagers believe in moral absolutes.[4]

CHRISTIAN STUDENTS RENOUNCE THEIR FAITH IN COLLEGE: And even more staggering, according to a major survey of college students across the United States, the percentage of Christians who no longer claim to be "born again" by their senior year is as high as 59%![5]

While these trends are alarming, we must remember that God's truth is more powerful than the false ideas capturing the minds of so many students. For years, the Christian community has drawn a line between the *sacred* and the *secular*. Christians have been encouraged to focus only on "sacred" activities (like going to church, praying, or reading your Bible) and avoid "secular" activities (such as politics, film-making, science, or philosophy). The result is that Christians have withdrawn from the very institutions that have the most influence for shaping society. We have stepped into "holy huddles," and refused to participate in the larger culture. The results have been predictable: without the salt and light of the Bible, society has grown tasteless and dark.

In reality, no such sacred/secular distinction exists. Through *Lightbearers*, we want you to see that every area of life is ultimately sacred, even politics and filmmaking. This curriculum operates on the premise that every generation must be prepared to undertake a pro-active Christianity—one that seeks to *redeem* culture as part of God's creation, rather than *reject* it.

But What Is a Lightbearer?
Did you know that the Bible refers to you as a *Lightbearer*? You may be wondering what that means. To find out, you need to ask three questions:

[2] James C. Dobson and Gary L. Bauer, *Children at Risk: The Battle for the Hearts and Minds of Our Kids* (Dallas: Word, 1990), 19–20.

[3] This study was done in 1994, with a total of 3,795 Christian youth from 13 different mainline denominations. See Josh Mcdowell and Bob Hostetler, *Right from Wrong* (Dallas, TX: Word Publishing, 1994), 251–253, 264–265.

[4] http://www.barna.org/cgi-bin/PagePressRelease.asp?PressReleaseID=106&Reference=C

[5] This study was originally done in 1989 by Gary Lyle Railsback, "An Exploratory Study of the Religiosity and Related Outcomes Among College Students," Doctoral dissertation, University of California at Los Angeles, 1994. Railsback did a follow up study in 2001 and found the percentages had increased. The greatest losses were at Catholic universities, reporting that 59% of Christian freshmen who had indicated being "born again" no longer claimed to be "born again" by their senior year, Many Protestant universities showed a 31% loss, with secular universities falling in-between these two extremes.

- What is the light that you bear?
- What is the source of the light?
- What should you do with the light?

First, what is the light that you bear? The "light" is not some vague emotion a Christian might feel. According to the Scriptures, the light that Christians carry is something very specific and extremely special. It is the "gospel of the glory of Christ" (2 Corinthians 4:4, NIV), the good news that Jesus is the Savior of the world! Bearing this light means proclaiming the glory of Jesus as God's only Son.

Second, what is the source of the light? The light you bear comes from your relationship with Jesus Christ. You could think of yourself as a reflector of His light. In John 8:12, Jesus said, "I am the light of the world. He who follows Me shall not walk in darkness, but have the light of life" (NKJV). Jesus is the source of your light, which is the light of life—both eternal life when you die, and a meaningful life here and now. "For it is the God who commanded light to shine out of darkness, who has shone in our hearts to give the light of the knowledge of the glory of God in the face of Jesus Christ" (2 Corinthians 4:6, NKJV). Think of it this way: the light of Jesus Christ that reveals the glory of God is shining in your heart!

And third, what should you do with the light? Shine it, of course. Jesus told His followers, "You are the light of the world. A city that is set on a hill cannot be hidden. Nor do they light a lamp and put it under a basket, but on a lampstand, and it gives light to all who are in the house. Let your light so shine before men, that they may see your good works and glorify your Father in heaven" (Matthew 5:14–16, NKJV). You have a purpose in life. Part of that purpose is to be a witness for God, like a lighthouse on a dark, stormy night—shining light all around you for others to see. In this way, other people can see the glory of Jesus and learn how to follow Him too.

Have you ever been in a dark room when a door opened and light suddenly streamed in? If you have, then you know that light always displaces darkness. Darkness has no power in itself. Light, however, always conquers or overcomes darkness. According to the Bible, light symbolizes the life and testimony that you live before others. And with the light of Jesus Christ burning brightly in you, no worldly darkness of sinfulness or selfishness can overcome you. God wants you to allow the light of Jesus to shine forth so others can watch you and learn to walk in His ways. This brings Him glory.

A Lightbearer, then, is a follower of Christ who is allowing the light of God's truth to shine through him or her to others. This means shining His light not in just a few areas of your life, but in every area.

It's easy to have too small an idea of what it means to be a Christian. Living as Jesus wants you to live is not just something you do on Sundays, like going to church. It's also not just being kind to people. Nor does it simply mean you will go to heaven when you die. Being a Christian means so much more. God's plan for you is much broader and deeper—He wants you to understand His desires for you in every area of your life.

Lightbearers provides a constructive "rite of passage." Through it, we want to pass the torch to you, the next generation, by explaining the mistakes of the past and endowing you with the responsibility for shaping the future of the world.

Using This Manual

Before beginning this curriculum, it will helpful to understand its structure and layout.

UNITS: There are 10 units to this curriculum, plus an Introduction and Conclusion section at the beginning and end. The following elements are found within each unit:

1. **Table of Contents: At the beginning of each unit is a table of contents or section outline that lists the components and their corresponding page numbers.**

2. **180-day syllabus: At the beginning of each unit is a 180–day syllabus outlining your daily classroom and homework assignments.**

3. **Pre-Test: At the beginning of the curriculum, there will be a comprehensive multiple-choice exam that will help to measure the consistency of your worldview. This test will be taken again at the end of the course to measure how your thinking has changed because of this course.**

 4. **Videos: Each unit has corresponding video presentations and occasional outlines with fill-in-the-blank notes.**

 5. **Video Discussion Questions: Each video has a set of discussion questions. These questions will be completed and discussed after watching each presentation.**

 6. **Readings: Each unit has a primary reading assignment called** *A World of Ideas***, as well as assigned chapters from the book** *How to be Your Own Selfish Pig***. A few additional readings are also assigned throughout the curriculum and are included in the student workbook.**

 7. **Reading Discussion Questions: Each reading assignment has an accompanying set of discussion questions. These questions will be completed and discussed after each reading.**

 8. **Learn to Discern Quizzes: These quizzes will test your understanding of the Christian worldview.**

 9. **Journal: During this class, you'll have the opportunity to keep track of your spiritual, intellectual, and emotional growth using the** *Journal* **section in the back of your workbook. Use this to record your thoughts about anything, whether prayer requests, a Scripture passage you want to remember, important events in your life, etc.**

 10. **Paragraph Assignments: Using a checklist as a guide, you will write a paragraph summarizing what you have learned about the Christian worldview in each discipline.**

11. **Presentation Assignments: Each unit will contain an assignment that will ask you to research various topics or participate in various activities. You will then write a half-page to one-page summary of your findings and/or experience and then present these findings to the class, as well as turn in your summary for a grade.**

 12. **Exercises: Each unit contains exercises that reinforce the subject matter being taught in each unit. These will be explained fully by your teacher.**

13. **Test Review: Toward the end of each unit there is a day to review all the concepts covered in that unit before taking the test.**

14. **Unit Tests: At the end of each unit is a unit test. The questions for these tests may be matching, multiple choice, true/false, fill-in-the-blank, or short answer. Each test is based on the textbook, video, and essay discussion questions.**

15. **Comprehensive Exam: At the end of the Conclusion Unit, there will be a comprehensive multiple-choice exam covering all the materials from the course. Questions for the comprehensive exam are taken from the video, textbook, and essay discussion questions throughout the entire course.**

16. **Post-Test: At the end of the curriculum, there will be a comprehensive multiple-choice exam that will help to measure the consistency of your worldview. This is the same test taken at the beginning of the course.**

BIBLE TRANSLATIONS: For this curriculum, we have chosen to alternate between the New King James Version, the New International Version, and the Holman Christian Standard Bible. Others may be used as well, but will be noted.

ADDITIONAL RESOURCES

SUMMIT HOMEPAGE: Online hub for Summit's conferences, curriculum, and resources is www.summit.org.

SUMMIT'S TRUTH & CONSEQUENCES: A free monthly e-news article that reviews current issues from a worldview perspective. To sign up, visit the RESOURCES page at www.summit.org.

THE SUMMIT JOURNAL: A free monthly review of the news and cultural events, edited by Dr. David Noebel. To sign up, visit the RESOURCES page at www.summit.org.

SUMMIT'S WEBSTORE: For the most up-to-date selection of worldview-oriented books, videos, and CDs covering such topics as apologetics, Darwinism, Relativism, Pluralism, Skepticism, and many others, visit visit the STORE page at www.summit.org.

SUMMIT CONFERENCES: To learn more about our intensive educational conferences analyzing the major worldviews of our day and developing a Christian worldview, visit visit the CONFERENCES page at www. summit.org.

LIGHTBEARERS

Introduction

A Summit Ministries Curriculum

Day	INTRODUCTION: syllabus & outline	SW	✓
1	Read **Preparation Section**... Take **Pre-Test**..	i ---	
2	Watch **"re:View: Numb"** Video.. Review **"re:View: Numb"** Video Discussion Questions..................................... Watch **"re:View: Culture TS"** Video.. Review **"re:View: Culture TS"** Video Discussion Questions............................	--- 3 --- 4	
3	Read *A World of Ideas* Reading...	5	
4	Read *A World of Ideas* Reading... Review *A World of Ideas* Reading Discussion Questions.................................	Ditto 12	
5	Review *A World of Ideas* Reading Discussion Questions................................. Assign **The Evaluator** [Assignment Due on Day 11]..	Ditto 13	
6	Watch **"re:View: Ultimate Questions"** Video... Review **"re:View: Ultimate Questions"** Video Discussion Questions............... Watch **"re:View: Ultimate Questions TS"** Video... Review **"re:View: Ultimate Questions TS"** Video Discussion Questions.........	--- 14 --- 15	
7	Read *How to Be Your Own Selfish Pig* Reading (Ch. 1)...................................	---	
8	Read *How to Be Your Own Selfish Pig* Reading (Ch. 2)................................... Review *How to Be Your Own Selfish Pig* Reading Discussion Question (Ch. 1 & 2).....	--- 16	
9	Review *How to Be Your Own Selfish Pig* Reading Discussion Question (Ch. 1 & 2).....	Ditto	
10	Watch **"re:View: Worldviews"** Video.. Review **"re:View: Worldviews"** Video Discussion Questions............................ Watch **"re:View: Worldviews TS"** Video.. Review **"re:View: Worldviews TS"** Video Discussion Questions.....................	--- 18 --- 19	
11	Turn in & Share **The Evaluator** Presentation Assignment................................	---	
12	Complete **Biblical Application** Exercises... Take **Learn to Discern** Quiz...	20 ---	
13	Prepare **Introduction** Test...	---	
14	Take **Introduction** Test..	---	
15			

re:View: Numb
Video Discussion Questions

Synopsis: Sometimes we glide through life and don't even notice what is around us. This film is a glimpse into the day of an average guy like that, with one exception—from the moment he gets up until the time he goes to bed, his life will subtly change with every wave of influence.

1. **What is the film about?**

2. **How did the main character react to what was happening around him?**

3. **What are examples of things that changed as a result of the influences around him?**

4. **What do each of these examples represent in today's popular culture?**

5. **What do you think the TV analyst meant when he said, "The question then becomes: What are we going to do? Are we going to sit here and be numb, or are we going to do something about it?"**

re:View: Culture TS
Video Discussion Questions

Synopsis: Whether we recognize it or not, our culture is the major influencing factor on our behavior, values, and beliefs. Our goal as wise believers is to knowledgeably critique culture's values, rather than uncritically absorb them. The first step in making life changes is to recognize how profoundly culture shapes us in ways we probably don't even realize.

1. **What did Dr. Brown mean when he mentioned the fish in the ocean?**

2. **Culture has a major influence on what three things?**

3. **What is popular culture?**

4. **Why is popular culture so influential?**

5. **How is "the right to choose" seen as the most important value in our culture?**

The film and Teaching Segment you just watched, as well as the discussion materials, are part of a curriculum project produced by Cedarville University and re:Films. This study is designed for either a 13-session series or an abbreviated 7-session study. Consisting of seven award-winning short films, video teaching segments, and a resource-packed website, this revolutionary series will cause students to evaluate their world, discerning and engaging culture with a defined purpose. Tell your Pastor and Youth Pastor about this curriculum and have them visit www.re-films.com for more information.

A World of Ideas:
What is a Worldview?

Objects on this page are no smaller than they appear. If you can read this, you are too close to your workbook.

KEYS TO UNDERSTANDING

Key Question: What is a worldview?
Key Idea: Everyone has a worldview
Key Terms: popular culture, worldview
Key Verses: Romans 12:2 and 2 Corinthians 10:5

"Do not be conformed to this age, but be transformed by the renewing of your mind, so that you may discern what is the good, pleasing, and perfect will of God" (Romans 12:2, HCSB).

"We demolish arguments and every high-minded thing that is raised up against the knowledge of God, taking every thought captive to the obedience of Christ" (2 Corinthians 10:5, HCSB).

Thinking about Thinking

Christine woke so suddenly she banged her head on the bookshelf. Rubbing her head groggily, she counted the sleeping bags scattered on the floor around her. Four. And they were all still asleep. No one was playing jokes on her or calling her names. It must have been a dream.

Christine sighed and leaned back on her elbows. Her girlfriends would never do that to her. They'd all sworn that "forever friend" pact back in first grade, and nobody had broken it since. Maybe it had been that late-night movie...on screen the nasty pranks were funny, but in the dream it had been her friends ganging up against her. That hurt, even though she knew they'd never do that in real life.

It started her thinking. Maybe there were some lessons they could learn from that movie, even if it was just a silly comedy. Wide-awake now, she crawled out of her sleeping bag and went to take a shower to clear her head.

Later, when everyone had gathered in the kitchen for pancakes, Christine told the girls about her dream.

"Don't worry about it, Christine," Lydia said, laughing. "Movie stuff never affects real life."

"Yeah," chimed in Michelle, "we like each other too much to let something like a movie or a dream mess up our friendship."

"But don't you think that movies sometimes teach us things?" Christine pressed. "I mean, in the dream I really felt picked on...and I didn't like it."

"Chrissy, you're just reading too much into all this," Kelly said. "It was just a movie...you know... entertainment?"

"That's right," said Ashley. "Movies are supposed to be mindless and fun. You just leave thinking for the rest of life. Right?"

Beliefs and the Common Cold

Thinking can be hard work. If you were to ask one of your friends about his or her philosophy of life, you would probably get a blank stare. But if you ask what he or she believes about something more specific, like how life appeared on earth, you would probably get some sort of answer, even if it's not all that clear. If you go even further and ask your friends *why* they believe what they believe, then you will probably find out that they just don't have good reasons for their beliefs.

Often people get their beliefs the same way they catch colds—by being around other people! And the more we are around other people, the more their beliefs influence us and become our own.

That's the power of friends, family, and our larger society. It is primarily through these sources that we pick up our ideas about life. Increasingly, it is popular culture that has become the loudest voice that we hear. **Popular culture** describes the predominant ideas, values, and beliefs transmitted through movies, video games, music, television, books, magazines, radio, advertising, and the internet.

Popular culture offers us short "sound bites" that many people take for the truth. You might think of phrases like "you should be tolerant" or "that may be true for you, but not for me." When repeated often enough, slogans like these generally become accepted as cultural truth, regardless of whether they are actually based in reality. We will evaluate common sayings like these later in this course, but for now the point is that we all tend to accept these without thinking about them.

"In Colossians 2, the Apostle Paul warns believers to not allow false ideas to capture or take over their minds. This means that we must be on our guard, constantly evaluating what we hear, see, and think. Do our thoughts line up with God's thoughts? Not only that, but we are told to understand ideas and the truth so that we can help others see where their ideas are wrong."[1] This is what being a Lightbearer is all about.

Again, the Apostle Paul said: "We use our powerful God-tools for smashing warped philosophies, tearing down barriers erected against the truth of God, fitting every loose thought and emotion and impulse into the structure of life shaped by Christ" (2 Corinthians 10:5, THE MESSAGE).

Because so much of life today revolves around fast-paced music videos, action-packed movies, popular TV programs, and intriguing print media, you've learned to experience the world through your emotions, instead of processing the information with your mind. With images and sounds moving so quickly, it's hard to take the time to think very deeply about the ideas that are coming at you. Even when you want to examine those ideas, you may not really know how. Sometimes you don't even know the right questions to ask to get started!

That's why Christians especially need to slow down the pace a little and spend time learning how to think about the big questions in life. More importantly, we need to make sure we're developing consistent answers that match up with God's ideas as expressed in the Bible. This means we need to "renew our minds" according to God's truth (Romans 12:2), which leads to transforming our behavior. In this way God's light shines more brightly in our hearts and minds. As the psalmist explains, "Your word is a lamp to my feet and a light for my path" (Psalm 119:105, NIV).

Throughout this course, you will explore the Christian worldview—the ideas that come from the Bible—and examine how those ideas are better *in every way* than any you can pick up from popular culture. Also, you will discover answers to the questions you may be asking about life in general, and learn how God's answers will bring you the most fulfillment and joy. The more you study God's answers, which are found in His perfect Word, the better you will become at being a Lightbearer—helping other people see His light and understand why God's thoughts are higher and better than our thoughts (Isaiah 55:9).

Popular Culture: A collection of values, themes, ideas, and behavior popularized mainly through media and technology. The most visible forms of popular culture are seen in television, movies, music, the internet, etc.

What is a Worldview?

If you are to be a Lightbearer, then you need to understand some things about why God made the world and how you fit into His plan. To do this, you need to broaden your understanding of what it means to live as Christ wants you to live. You need to step out of your limited human perspective and think about the bigger questions of life. This means learning to think in terms of a worldview.

What is a worldview? Simply put, it is the way you view the world. Your view of the world includes:

- Your most basic beliefs about life and the world
- Your answers to the big questions of life
- How you interpret what you encounter in life and the world
- The starting point for your decisions and actions

A **worldview** consists of our most basic beliefs, which shape our view *of* and *for* the world and form the basis for our decisions and actions. The fact is everyone has a worldview, a way of making sense of the world. To help you understand how a worldview works, think about the following illustrations. First, a worldview is like a fruit tree. If you were to draw a fruit tree, you would probably draw a trunk and some fluffy branches bearing fruit at the end. But what part of the tree channels nutrients to the branches so that they can produce fruit? The roots. The roots are a vital part of the tree, and provide nourishment for producing the fruit. If there were no roots, there could be no fruit.

In a similar way, a worldview is an interconnected set of ideas. Jesus described the connection between what a person believes and how he or she behaves this way, "By their fruit you will recognize them" (Matthew 7:16, NIV).

Also like a tree, everyone's worldview begins at the same place—with the roots. The roots represent your beliefs about God. These beliefs about God are the sap that travels up the trunk and out the branches to produce the fruit—the ideas—about all other areas of life.

The connection between root ideas about God and the resulting fruit can easily be seen in this way. Take, for example, the people who do not believe that God exists. When facing a moral dilemma, they cannot look to God for answers; they can only look within themselves or to others. Therefore the answers *will change* from person to person or culture to culture. On the other hand, if God exists, then our moral choices must be based in His *unchanging* character (which has been shown to us in the Bible). As you obey the commands found in the Bible, you have a reliable way to understand how you should live.

Another way to illustrate a worldview is to consider a pair of eyeglasses. Have you ever put on someone else's glasses? If the prescription for the glasses is not the right one, what you see will be a distorted view of what is in front of you. In other words, without the right prescription, glasses will not help you see the world more clearly. Instead, they will keep you from seeing the world as it truly is.

Worldview: Our most basic beliefs that shape our view of and for the world and form the basis of our decisions and actions.

It's the same with a worldview. Just as eyeglasses can either help or hinder your sight, a worldview will either help or hinder your understanding of the world. For example, two people looking at a giraffe's long neck may think about the complex arrangement of the giraffe's heart, arteries in its neck, and the tissue surrounding its brain. They may both be aware that the giraffe doesn't blow its brains out when it lowers its head to get a drink of water because of the pressure valves strategically placed along its neck. Yet one person, if he or she does not believe in God, may conclude the giraffe got its long neck as a result of a natural, evolutionary process over vast stretches of time. The other person, starting with the idea that God created each kind of animal, interprets the giraffe's neck as clear evidence of God's special design. So, like a set of prescription glasses, each person's ideas act as a lens through which he or she interprets the world.

A worldview is like a pair of eyeglasses—you need the right worldview to see and understand the world as it really is.

From these illustrations, you can learn two things about a worldview: first, that a worldview is like a fruit tree—what you believe about God is like the sap that nurtures how you think about everything else in life. Second, that a worldview is like a pair of eyeglasses—you need the right worldview to see and understand the world as it really is.

Asking the Right Questions

Do you remember when you were about four or five years old? If you were like most children at that age, you asked a lot of questions. As your awareness of your neighborhood, city, and world began to grow, so did your curiosity. You wanted to know why and how things work or came to be, so you asked questions like *Why is the sky blue? Will my dog go to heaven?* and *What is God like?* You learned about the larger world around you by asking questions.

As it turns out, people have been asking certain kinds of questions from the dawn of recorded history. They wanted to know how they fit into the story of their world, culture, and family. So they asked questions like *How did life get here? What is wrong with the world?* and *Can we make the world better?*

Christians have thought about these questions too and have looked to the Bible for answers. What is found there is the unfolding story of God, His continued involvement with everything that He made, and His control over human history. This story is laid out for us in God's word, and can be understood in three main themes: Creation, Fall, and Redemption.

The Bible begins with the beginning of everything—everything, that is, except God. He was already in the beginning, since He has always existed, and He brought all things into existence. Thus, all things (and all people) are utterly dependent on God. This is the first theme: the Creation.

To really understand who we are and what our place is in God's creation, we must understand that God has placed every human being in four primary relationships. All people are in these relationships whether or not they realize that they are. First, you are in a relationship with God, your Creator. This is the most important relationship anyone has, since our very existence is dependent on Him and since He is the absolute Ruler of the universe in which we live. God desires a relationship of authentic obedience and love from each and every one of the people He made.

Second, we are in a relationship with ourselves. That may sound strange, but this is one of the things that make humans so different from animals. Humans and animals both exist, but humans know they exist—we wonder why we exist, and we try to make sense of our own lives. According to the Bible, God gave humans their identity when He created us in His image. This means that no matter what you hear from others about yourself or what you feel about yourself, you have purpose and value as a special creation of God.

Third, each and every one of us finds ourselves in relationships with others who also bear God's image. We have family, friends, teachers, bosses, and acquaintances. Even more than that, however, the relationships between humans are the key pieces of our (or any) society. For example, human relationships are the key ingredients of families, churches, and governments (the three primary social institutions).

Finally, every human is in a relationship with the rest of creation. This means we need to ask questions like *Do we have a responsibility for the animals? If so, what is that responsibility? What about the environment? How should we treat it? What can we use for our benefit? What needs to be protected?* During Creation, God placed His image bearers in charge of everything else He had made. We were told to care for God's creation and be productive with it.

The Bible tells us that God created all things as "very good" (see Genesis 1). In other words, God's creation was a brilliant design! At that time, each of the four relationships were functioning together in harmony. However, this ideal situation did not last.

When our first human parents chose to disobey God, death came into the world as the consequence of their sin. In other words, something has gone very wrong with God's very good creation. This is known as the Fall, and it has impacted each of the four relationships that God established. First, humans fell from full fellowship with a holy God through their sin (Genesis 3). Rather than obeying and loving God as we ought, there is a separation between mankind and God due to our sin. Second, humans fell in their ability to fully reflect God's image. Third, our relationships with other image bearers has fallen also. There is often conflict in our homes, churches, or governments. In fact, sometimes these conflicts even turn violent. For example, immediately after the Bible talks of the Fall (Genesis 3), it records a family murder (Genesis 4). Finally, humans fell in their ability to take care of and rule over the rest of the creation. Droughts, earthquakes, and other disasters often occur. Weeds grow instead of plants, and our best plans sometimes just don't work out right. Our ability to be responsible for the creation has been frustrated by the effect of sin.

But God did not leave mankind or His world in this fallen condition. He devised a plan to bring humanity back into a special relationship with Himself and restore the relationships humanity has with others and the creation. He did this by having His own son, Jesus, pay the penalty for mankind's sin. When the time was right, Jesus came to earth to die in our place, paying the price for our sin and removing our separation from God. This part of God's plan is called Redemption, meaning that God paid in full for our sins so we can experience fellowship with Him once more (Genesis 3:15, 21; John 3:16–21; Acts 17:24–31). When we are in a right relationship with God, we can fully understand who we are and how to relate to others personally and socially, and we can seek to be agents of His kingdom here on earth. Further, the Bible speaks of a time when, through Christ, all wrongs will be made right.

This three-step progression—creation, fall, redemption—shows us why the world is the way it is. And if this story is the story of the world, it is also your story. Have you really embraced this story? Through Jesus' death on the cross, the door is now open for you to return to the ideal relationship with God that He intended in the beginning. But first you need to believe that Jesus' death was personal, for you and your sins, and accept His gift of salvation.

It is your relationship with God that has the most impact on how you live each day, so it is the first relationship that needs to be developed once you believe in Jesus as your savior. And once your relationship with God is restored through Jesus Christ, you can have renewed relationships with yourself (recognizing that you are created in His image and that your task is to glorify Him in everything that you do), with others (treating those around you as people who also bear the image of God and need to hear the message of salvation and grow stronger in their relationship with God), and even with the earth (wisely caring for the earth as a steward, responsible to God).

In this course, you will study these foundational questions and relationships, as well as other life issues, by asking key questions related to specific areas of life. You will discover that the biblical answers to these key questions form a *consistent* and *comprehensive* view of life.

People form a worldview based on their answers to the following questions:

- What about God? – *Theology*
- What is true and how do we know? – *Philosophy*
- How should we behave? – *Ethics*
- What is the origin of life? – *Biology*
- What is human nature? – *Psychology*

- What makes a healthy society? – *Sociology*
- What is the basis for law? – *Law*
- What is the purpose of government? – *Politics*
- How should we use our resources? – *Economics*
- What is the meaning of history? – *History*

The answers you choose for these questions are interconnected and come together to form an overall system of beliefs—a worldview. Your worldview does not simply determine what you think the world *is* like; it determines what you think the world *should* be like. Therefore your worldview will dictate your actions and responses to every aspect of life.

This curriculum focuses on each of these ten key questions, one at a time. In this way, you will learn that the answers to these questions reveal how God wants you to live in His world. But God hasn't left you without help in finding out the answers to these questions. He gave you His written Word as a guide to the truth. Only by searching the Bible for His answers will you be able to understand His overall plan for the world and His purpose for how you should live.

Developing Your Worldview

But how can you develop your worldview when there is so much "truth" available today? We live in an era where confusion is commonplace, and any solid statements about truth are often frowned upon or swept away as mere opinion. What should you believe about God? What is truth? What is good? There are so many answers to these questions that it can make your head spin! How in the world are you supposed to get things straight, given the many beliefs that our culture throws at you? In this world of conflicting ideas, how can you develop a Christian worldview instead of just going along with the crowd?

Developing your worldview will take some time and effort. As you work your way through this course, you will find out where your ideas may be unclear or mistaken and you will have the opportunity to develop clear, solid ideas from the source of all truth, the Bible.

A Biblical Christian Worldview

As you learn more about the biblical answers related to our key questions, you will begin to see just how the Christian worldview is relevant to *all* of life. It makes sense that Christianity would be relevant to all of life—it's the one worldview entirely based on how God designed and created the universe. True truth exists, and it has its sole foundation in the unchanging character of God. Once you know and understand God's truth, you can live as a Lightbearer in the midst of a very confused culture.

Today, however, many Christians have turned away from a biblical foundation and have forgotten how to think and how to carefully analyze competing ideas. As a result, their light, which is supposed to shine brightly throughout society, has grown dim.

Francis Schaeffer, a Christian philosopher, blamed the Christian community for America's shift away from God. Schaeffer saw that Christians had forgotten that following Jesus impacts every aspect of life—that Christianity is a comprehensive world and life view. Instead, they turned their attention to a few "bits and pieces"[2] of life's key questions. By focusing only on their private relationship with Jesus, Christians have lost sight of the importance of shining the light of Jesus Christ into philosophy, ethics, politics, economics, the mass media, the sciences, entertainment, and other areas.

Schaeffer went on to explain that Christians have very gradually "become disturbed over permissiveness, pornography, the public schools, the breakdown of the family, and finally abortion. But they have not seen this as a totality—each thing being a part, a symptom of a much larger problem. They have failed to see that all of this has come about due to a shift in worldview—that is, through a fundamental change in the overall way people think and view the world and life as a whole."[3]

But many of Schaeffer's warnings came too late. Because Christians in the past few decades have been content to remain isolated and not become involved in the larger culture, many people have turned away from a Christian worldview and embraced other non-Christian worldviews instead. As a result, Christians today have an uphill battle in trying to regain a positive influence for good in our society.

The Consequences of Ideas

It has been said that ideas have consequences[4] and bad ideas have bad consequences. Ideas affect more than just our minds—people will help or harm others based on what they believe is good and right. And if a whole society begins to believe wrong ideas, it will probably move in the wrong direction.

Take for example the nation of Germany. Before World War II, the Germans had for the most part built their society on a Biblical Christian worldview. But when Hitler took control of the country in the 1930s, he began propagating hatred for Jews. Because he was powerful, the German people failed to take a strong stand for God's truth that everyone is created in God's image. Many remained silent and allowed Hitler to influence the entire nation, leading it into a holocaust against the Jews and plunging most of the world into a global war as other nations fought to stop him.

When Christians do not speak up and participate in society, their light becomes dim and darkness fills the void, often with tragic consequences.

Without a comprehensive and consistent worldview, Christians are as likely as anyone to adopt the beliefs and practices of those around them. We see evidence of this happening today throughout a number of former Christian-centered nations. Recent surveys show that an increasing number of people who claim to be Christians deny that there are binding moral standards of behavior or absolute truth. But that doesn't make sense. How can someone claim to believe in Jesus and His teachings, but also claim that everyone can decide for himself or herself what is right or wrong or true? This makes Jesus' teachings irrelevant to everyday life. In the end, many people simply do what is right in their own eyes, falling into the same trap as the ancient Israelites (Judges 17:6; 21:25).

If you are serious about developing a Biblical Christian worldview, then you need to pay close attention to how the Bible applies to every idea that comes into your mind. Jesus claimed that He is "the way, the truth, and the life" (John 14:6, NKJV). To become a true follower of Jesus, you will need to think and act in each situation just as He would act. That is no trivial matter.

The Bible demonstrates a comprehensive faith and worldview. When your Christian worldview is well developed, you will know how you should act, just like the men of Issachar, a small tribe of ancient Israel. We read in 1 Chronicles 12:32 how these men "understood the times, and knew what Israel ought to do" (NIV). Even though they were the smallest tribe among their brothers, they provided leadership for the entire nation because they understood the ideas of their culture and how God wanted them to respond. It was as if they had a newspaper in one hand and the Bible in the other—they read the events of the day through the "glasses" of God's truth. This biblical worldview knowledge qualified them for leadership.

Christians can do the same today. If you understand and are confident in the truth of the Christian worldview, you can provide today's Christians with the wisdom necessary to lead our nation and spread "the faith which was once for all delivered to the saints" (Jude 3, NKJV).

This is what it means to be a Lightbearer. Are you ready to let your light shine into a darkened world? Your friends, neighbors, and nation desperately need to see God's light shining through you. Maybe God is preparing you to understand the times in which we live so that you will know what to do.

Endnotes

[1] Norman L. Geisler and William D. Watkins, *Worlds Apart* (Grand Rapids, MI: Baker Books, 1989), 11.

[2] Francis A. Schaeffer, *A Christian Manifesto* (Westchester, IL: Crossway Books, 1981), 17.

[3] Ibid.

[4] See Richard M. Weaver, *Ideas Have Consequences* (Chicago, IL: University of Chicago Press, 1984).

A World of Ideas
Reading Discussion Questions

1. What point did the story about Christine's sleep-over make?

2. How do most people get their beliefs? Is this bad?

3. What is a worldview? What two illustrations can help you see the effect a worldview can have on your life?

4. How is a worldview both a view *of* and *for* life?

5. What three-step progression describes the big picture of the Bible?

6. What four major relationships do Christians experience?

7. What did Francis Schaeffer see as the main problem with this culture?

8. Reflection Question: How do the different people you turn to in your life (parents, friends, neighbors, pastors, cultural icons, etc.) answer some of life's most important questions?

9. Reflection Question: What does the phrase "ideas have consequences" mean?

The Evaluator
Presentation Assignment

Pick a favorite TV show, movie, song, game, website, book, or magazine that you were recently exposed to and evaluate it to see what key worldview concepts it is based on. The purpose of this assignment is to help you take a step back and objectively evaluate a form of entertainment that appeals to you. Take your time and think about the questions being asked. You may be surprised at some of your answers.

1. What TV show, movie, song, game, website, or reading material are you evaluating?

2. What is it about this form of entertainment that attracts you? Why do you like this particular style, genre, or show more than others? (If it is because your friends do, why do they listen to or watch it?)

3. How does this kind of entertainment make you feel?

4. What are the major messages being sent through this entertainment? Do you agree or disagree with them? What subtle messages are put forth in this entertainment?

5. Do the themes of this entertainment reflect reality? Do they gloss over evil?

6. How do the messages compare with your personal values, what you know to be right and wrong?

7. Do you think these messages have any effect on how close you feel to your family, friends, or God? Why or why not?

8. What might happen if someone took these messages literally? What might happen if you imitated the lifestyles and choices of the characters portrayed in this entertainment?

9. How does it make you feel to know that by supporting this entertainment you are supporting the ideas it is promoting?

10. Would you feel comfortable if Jesus listened to or watched this with you? What do you think He would say about it? Does the Bible say anything about entertainment like this? If so, what?

re:View: Ultimate Questions
Video Discussion Questions

Synopsis: Taking tests—no one enjoys it. But what if you didn't know what the test was about or why you were there? What if you couldn't leave or find a way out? Sitting in a high school gymnasium with endless rows of desks, Nick discovers that there are some questions that everyone has to answer.

1. **Where did Nick try to go? Did he succeed? Why or why not?**

2. **What were the four questions on the test?**

3. **Why didn't the other students help him answer the questions?**

4. **Why was it important that he come back and sign his name on the test booklet?**

5. **What are some of the big questions we ask in life?**

re:View: Ultimate Questions TS
Video Discussion Questions

Synopsis: Everybody answers the ultimate questions from the test of life. While the questions do not always occupy our minds, they are inescapable. How you answer them determines the foundation for your life.

1. What are the four ultimate questions?

2. What makes these questions ultimate?

3. What is popular culture?

4. Why is it wrong to think it doesn't matter what the answers to the ultimate questions are?

How to Be Your Own Selfish Pig
Reading Discussion Questions

Chapter 1: Don't Ask Questions

1. What is the big question Sally and Matthew are asking?

2. What does the title of this chapter mean?

3. What are the elements of a person's philosophy of life?

4. Why do so few people engage in thinking?

5. What incident caused Susan to clarify her faith?

6. When Susan started questioning, what was her father's reaction?

7. When Francis Schaeffer encouraged his daughter to seek answers, what did she realize?

8. What further explanation did Francis Schaeffer give to Susan about questions?

9. Francis Schaeffer said, "No man can live without a _____, therefore, there is no man that is not a philosopher."

10. To what does Susan compare a worldview?

11. According to Dorothy Sayers (page 19), when do we usually begin to question our faith?

12. Why was this book written?

13. Reflection Question: What are your roots? What is it you hang onto to keep yourself going day after day?

14. Reflection Question: Do you believe the things your parents tell you? Why or why not? What about the things you pick up from television or your friends? Are your reasons for believing what you believe good ones?

15. Reflection Question: Do you know what is really true? Do you want to know the truth? What will it take for you to look for answers?

16. What popular view do Mr. and Mrs. Briggs hold?

17. What does the title of this chapter mean?

18. Why is this thinking an error?

19. Susan points out two important facts about beliefs. What are they?

20. What do your beliefs affect?

21. What does the story about the keys have to do with the purpose of this book?

22. The box at the end of this chapter talks about flying in the dark. How does a pilot's trip over the Alps in the dark compare to how you live your life?

23. Reflection Question: Do you think there is a key to reality? Is it the same for everyone, or are there many keys that could work?

24. Reflection Question: Do you believe that some things are true and others are false, that some things are right and some are wrong? Why?

25. Reflection Question: What if there were no such thing as truth? How would that affect your life? How would you be able to make a decision about anything?

re:View: Worldviews
Video Discussion Questions

Synopsis: When a bank is robbed in a small town, it is Chief Detective Howard's job to investigate the case. When police arrive at the scene, they find surveillance lines cut and no clues left behind. Will statements from the witnesses solve the case? One robbery. Six witnesses. Two robbers. Or maybe it was three?

1. Could the detective determine what had happened from the testimonies of the witnesses? Why or why not?

2. Did the detective ask everyone the same questions? Did the answers match?

3. How is it possible for everyone to answer differently?

4. From their answers, what information can you determine about each of the witnesses?

re:View: Worldviews TS
Video Discussion Questions

Synopsis: A worldview is a category of consistent answers to the four ultimate questions. There are three main answers (worldviews): Naturalism, Transcendentalism, and Theism. Every person has a worldview, whether he or she recognizes it or not.

1. Who has a worldview?

2. What are the two roles of a worldview?

3. How did Dr. Brown define the two roles?

4. Someone once said, "Find a worldview that fits you and then live it passionately." What is wrong with this statement?

5. What's the difference between the role of an artist and an architect?

Biblical Application
Exercise

Often we are told to "apply" biblical truth to our lives. But what is biblical application? Well, it is practicing the truths that you have learned through God's Word; it is *doing something about what you read*. How do you translate what you read into daily practice? The following three steps will help yo make biblical application a reality in your life.

First, read the Scripture passage in its larger context. It's always best to read a whole passage at a time, not just a verse or two. This is because if you just focus on one or two verses you are more likely to miss the overall point of the passage. You need to *understand the author's words within the larger context* of what he is saying. This means grasping the bigger picture of what you are reading.

Second, read for understanding, not just recall. In other words, *ask questions as you read*. What style of literature is this (history, poetry, direct teaching, prophecy, etc.)? Who is doing the talking? Who is the author talking to? What event is taking place? What happened before and after this event that might have a bearing on why this event is important? Be sure to look up the definition of words you don't understand. Also, think about whether there are general principles or timeless truths that can be derived from this passage. What principle can you apply to your own life?

Finally, you should plan a strategy to change your behavior. This means seeking out ways to actually *put God's truth into practice*. It means planning how to be obedient. As a result of what you have learned, what will you do differently today, this week, or as a new pattern for your life into the future? Is it a change in attitude? Or maybe a more godly way of treating other people? How about, through the power of the Holy Spirit, changing a bad habit that you know is not pleasing to God?

To simplify this process a little, remember that: first, you read; second, you understand; and third, you say, "Now what? How will I be different because I know this? What will I do about what I know?"

It is this step of applying the Bible to your life by making changes to your behavior that sets you apart as a Lightbearer. James give us clear direction when he wrote:

Do not merely listen to the word, and so deceive yourselves. Do what it says. Anyone who listens to the word but does not do what it says is like a man who looks at his face in a mirror and, after looking at himself, goes away and immediately forgets what he looks like. But the man who looks intently into the perfect law that gives freedom, and continues to do this, not forgetting what he has heard, but doing it—he will be blessed in what he does (James 1:22–25, NIV).

Applying God's truth to life is the dividing line between those who read the Bible but stay the same and those who read the Bible and live differently. Someone once asked, "If you were put on trial for being a follower of Christ, would there be enough evidence to convict you?" What about you? Have people ever wondered why you were kind to them even when they were unkind to you? Has anyone ever asked about your moral choices because your standards are different? This "fruit" of your salvation can only grow from a heart changed by the Bible and the Holy Spirit.

One of the application skills you should develop is the ability to paraphrase or summarize the Scripture verses that you read. By putting them into your own words, you can wrestle with them long enough to know that you fully understand what God is saying. Let's work through the process step-by-step, using Philippians 2:5–11 as an example.

1. **Paraphrase**—If you were to paraphrase this passage, it might look something like this:

    In your relationships with one another, have the same attitude of mind Christ Jesus had: Who, being in very nature God, did not consider equality with God something to be used to his own advantage; rather, he made himself nothing by taking the very nature of a servant, being made in human likeness. And being found in appearance as a human being, he humbled himself by becoming obedient to death—even death on a cross! Therefore God exalted him to the highest place and gave him the name that is above every name, that at the name of Jesus every knee should bow, in heaven and on earth and under the earth, and every tongue acknowledge that Jesus Christ is Lord, to the glory of God the Father. (Today's New International Version)

2. **Bridge**—Now you need to bridge this truth into our world of today. They are not just dusty words written to people who are long dead. The words of the Bible are living and active for your life today. So what is God telling His people that He wants them to do? It might look like this:

    The humility Jesus demonstrated needs to become a vital part of my life. Just as He took on the role of a servant, so I should look for ways that I can serve others and obey God's commands. My ultimate goal should be to bring as much glory to God as possible.

3. **Strategy**—Now you need to work out your strategy, a specific, concrete plan that you can follow so that the passage of Scripture will actually *change the way you think and the way you behave*. For example, you can:

    • Make a list of practical ways you are demonstrating humility and a servant's heart right now.
    • Pray and ask God to show you how you can express humility to your family, friends, and peers.
    • Make a list of things you are "grasping"—needlessly struggling to hold on to or control— and ask God to give you the trust to put these things in His hands.
    • Praise God for the ways He is gaining glory in the world.
    • Memorize these verses as a reminder of the kind of person God wants you to be.

When you pursue God like this, you are allowing Him to remake your character and He is glorified! At the end of every day, take an account of your successes and failures. When you fail, ask for God's forgiveness. Begin each day with new enthusiasm and commitment. As a result, you will sense a growing awareness of walking with God and greater ability to respond to life's challenges in a way that is honoring to Him.

Exercise #1

Here is an opportunity to practice the steps for biblical application that we've just outlined. Imagine that while you are doing your personal devotions, you come across James 3:13–18. As you are reading this passage, you recall a recent encounter with a friend where you got angry and said some unkind things.

Work on applying what you learn from this passage by using the following suggestions:

1) Paraphrase: First, pray, asking the Holy Spirit to help you understand God's Word as you read James 3:13–18 several times. Then paraphrase the verses by putting them in your own words.

2) Bridge: Write out how the main idea of this passage applies in today's world.

3) Strategy: Write out a practical strategy. Remember, your strategy needs to be something to help change your mindset or behavior. It needs to be so specific that you can say, "Yes, I did this" or "No, I haven't done that yet." For example, from this passage, you may decide to search the Scriptures to compare godly wisdom with worldly wisdom. Then, take a daily account of how well you are doing in accomplishing your strategy. Ask God to forgive your failures, and give Him the glory if you succeed.

Here is space for completing this exercise:

Paraphrase:

Bridge:

Strategy: I will . . .

Exercise #2

Here is another opportunity to practice applying Scripture for life change, using a passage from Ephesians 4:1–16:

Paraphrase:

Bridge:

Strategy: I will . . .

LIGHTBEARERS

Unit One

A Summit Ministries Curriculum

DAY	UNIT 01: syllabus & outline	SW	✓
1	Read *A World of Ideas* Reading..	25	
2	Read *A World of Ideas* Reading..	DITTO	
3	Review *A World of Ideas* Reading Discussion Questions........................	33	
4	Review *A World of Ideas* Reading Discussion Questions........................ Assign **Theology Paragraph** [Rough Draft Due on Day 8]....................	DITTO 34	
5	Watch **"re:View: Check"** Video.. Review **"re:View: Check"** Video Discussion Questions.......................... Watch **"re:View: Naturalism TS"** Video Review **"re:View: Naturalism TS"** Video Discussion Questions.............	--- 35 --- 36	
6	Complete **Attributes of God** Exercise #1.. Complete **Attributes of God** Exercise #2.. Complete **Jesus** Exercise.. Assign **Theology in Movies** [Assignment Due on Day 11].....................	37 38 40 41	
7	Watch **"re:View: Reset"** Video.. Review **"re:View: Reset"** Video Discussion Questions.......................... Watch **"re:View: Transcendentalism TS"** Video.................................. Review **"re:View: Transcendentalism TS"** Video Discussion Questions.......	--- 42 --- 43	
8	Turn in **Theology Paragraph** Rough Draft [Assignment Due on Day 13]....... Read *How to Be Your Own Selfish Pig* Reading (Ch. 5).........................	--- ---	
9	Review *How to Be Your Own Selfish Pig* Reading Discussion Questions (Ch. 5)...........	44	
10	Watch **"re:View: Help"** Video.. Review **"re:View: Help"** Video Discussion Questions........................... Watch **"re:View: Theism TS"** Video.. Review **"re:View: Theism TS"** Video Discussion Questions...................	--- 45 --- 46	
11	Turn in & Share **Theology in Movies** Presentation Assignment..............	---	
12	Complete **The Trinity** Exercise..	47	
13	Turn in **Theology Paragraph** Assignment.. Take **Learn to Discern** Quiz.. Prepare **Unit 01** Test..	--- --- ---	
14	Take **Unit 01** Test..	---	
15			

Objects on this page are no smaller than they appear.

If you can read this, you are too close to your workbook.

A World of Ideas:
What About God?

KEYS TO UNDERSTANDING

Key Question: What about God? (Does God exist and what is God like?)

Key Ideas: God has revealed Himself in the created universe and His revealed words, the Bible.

Key Terms: theology, atheism, theism, pantheism, general revelation, causal argument, design argument, mind argument, moral argument, special revelation, trinitarianism, monotheism, deism

Key Verse: Genesis 1:1

"In the beginning God created the heavens and the earth" (Genesis 1:1, NIV).

A Close Encounter of the God Kind

Making sense of the world is a pretty big task. Sometimes you may feel confused when trying to understand why people act in certain ways and why things happen the way they do. Having a well-thought-out worldview helps you make sense of the world and your experiences in it.

The Introduction described worldviews using the illustration of a fruit tree. Just like a tree draws nourishment from its roots, the root system of everyone's worldview begins by answering the question *What about God?* When you ask that question, you are dealing with the subject of *theology.* It sounds like a big word, but it comes from two Greek words—*theos,* meaning God, and *logos,* meaning knowledge. So **theology** is simply the study of what we can know about God. Or, to put it another way, theology answers the key questions *Is there a God?* and *What is God like?*

Theology: The study of what we can know about God.

In this chapter you will look into both questions. In the process, you will:

. . . experience what it's like to have pizza with an atheist
. . . make the connection between watches, minds, morals, and God
. . . learn that God has a special message for you
. . . discover how God has personalized that communication in the person of Jesus Christ

To start finding out more about the roots of the Christian worldview, read on!

Lunch with an Atheist

One Saturday, you're out for pizza with a group of friends and discover that one of the gang has brought along someone you don't know. Being the charming, outgoing person you are, you strike up a conversation with the new guy, Skip.

As you're munching your pepperoni pizza with extra cheese, Skip tells you that his parents sued the last school he attended because the coach said a prayer before each football game. He also shows you his membership card to a national atheist association. You take a bite of pepperoni and weakly mumble that you lead your football team in prayer before each game.

Skip then asks you a question that makes you choke on your crust and leaves a string of mozzarella cheese dangling from your mouth. "So, you're a Christian. Tell me, how do you know there is a god?" At that precise moment, the entire restaurant grows strangely silent and every person in the room turns and looks at you!

Now . . . what do you do? You may wish you could drop to your knees and pray that God would answer Skip with a booming voice from heaven. Or that you could at least whip out your cell phone, call your youth leader, and let him talk to Skip. But Skip's question is a great starting point for leading you—and him—to some real answers about God.

What he's really asking is *How do you know that God is real?* And, believe it or not, there are some very convincing answers to that question.

Does God Exist?

People have always wondered about God. Over the centuries, mankind has come up with different answers to the question of whether God exists. One answer is that God does not exist, which is the answer of **atheism**. On the other hand, the vast majority of people throughout history have answered that God does exist. If you believe God exists, you believe in **theism**.

But if you say that God exists, you need to answer another question: *What is God like?* There is basically two ways to answer this question. One answer is that God is in everything. In other words, He is not separate from the world of nature. This is the answer of **pantheism**, which includes many of the Eastern religions like Hinduism and Buddhism.

As it turns out, the Christian worldview provides answers to both of these theological questions. Christianity claims that God exists and has chosen two primary ways for revealing Himself to us. The first is through what He has created. As you consider the universe, our solar system, the planet on which we live, life itself, and the uniqueness of humanity, it is natural to conclude that such a complex arrangement of matter can only have come from a supernatural source—God.

The second way God reveals Himself to us is through the Bible. In the Bible we find out not just that He exists, but also details about the character and personality of the Creator of the universe. We learn, for instance, that God desires a relationship with His highest creation—mankind.

The content of Christian theology, then, rests on two foundations: *general revelation* and *special revelation*. General revelation is God's communication, through nature and conscience, regarding His existence. Special revelation is God's more specific communication, through the Bible and Jesus Christ, about salvation and His nature. One theologian had this to say about these two forms of revelation:

Atheism: The belief that God does not exist.

Theism: The belief that God does exist.

Pantheism: The belief that God is and is in everything.

On the one hand, general revelation is God's communication of Himself to all persons at all times and in all places. Special revelation, on the other hand, involves God's particular communications and manifestations which are available now only by consultation of certain sacred writings [i.e., the Bible].[1]

General Revelation

General revelation is God's communication to humanity through nature, conscience, and rational thought. For example, the immensity of the universe demonstrates that God is very powerful, the complexity of the human body shows that God is a masterful Designer, and the fact that humans alone have the ability to reason reveals the existence of an ultimate Mind.

Psalm 19 confirms that the universe shows certain characteristics of the Creator:

The heavens declare the glory of God; and the firmament shows His handiwork.
Day unto day utters speech, and night unto night reveals knowledge.
There is no speech nor language where their voice is not heard.
Their line has gone out through all the earth, and their words to the end of the world (Psalm 19:1–4, NKJV).

Every person on Earth can hear and understand what nature is saying. In a loud voice, creation screams "God Is!" People like Skip (in our story above) may not care to admit it, but the universe itself provides strong evidence there is a God.

In Romans 1:20, the Apostle Paul said that because nature speaks so plainly, there is no excuse for anyone not to believe in God. "For since the creation of the world God's invisible qualities—his eternal power and divine nature—have been clearly seen, being understood from what has been made, so that men are without excuse" (NIV).

This is why throughout history we find cultures that believe in a Supreme Being. Nature compels them to believe that God exists. So, using Romans 1:20, answer the following questions:

General Revelation: God's communication with mankind, through nature and conscience.

- How long has God been known?
- What has He made known?
- In what ways do you think the universe displays God's "eternal power"?
- In what ways is God's "divine nature" shown?

More Reasons to Believe in God

In addition to the general revelation found in nature, there is another way to discern that God exists. That way is by using your mind to make sense of what you see around you. Over the centuries, Christian theologians and philosophers have come up with several logical arguments for believing in God's existence. These include: 1) the fact that the universe came into existence, 2) the designed features found in living things, 3) the fact that our minds are made for thinking, and 4) the existence of a universal moral law.

ARGUMENT #1: THERE'S SOMETHING RATHER THAN NOTHING

The **Causal argument** considers how the cosmos (i.e., the universe) came to be. This argument simply contends that anything that begins to exist must have been caused to exist by something else. Therefore, the existence of the universe must have been caused to exist by something else. Just like a ten-story building cannot pop into existence without someone building it, the universe cannot pop into existence without something (or someone) creating it.

But what would be powerful enough to cause the universe? Some people believe that *nothing* caused the universe. But how could *nothing* cause *something* to do *anything*? That is just not reasonable. Therefore, there must be a better answer.

Other people suggest that the universe has always existed. What's wrong with that answer? Very simply, it contradicts scientific evidence. For example, scientists tell us that the universe has a limited amount of usable energy. Yet, if the universe had always existed—if it had existed for an *unlimited* amount of time—then its *limited* energy would have been used up by now.

For example, the average car can only go about 300 miles on a tank of gas. If we were driving down the highway and you asked me how long we had been driving and I said "forever," wouldn't you wonder why we hadn't run out of gas yet? Similarly, since all of the limited energy in the universe hasn't been used up yet, then the universe must have came into existence at some point in time. That means we are back to needing a cause for the universe.

So what can you conclude from this line of thinking? If the universe has not always existed, and if it is unreasonable to think that *nothing* caused it to exist, then we are left with the idea that something outside of the natural universe—something *supernatural*—must exist. This *supernatural* something, as the only thing not limited by the laws of the universe, must also be the cause of the universe. This something would need to be more powerful than all the energy in the entire universe; in fact, it must be supremely powerful. Only the all-powerful God of the Bible fits this list.

Causal Argument: Anything that begins to exist must have been caused to exist by something else.

ARGUMENT #2: THERE'S DESIGN INSTEAD OF CHAOS

But there is another compelling reason to believe in God. It is called the **design argument**, also known as the "teleological argument." (You already know that *logos* means knowledge; the root *teleos* means something perfect or complete.)

The design argument makes the case that if something exists that is clearly designed, then it must have a designer. For example, if you stumble across a watch in the woods, you wouldn't think it just popped fully formed into existence or arose by accident from a combination of random natural forces, such as wind, lightening, or gravity. You would think a watchmaker designed it and that someone probably lost it while walking in the woods.

If it is not possible for a watch to come into existence through the process of simple natural laws, then something like the human body, which is immensely intricate and complex, has much less chance of coming into existence through purely natural processes. If a watch designer is required for a watch to exist, then doesn't the watchmaker (indeed, all humanity) also need a designer? If you wouldn't believe that watches could exist without watchmakers, then how could you believe that humans can exist without a "human-maker"? Again, this human-maker must be something supernatural, outside of the natural universe, and immensely powerful, i.e., someone like God.

Design Argument: If something exists that is designed, then it has a designer.

These observations from design suggest that the universe was created by a super-intelligent Designer. This provides additional reasons to believe that an Intelligent Designer (i.e., God) must exist.[2]

ARGUMENT #3: THERE'S MIND NOT JUST MATTER

Not only did God place clues to His existence in nature, but He also gave mankind a mind made in the image of His so that we could reason, something no animal on earth can do. Christian author C.S. Lewis gave radio broadcasts and wrote books defending why it is reasonable to believe in God. One of his reasons involved the **mind argument**. "Suppose," contends Lewis, "that there is no intelligence behind the universe. In that case, nobody designed our brain for the purpose of thinking. Thought is merely the random by-product of atoms within our skull. But if so, how can I trust my own thinking to be true?" asks Lewis.[3]

Lewis has a good point. Think about "thinking" for a moment. The very fact that you are *thinking* raises an important question: *Where do your thoughts come from?*

Check the answer you think best completes this sentence: "My thoughts are the result of…

- ☐ electrical impulses between the synapses of the cells in my brain."
- ☐ the Force, the same energy that permeates all living things."
- ☐ myself —my soul—initiating the thought that animates my brain."
- ☐ I try not to think—it gives me a headache."

Why does Lewis insist that we could not trust our own thoughts if they are the by-products of random processes found in nature? To better grasp Lewis's point, think again about a computer program. What if a monkey typed away on a keyboard in an effort to create a computer program? Do you think the program would work? Obviously not! That's because a monkey would be hitting random keys, not having an end purpose in mind. The same is true when it comes to your mind. It seems to be *programmed* to think. A thinking mind could not possibly come about by a random process of molecules bumping into each other.

Your mind is more than just the chemical processes of the "gray matter" in your brain. If a surgeon opened your skull and searched everywhere throughout your brain, he would never find a thought, idea, or feeling. That is because there is more to your mind than just your physical brain—there is a part that goes beyond simple matter. The Bible refers to this immaterial part of you as your "soul." And since the end result (your thinking mind) needs a sufficient cause, there must be an intelligent God who created your ability to think. Therefore, the existence of thinking minds implies the existence of a Divine Intelligence.

Mind Argument: If there is no intelligence behind the universe, then our thoughts are only by-products of matter and we have no reason to trust them.

Argument #4: There's Right and Wrong

In addition to your mind, consider the concepts of right and wrong. The **moral argument** for God rests on the fact that moral laws exist and are known by human beings.

To illustrate the logic behind the moral argument, think about this scenario. Suppose you find a fenced-off piece of land in the forest. If the owner of the land didn't put up a "No Trespassing" sign there, then it is fine for you to cross the fence and keep walking, right? It is legal to walk wherever you want. If, however, the owner *did* put up a "No Trespassing" sign so that you would not walk on his land, then it is not legal for you to walk wherever you want, because he has the authority to make this demand.

Well, the same thing is true of moral laws and God: if God is not the creator of moral laws, or if He does not care if you follow them, then it is okay for you to do whatever you want. But if God has created moral laws and cares if we follow them, then it is not okay for you to do whatever you want.

This question of right vs. wrong is not new. People in every place and time have known deep down that certain things are right and certain things are wrong.

- Torturing innocent children for fun...wrong
- Helping a child who is lost...right
- Stealing bread from the hungry...wrong
- Warning someone that their house is on fire...right
- Intentionally infecting someone with a deadly disease...wrong
- Claiming to be the emperor of the universe...wrong
- Screaming fire in a crowded movie theater...wrong
- Helping an elderly person cross a street...right

But where do these ideas of right and wrong originate? There are only two possibilities: either they come from nature or they come from God. Does it make sense to say that morals originated from a bunch of molecules? No! This is just as silly as saying that a clock can pop into existence out of thin air.

If this is not the case, then God—the Moral Lawgiver—must be the originator of moral laws, and He must care whether or not we follow His rules. This, in fact, is what the Apostle Paul explained to the believers in Rome when he wrote that "the requirements of the [moral] law are written on their hearts, their consciences also bearing witness, and their thoughts now accusing, now even defending them" (Romans 2:15, NIV). Because of the existence of moral laws, the only logical conclusion is that they exist because of a Lawgiver.

Moral Argument: Since moral law exists, there must be a moral law-giver.

Special Revelation

According to the Bible, the destiny of human beings involves either salvation or condemnation (John 3:16–21). While general revelation demonstrates that God exists and reveals certain broad aspects of God's nature, it is through special revelation that the question *What is God like?* is answered. The Bible reveals both God's character and the good news of salvation in detail (Romans 10:14).

Special revelation is expressed through such events as miracles, dreams, and visions (Hebrews 2:4), as well as through words given to prophets and apostles (Hebrews 1:1). Many of these revelations have been recorded in the Bible, God's inspired word (2 Timothy 3:16). In addition, the ultimate special revelation is Jesus Christ Himself. If you really want to know what God is like, all you need to do is look at the person of Jesus.

God, who...spoke in time past to the fathers by the prophets, has in these last days spoken to us by His Son, whom He has appointed heir of all things, through whom also He made the worlds; who being the brightness of His glory and the express image of His person, and upholding all things by the word of His power, when He had by Himself purged our sins, sat down at the right hand of the Majesty on high (Hebrews 1:1–3, NKJV).

Special Revelation: God's communication of Himself and His will to particular people through His word and Jesus Christ.

The teachings and actions of Jesus have been recorded in the Bible so that we can know about God (John 20:30–31), as well as how we should live as followers of Jesus (2 Timothy 3:16–17). Thus, Christians should not treat the Bible like any other book, for it is not like any other book. Rather, the Bible is the Word of God given to human beings, not merely the words of human beings.

What is God Like?

Even those who agree that God does exist (including Muslims, Jews, Mormons, and Christians) often disagree about what God is actually like. The Bible informs us that God is the creator of the universe, life, and morality. But more than that, we find that He is personal, He is three-in-one, He is involved in the world, He is a judge, and He is a redeemer. Let's explore each of these characteristics of God.

CHARACTERISTIC #1: GOD IS PERSONAL

Some transcendentalists believe that everything and everyone is in reality god (or at least a part of god). This belief, as mentioned earlier, is known as pantheism. However, other transcendentalists believe that god is an impersonal force, something like electricity. (This idea is presented in the *Star Wars* films.)

In contrast, Christians affirm that God is not an impersonal force, but a personal being. Personal beings possess qualities such as self-awareness, the ability to make choices, and the ability to experience feelings like happiness, loneliness, or anger.

In the Bible, God's personhood is revealed in the fact that He is self-aware (Exodus 3:14), that He speaks (Hebrews 1:1–3), that He has a will to choose (Matthew 6:10), and that He feels emotions such as love (John 3:16). This list could be multiplied to include additional attributes and actions of God, each of which would combine to reveal His magnificent personality.

God does not have a physical body, but that does not make Him any less of a person. Personal traits are not tied to bodies. If a person lost a foot or a hand, it would diminish his or her body, but it would not make him or her any less of a person. And because we are created in God's image, we share such traits of personhood. This means that you can have a personal relationship with the Creator of the universe, but you cannot have a relationship with a thing, like a rock, a tree, or electricity.

CHARACTERISTIC #2: GOD IS TRIUNE

One distinctive feature of the Christian worldview is the belief that God is three persons in one being, known as **Trinitarianism**. This idea is summarized in an ancient Christian statement of faith, the Athanasian Creed: "That we worship one God in Trinity, and Trinity in Unity; neither confounding the Persons; nor dividing the Substance."[4] Since this statement is a little hard to understand, let's break it down into its parts.

Trinitarianism: The biblical teaching that there is one God who exists as three persons: Father, Son, and Holy Spirit.

The first key element of this creed is that there is only one God. This is called **monotheism**, the belief that only one God exists (*mono* means one, and *theos*, as you already learned, means God). The second key element is that the Father, Son, and Holy Spirit are three distinct persons. This means that they can communicate with each other. This also means that they are not just one person pretending to be three persons, or one person simply appearing throughout history in different forms. Neither of these explanations is complete.

In order to explain the idea of the Trinity, ancient Christians constructed a triangular diagram. As you can see from the diagram, only the center circle is labeled "God." This is because there is only one God (Isaiah 44:6–8). Yet the diagram illustrates that the Father is God (Matthew 6:9), the Son is God (John 1:1), and the Holy Spirit is God (Acts 5:3–4). The diagram avoids confusing the persons of the Trinity by showing that the Father is not the Son (Matthew 3:16–17), the Son is not the Spirit (John 16:13), and the Spirit is not the Father (John 14:16).

Some people object to the idea of the Trinity because the word itself does not occur in the Bible. This is true; but the word *Bible* does not appear in the Bible either. Ultimately, where the term came from is irrelevant to whether the idea is true or not. What is important is not the word that is used, but the teaching. Through reason, Christians have concluded that the Bible teaches there is one God who has revealed Himself as three persons. *Trinity* is simply a useful word we employ to summarize this concept.

Others object that God cannot be Three-in-One because it is hard to understand. How can someone be three and yet one at the same time? Actually, Christians do not say that God is one person and three persons at the same time. That would be a logical contradiction. The doctrine of the Trinity states that God is three *persons* in one *essence.* Of course, that idea is still hard to understand. But frankly, there are many things in life that are difficult to understand. If we cannot fully understand the creation around us, or even why other people do what they do, we should not panic if we cannot fully understand the Creator, who is so far beyond our abilities in strength, power, holiness, and thought. It comes down to the fact that this is how God has chosen to reveal Himself, and we can take His word on that.

In summary, Christians believe that there is only one God who exists as three persons (one *what* and three *who's*). This idea is summed up by the Apostle Paul. As he finished his second letter to the Corinthians, Paul wrote this closing comment, "The grace of the Lord Jesus Christ, and the love of God, and the communion of the Holy Spirit be with you all" (2 Corinthians 13:14, NKJV).

> **Monotheism**: The belief that only one God exists.

CHARACTERISTIC #3: GOD IS INVOLVED

Another idea people consider is whether God cares about what we do. Maybe God is the Creator in the sense that He wound up the universe like a clock and then left everything, including human life, to run under its own power.

Deism is the belief that although God exists, He is not involved in the universe or human history. Thus, there are no miracles (events where God supernaturally intervenes in the natural course of history) and there is no special revelation (so Jesus is not God and the Bible did not come from God).

The biblical description of God stands in contrast to this perspective. Not only is He the Creator (Genesis 1:1), but He also hears when we pray (1 John 5:14), and even entered frail human life so that He might redeem His people from their sins (Philippians 2:6–8). One of God's great promises to His people is that He will never leave us nor forsake us (Deuteronomy 31:6, 8; Hebrews 13:5). Instead of thinking about God as an impersonal force or a removed deity, we should realize that God loves us so much that although He is bigger than the universe, He is still with us at all times.

> **Deism**: The belief that God created the universe, but that He is no longer with His creation.

CHARACTERISTIC #4: GOD IS JUDGE

The judgment of God is not a popular subject, even among Christians. While many people enjoy thinking about the love of God, they don't like the idea that God is also a God of wrath (Romans 1:18). However, you cannot read far in the Bible before seeing that God's holiness involves both love and judgment.

Because God is by nature holy, He cannot tolerate sin. In fact, His holiness is the exact opposite of sin. After Adam and Eve violated God's command and ate from the tree of the knowledge of good and evil, God judged their disobedience by expelling them from His presence in the garden of Eden (Genesis 3:23–24). Other demonstrations of God's judgment are recorded in the Bible, including the Flood (Genesis 6:17–7:24), the destruction of Sodom and Gomorrah (Genesis 19), the striking down of Nadab and Abihu (Leviticus 10:1–7), the fall of the Canaanites (Leviticus 18–20), and the eventual fall of both Israel (2 Kings 17) and Judah (2 Chronicles 36). In each case, God was motivated by His holy nature and steadfast word to judge sin.

Though God is a Judge, He is always fair and righteous. He is not a big bully just waiting for any opportunity to squelch your fun. God is truly interested in seeing good prevail over evil. Yet God does not take pleasure in the judgment of the wicked (Ezekiel 33:11). Although His holiness must be fulfilled, God also wants to show mercy.

> The LORD, the LORD God, merciful and gracious, long-suffering, and abounding in goodness and truth, keeping mercy for thousands, forgiving iniquity and transgression and sin, by no means clearing the guilty… (Exodus 34:6–7, NKJV).

CHARACTERISTIC #5: GOD IS REDEEMER

There is only one thing that can protect humans from the holy wrath of God on the final Day of Judgment—God's mercy. In the most awesome display of His mercy, God provided an advocate for us, someone who, though without sin, became sin for us (2 Corinthians 5:21). The central theme of redemption is the love of God: "For God so loved the world that He gave His only begotten Son, that whoever believes in Him should not perish but have everlasting life" (John 3:16, NKJV).

Indeed, God's love for sinners is demonstrated by Jesus Christ's death (Romans 5:8). God's love knows no social, racial, or gender boundaries. God loves the rich and poor, old and young, males and females of all nationalities and races. Jesus was not sent to earth simply to be a good teacher or example, but to redeem people from their sins. All who receive Jesus Christ (John 1:12) and believe in Him (John 3:16) will escape from God's wrath and have eternal life, because the penalty for their sins has been paid in full. Those who believe in Jesus will not be condemned (Romans 3:24) and are no longer controlled by sin (Romans 6:11).

Conclusion

The Christian worldview holds that God has revealed Himself in three ways: 1) through the created order, 2) through His inspired word, the Bible, and 3) through the incarnate Son of God, Jesus Christ. From the Christian perspective, the foundation for everything in life is the opening phrase of the Bible, "In the beginning God…" (Genesis 1:1). Christian theology teaches that God is an intelligent, powerful, loving, just, and holy Being. Not only that, but God exists as a Trinity: Father, Son, and Holy Spirit (i.e., three persons, but one Divine essence). Christianity further proclaims that God took upon Himself human form in the person of Jesus Christ and died for our sins.

As Christians, we worship a God who is both Mind and Heart, who with intelligence and power created the world, yet also loves mankind so much that He sent His son to die so people can reconnect with Him. But this holy and righteous God stands in judgment of our actions as well, most importantly whether we have chosen to accept Jesus' death as payment for our sins. Christian theism declares that God exists, is triune, is personal, is holy yet merciful, created the universe, and loved us enough to send His son to die for us. And to top it off, God is a communicating God who speaks through the general revelation of creation and the special revelation of the Bible and Jesus Christ.

Now that you have all this information about God, the question you need to ask yourself is *are you listening?* When you examine a cell in biology, when you walk through the park, when you study the Bible, when you care for someone in need, are you looking for evidence of God's existence and seeking to glorify Him by your actions? Samuel's response to God makes for a great heartfelt prayer: "Speak, for Your servant is listening" (1 Samuel 3:8–10, HCSB).

Endnotes

[1] Millard J. Erickson, *Christian Theology*, three volumes (Grand Rapids, MI: Baker Books, 1983), 1:153.

[2] We will go into more detail on "intelligent design" in the chapter on Biology.

[3] C.S. Lewis, *Broadcast Talks* (London, UK: B. Bles, 1944), 37–8.

[4] As provided in Wayne Grudem, *Systematic Theology: An Introduction to Biblical Doctrine* (Grand Rapids, MI: Zondervan, 1994), 1170.

A World of Ideas
Reading Discussion Questions

1. What is theology? What questions does theology seek to answer? What is the key idea of Christian theology?

2. What are the three primary ways that people answer the question *Does God exist?*

3. In what three ways has God revealed Himself to us?

4. What are four rational or logical arguments for God's existence?

5. What are some of the characteristics we learn about God from Scripture?

Theology Paragraph
Assignment

*As you continue your study, write your own paragraph titled **My Christian Worldview of Theology**. You will be able to correct it, add to it, put it into your Lightbearers Journal, and memorize it. Below is a checklist to help you with this assignment.*

☐ The paragraph states that you believe that God exists.

☐ It stresses the importance of both special and general revelation as the only reliable ways to clarify your knowledge of God, since He is the God of the Bible and creation.

☐ It includes the various ways to show why it is reasonable that God exists.

☐ It includes some of the characteristics of God that we learn from the Bible.

☐ It includes the importance of a personal relationship and trust in Jesus Christ.

☐ It emphasizes the importance of personal application of Scripture for continued spiritual growth.

re:View: Check
Video Discussion Questions

Synopsis: Scott lives life for the moment—at least while he can. Take a peek inside his head as he discovers that his relationship with Julie isn't what it used to be. He had painted the perfect relationship—why couldn't she just live within the boundaries? Can the world really revolve around one person?

1. **What is Scott struggling with?**

2. **How does he eventually resolve the struggle?**

3. **How would you describe Scott's relationship with Julie? With others in the world?**

4. **What are some things Scott says that reveal his view of life in the world?**

5. **What do you think Scott represents? What does Julie represent?**

re:View: Naturalism TS
Video Discussion Questions

Synopsis: The first of the three worldviews we'll study is Naturalism, which teaches that there is no God and that I am in control of my life. There are no ultimate consequences nor any accountability for my choices, but there is also no ultimate meaning or purpose in life.

1. **What are some of the specific forms that Naturalism takes?**

2. **Why is Naturalism called "the world as we see it"?**

3. **If Naturalism is true and there is no God or life after death, then what difference would it make in my life?**

4. **If Naturalism is true, then how should I live?**

The Attributes of God
Exercise #1

As a class, define the following attributes of God.

1. **Eternal**

2. **Faithfulness**

3. **Goodness**

4. **Grace**

5. **Holiness**

6. **Immutability**

7. **Independence**

8. **Patience**

9. **Love**

10. **Mercy**

11. **Omnipotent/Sovereign**

12. **Omnipresent**

13. **Omniscient**

14. **Righteousness/Justice**

15. **Wisdom**

The Attributes of God
Exercise #2

Using the words just defined, match the following verses with the word that best defines the attribute being described or referred to. All verses are from the New International Version.

1. "For as the Father has life in himself, so he has granted the Son to have life in himself" (John 5:26).

2. "I the LORD do not change. So you, O descendants of Jacob, are not destroyed." (Malachi 3:6). "Every good and perfect gift is from above, coming down from the Father of the heavenly lights, who does not change like shifting shadows" (James 1:17)

3. "Before the mountains were born or you brought forth the earth and the world, from everlasting to everlasting you are God." (Psalms 90:2). "But you remain the same, and your years will never end" (Psalms 102:27).

4. "Where can I go from your Spirit? Where can I flee from your presence? If I go up to the heavens, you are there; if I make my bed in the depths, [a] you are there. If I rise on the wings of the dawn, if I settle on the far side of the sea, even there your hand will guide me, your right hand will hold me fast." (Psalms 139:7–10). "Am I only a God nearby," declares the LORD, "and not a God far away? Can anyone hide in secret places so that I cannot see him?" declares the LORD. "Do not I fill heaven and earth?" declares the LORD." (Jeremiah 23:23–24)

5. "He said, 'Lord, you know all things; you know that I love you'" (John 21:17b). "Nothing in all creation is hidden from God's sight. Everything is uncovered and laid bare before the eyes of him to whom we must give account" (Hebrews 4:13).

6. "How many are your works, O LORD! In wisdom you made them all; the earth is full of your creatures." (Psalms 104:24). "Praise be to the name of God for ever and ever; wisdom and power are his. He changes times and seasons; he sets up kings and deposes them. He gives wisdom to the wise and knowledge to the discerning" (Daniel 2:20, 21b).

7. "You are forgiving and good, O Lord, abounding in love to all who call to you" (Psalms 86:5). "Give thanks to the Lord, for he is good; his loves endures forever" (Psalms 118:29).

8. "For God so loved the world that he gave his one and only Son, that whoever believes in him shall not perish but have eternal life" (John 3:16). "Whoever does not love does not know God, because God is love" (1 John 4:8).

9. "But you are a forgiving God, gracious and compassionate, slow to anger and abounding in love. Therefore you did not desert them," (Nehemiah 9:17b). "And are justified freely by his grace through the redemption that came by Christ Jesus" (Romans 3:24).

10. "Therefore God has mercy on whom he wants to have mercy, and he hardens whom he wants to harden." (Romans 9:18). "But because of his great love for us, God, who is rich in mercy, made us alive with Christ even when we were dead in transgressions—it is by grace you have been saved" (Ephesians 2:4–5).

11. "The LORD is slow to anger, abounding in love and forgiving sin and rebellion. Yet he does not leave the guilty unpunished; he punishes the children for the sin of the fathers to the third and fourth generation" (Numbers 14:18). "Or do you show contempt for the riches of his kindness, tolerance and patience, not realizing that God's kindness leads you toward repentance?" (Romans 2:4).

12. "Who among the gods is like you, O LORD Who is like you— majestic in holiness, awesome in glory, working wonders?" (Exodus 15:11). "Holy, holy, holy is the LORD Almighty; the whole earth is full of his glory" (Isaiah 6:3b).

13. "Righteousness and justice are the foundation of your throne" (Psalms 89:14). "The LORD is righteous in all his ways and loving toward all he has made" (Psalms 145:17). "Since you call on a Father who judges each man's work impartially, live your lives as strangers here in reverent fear" (1 Peter 1:17).

Jesus
Exercise

Today there is a lot of confusion about who Jesus Christ is. Some say that He is just a good man, or just a prophet (but not God). Some even say that He is savior, but that He is only one of many saviors. So who is this Jesus?

This is one of the most important questions that you will ever answer, because it affects your view of God's love for His people (how He views us), God's revelation to His people (how He has communicated to us), and God's expectations for His people (how we are to live). It affects how we view ourselves, how we view others, how we view nature, how we view the future, and how we view the meaning of life.

Sounds serious, doesn't it? This is because it is. Discovering the true answer to this question is one of the main purposes of this class. Hopefully by the end of it you will have a greater understanding of Jesus Christ, so that you will be better equipped to explore this question for yourself and able to give an answer to those who ask you this same question.

For this exercise, your assignment is to look at the following verses and write down what they say about Jesus. There is one very important thing to remember, however, as you are reading: *read the verses in context.* This simply means that when you read a verse or a few verses, make sure that you consider the larger passage, chapter, book, etc. Make sure that you do not read it by itself. This is a very important principle to keep in mind for all Bible study, not just this class.

To give you an example of what this looks like, consider Matthew 7:1. This verse, "Judge not, that you be not judged," is commonly taken out of context. In other words, it is separated from the rest of what Jesus was saying in Matthew 5–7. In Matthew 7, Jesus is talking about how terrible it is to be a hypocrite. In Matthew 7:1, the idea that Jesus is conveying is that we must be very careful when we judge someone else, because if we are guilty of the same thing, then we are acting wickedly. He is not saying that we should never judge someone's actions to be right or wrong. He is saying that we should never be hypocritical enough to judge someone else's actions when we are doing the same thing they are.

If we remove a verse from the context in which it is found, then we can distort the meaning that God was intending to convey. This is why it is important to handle God's Word carefully.

Now that you have a better understanding of how to approach Scripture, look up the following references and write down what they say about our Lord Jesus Christ.

1. **Isaiah 53**

2. **Colossians 1:13–19**

3. **Philippians 2:5–11**

4. **Revelation 1:4–8**

Theology in Movies
Presentation Assignment

This assignment will give you practice discerning the various kinds of worldview messages you encounter every day in popular culture. Specifically, you will learn to spot how movies answer the question **What about God?**

You will be assigned to a group for watching a movie together. Watch the film with the purpose of looking for how the question of God is developed throughout the story. As you watch, have a pen and paper to record the scenes, what action is taking place, and what you learn about God through direct statements, implied comments, or actions by the characters. After watching the film, your group should discuss each person's observations. Finally, your group will prepare a short paper (1/2 page) giving a summary of your findings. This paper will be presented to the entire class by one member of your group. The following questions will guide you as you view and think about the movie.

1. What was your impression the very first time you saw this movie?

2. When you first saw the movie, did you recognize the theological content, or did you simply focus on the action scenes or overall story of the main character(s)?

3. How does the description of God in this movie compare with what we know about God from the Bible?

re:View: Reset
Video Discussion Questions

Synopsis: When Sonya is woken by a thud from the apartment next door, she decides to investigate. To her horror, she walks in on something she wishes she had never seen—pictures, videotapes, and newspaper clippings, all about her. Each decision leads to another ending, as the scenario keeps resetting.

1. **What is the film "Reset" about?**

2. **Why did the scenario keep restarting?**

3. **What happens at the end?**

4. **What if you had the ability to go back and "do over" your life? Would you want to?**

re:View: Transcendentalism TS
Video Discussion Questions

Synopsis: The second of the three worldviews is Transcendentalism, which is the natural bent of the human mind. We are not sinful, we are God! Transcendentalism has all the privileges of spirituality without any of the responsibility.

1. **What are some of the specific forms that Transcendentalism takes?**

2. **What are some common American versions of Transcendentalism?**

3. **Why is Transcendentalism such a popular worldview?**

4. **Why do you think so many celebrities are attracted to transcendental religions?**

How to Be Your Own Selfish Pig
Reading Discussion Questions

Chapter 5: You've Gotta Experience It Yourself

1. Sally wants to know God, to understand what He is like. What is the first thing Susan suggests?

2. What other source of information do we have about God?

3. How did Barbara encounter God once she asked Him to reveal Himself?

4. What about John's experience? Did it really exhibit aspects of God's nature?

5. Why does experience alone not tell you truth about God?

6. Experiences are important when they _____ what God has revealed to us about Himself and His character.

7. What helps you interpret experiences concerning God?

8. C.S. Lewis said: "_____ by itself proves nothing."

9. Reflection Question: Have you had an experience that you felt revealed something about God?

10. Reflection Question: Do you agree that it is important to interpret your experiences based on your knowledge of God and the Bible? Why or why not?

re:View: Help
Video Discussion Questions

Synopsis: Katie is a five-year-old on a mission to create the perfect peanut butter and jelly sandwich. All of the essential materials are present: a plate, knife, bread, peanut butter, jelly, and a glass of juice. All is well until Katie realizes that making a sandwich might be something easier said than done.

1. What was Katie trying to accomplish?

2. Was Katie ever in any danger? If so, give examples. Did she know she was in danger?

3. Was Katie asked if she needed help? Was help available all along? Did she eventually ask for help? Why?

4. What do you think Katie represents? What do you think the mom represents? The juice?

re:View: Theism TS
Video Discussion Questions

Synopsis: There is a powerful God who created the universe and us. He gives meaning, determines morality, and promises a specific destiny.

1. What are the five things that Theism explains?

2. Why do so many people not want to believe in God?

3. Why do many people think that believing in God restricts life?

4. What more could God do if He wanted more people to believe in Him?

The Trinity
Exercise

The Triune Nature of God

The Biblical Christian view of God is trinitarian. The word *trinity* is not found in the Bible. It was first coined by Tertullian as the best word to describe the nature and attributes of God in terms of three personalities existing in one God. To say that God is three Persons yet one God means that the Godhead (Acts 17:29) has revealed Himself as one God existing in three Persons: the Father (Romans 1:7), the Son (Hebrews 1:8), and the Holy Spirit (Acts 5:3–4).

The triune nature of God involves three persons, who are neither three gods nor three parts or modes of God. Each person of the Godhead is distinguishable in function and characteristics. Yet at the same time each is co-equally, co-eternally, and co-existently God. The doctrine of the Trinity does not support the idea of polytheism (meaning many gods) or tri-theism (meaning three gods in one). It also does not support the unitarian teaching that God is only one and not three Persons. Rather, it defines God as one God (monotheism) expressing Himself in a plurality of three Persons (Deuteronomy 6:4; 1 Corinthians 8:4; 1 Timothy 2:5).

The persons of the Godhead have been described in various terms, including "three distinct centers of consciousness," "three personalities," a "threefold manifestation," and "three divine essences, each constituting a Person."

The Relationships of the Trinity

The biblical view of the Trinity provides great insights into the nature of God. The inter-dynamics among the persons of the Godhead reveal that God Himself is a social being who is interactive, not static. In fact, this very dimension of God is reflected in the created order of people who, like God, are societal beings existing in various relationships. The eternal relationship of love, interaction, and communication that the Godhead exhibits is to be exhibited by people on earth.

Augustine has suggested that without the Trinity we could not experience fellowship or love in God, who has exhibited eternally a perfect, harmonious relationship among the members of the Godhead.

Scriptural Support for the Trinity

Though the word *trinity* is never used in Scripture, the indications of a triune God are found throughout its many pages. In the beginning, God and the Spirit of God were actively involved in the creation. The Hebrew word for God is Elohim, denoting a plurality of persons involved in the creation of the cosmos (Genesis 1:1–2; 1:26–27). At the baptism of Jesus, the Father, Son, and Holy Spirit were all present (Matthew 3:16–17). We are to carry out the Great Commission in the name of Father, Son, and Holy Spirit (Matthew 28:19). The apostolic benediction includes the grace of the Son, the love of the Father, and the communion of the Holy Spirit (2 Corinthians 13:14). Other Scripture references attest to the truth of the Trinity (Romans 8:9; 1 Corinthians 12:3–6; 1 Peter 1:2; Jude 20–21; Revelation 1:4–5).

The Work of Each Person of the Trinity

Though coequal in every respect, the persons of the Trinity fulfill unique roles. Regarding salvation, God the Father is the initiator of our redemption (John 3:16), because He sent the Son. God the Son is the accomplisher of the work of redemption by becoming God in the flesh and dwelling among humans on earth. God the Holy Spirit brings conviction of sin and applies the work of redemption to individuals. In essence, our salvation is the work of the Trinity (Titus 3:4–6).

Regarding revelation of truth, God the Father speaks His Word (Hebrews 1:1). God the Holy Spirit inspires and illuminates the Father's Word (John 16:7–8; 2 Peter 1:21). God the Son becomes the Word incarnate (John 1:1–2, 14) and is Himself the Truth (John 14:6).

The Mystery of the Trinity

A complete comprehension of the Trinity is essentially impossible. There is no parallel in human existence by which a comparison can be made. Ultimately, belief in the Triune nature of God, or in other doctrines we cannot fully understand, must rest on our faith in God and in the trustworthiness of His revealed Word.[*]

Read the following verses and answer the accompanying questions. As you work through this exercise, notice the connections, such as the fact that God the Father is called Lord and God, God the Son is called Lord and God too, etc. All verses are taken from the New International Version.

Our Lord God

1. Who is the Lord?

"Acknowledge and take to heart this day that the LORD is God in heaven above and on the earth below. There is no other" (Deuteronomy 4:39).

"There is no one like you, LORD, and there is no God but you, as we have heard with our own ears" (1 Chronicles 17:20).

2. Who is our God?

"Do any of the worthless idols of the nations bring rain? Do the skies themselves send down showers? No, it is you, LORD our God. Therefore our hope is in you, for you are the one who does all this" (Jeremiah 14:22).

3. Who is God?

"Blessed are the people of whom this is true; blessed are the people whose God is the LORD" (Psalm 144:15).

God the Father

4. How do we become God's children?

"See what great love the Father has lavished on us, that we should be called children of God! And that is what we are! The reason the world does not know us is that it did not know him" (1 John 3:1).

He came to that which was his own, but his own did not receive him. Yet to all who received him, to those who believed in his name, he gave the right to become children of God— children born not of natural descent, [a] nor of human decision or a husband's will, but born of God" (John 1:11–13).

5. Who is the Father

"[Y]et for us there is but one God, the Father, from whom all things came and for whom we live . . ." (1 Corinthians 8:6).

"Yet, O LORD, you are our Father. We are the clay, you are the potter; we are all the work of your hand" (Isaiah 64:8).

"Is he not your Father, your Creator, who made you and formed you?" (Deuteronomy 32:6).

---

[*] John Hay, *Building on the Rock*, Teacher Manual (Manitou Springs, CO: Summit Press. 2006).

6. **Who is our Father**

"Have we not all one Father? Did not one God create us?" (Malachi 2:10).

God the Son

7. **Who is Jesus?**

"'The virgin will be with child and will give birth to a son, and they will call him Immanuel' which means, 'God with us'" (Matthew 1:23).

"For to us a child is born, to us a son is given, and the government will be on his shoulders. And he will be called Wonderful Counselor, Mighty God, . . ." (Isaiah 9:6).

"The Word became flesh and made his dwelling among us. We have seen his glory, the glory of the One and Only, who came from the Father, full of grace and truth" (John 1:14).

"No one has ever seen God, but God the One and Only, who is at the Father's side, has made him known" (John 1:18).

"And there is only one Lord—Jesus Christ" (I Corinthians 8:6).

8. **Who is Jesus like? With whom is Jesus equal? Who will everyone say Jesus is?**

"Who, being in very nature God, did not consider equality with God something to be grasped, but made himself nothing, taking the very nature of a servant, being made in human likeness. And being found in appearance as a man, he humbled himself and became obedient to death—even death on a cross! Therefore God exalted him to the highest place and gave him the name that is above every name, that at the name of Jesus every knee should bow, in heaven and on earth and under the earth, and every tongue confess that Jesus Christ is Lord, to the glory of God the Father" (Philippians 2:6–11).

9. **Where is Jesus now?**

"...who has gone into heaven and is at God's right hand—with angels, authorities and powers in submission to him" (1 Peter 3:22)

10. **Where is Jesus seated?**

"But about the Son he says, 'Your throne, O God, will last for ever and ever, and righteousness will be the scepter of your kingdom" (Hebrews 1:8).

11. **Who is Jesus Christ?**

". . . from them is traced the human ancestry of Christ, who is God over all, forever praised!" (Romans 9:5).

God the Spirit

12. **Who is the Lord?**

"Now the Lord is the Spirit, and where the Spirit of the Lord is, there is freedom" (2 Corinthians 3:17).

13. What does God give?

"Therefore, he who rejects this instruction does not reject man but God, who gives you his Holy Spirit" (1 Thessalonians 4:8).

14. Where does God's Holy Spirit Live?

"Do you not know that your body is a temple of the Holy Spirit, who is in you, whom you have received from God?" (1 Corinthians 6:19).

15. How do you know the Spirit is a person?

"So, as the Holy Spirit says: 'Today, if you hear his voice, do not harden your hearts as you did in the rebellion, during the time of testing in the desert, where your fathers tested and tried me and for forty years saw what I did'" (Hebrews 3:7–9)

God the Father, the Son, and the Holy Spirit
16. What is asked of the Trinity in this verse?

"May the grace of the Lord Jesus Christ, and the love of God, and the fellowship of the Holy Spirit be with you all" (2 Corinthians 13:14).

Summary of Divine Attributes

Father, Son, and Spirit possess the same divine attributes. The Father is eternal (Genesis 21:33; 1 Timothy 1:17), the Son is eternal (John 1:1; 8:58; 17:5, 24; Hebrews 7:3; Revelation 22:13), and the Spirit is eternal (Hebrews 9:14). The Father is omnipresent (Jeremiah 23:24; Acts 17:27), the Son is omnipresent (Matthew 28:20), and the Spirit is omnipresent (Psalm 139:7–10). The Father is holy (Leviticus 11:45; John 17:11, the Son is holy (John 6:69; Acts 4:27), and the Spirit is holy (Romans 1:4; Ephesians 4:30). The Father is love (Psalm 136:1-26; Jeremiah 31:3; John 3:16; 1 John 4:8,16), the Son is love (John 15:9, 13; 1 John 3:16), the Spirit is love (Romans 5:5; Galatians 5:22; Colossians 1:8). The Father is omnipotent (Mark 14:36; Luke 1:37), the Son is omnipotent (Matthew 9:6; Luke 8:25; John 10:18), and the Spirit is omnipotent (Luke 1:35; Acts 1:8; 2:2–4, 17–21; 4:31–33).[**]

How They Work Together

God the Father sent God the Son to die for our sins. He sent the Holy Spirit to make us new and fill our lives with love, joy, and peace. Read the questions below. Then read the Scriptures that answer each question. If you have never received Jesus as your Lord and Savior, you may wish to do so now.

WHAT IS MY PROBLEM?
"But your iniquities (evil) have separated you from your God; your sins have hidden his face from you, so that he will not hear" (Isaiah 59:2).

WHAT DID GOD THE FATHER DO FOR ME?
"This is how God showed his love among us: He sent his one and only Son [a] into the world that we might live through him" (1 John 4:9, 14).

WHAT DID GOD THE SON DO FOR ME?
"He himself bore our sins in his body on the tree, so that we might die to sins and live for righteousness; by his wounds you have been healed" (1 Peter 2:24).

[**]Gordon Lewis and Bruce Demarest, *Integrative Theology* (Grand Rapids, MI: Zondervan Publishing, 1996), 273.

WHAT DID GOD THE HOLY SPIRIT DO FOR ME?

"[H]e saved us, not because of righteous things we had done, but because of his mercy. He saved us through the washing of rebirth and renewal by the Holy Spirit, whom he poured out on us generously through Jesus Christ our Savior, so that, having been justified by his grace, we might become heirs having the hope of eternal life" (Titus 3:5–7).

WHAT MUST I DO?

"This righteousness from God comes through faith in Jesus Christ to all who believe. . . God presented him as a sacrifice of atonement, [a] through faith in his blood" (Romans 3:22, 25).

"And everyone who calls on the name of the Lord will be saved" (Acts 2:21).

"Believe in the Lord Jesus, and you will be saved . . ." (Acts 16:31).

HAVE YOU?

LIGHTBEARERS

Unit Two

A Summit Ministries Curriculum

Day	UNIT 02: syllabus & outline	SW	✓
1	Read *A World of Ideas* Reading...	55	
2	Read *A World of Ideas* Reading...	Ditto	
3	Review *A World of Ideas* Reading Discussion Questions.............................	64	
4	Review *A World of Ideas* Reading Discussion Questions............................. Assign **Philosophy Paragraph** [Rough Draft Due on Day 8].........................	Ditto 65	
5	Complete **Wisdom** Exercise... Watch **"re:View: Seen"** Video.. Review **"re:View: Seen"** Video Discussion Questions............................... Assign **The Christian Influence on Science** [Assignment Due on Day 11 or 12]...........	66 --- 68 69	
6	Watch **"re:View: Response to Culture A"** Video....................................... Review **"re:View: Response to Culture A"** Video Discussion Questions....................... Watch **"re:View: Response to Culture B"** Video....................................... Review **"re:View: Response to Culture B"** Video Discussion Questions	--- 70 --- 71	
7	Research **Christian Scientists** Presentation Assignment.............................	---	
8	Read *Oh, Those Amazing Feats* Reading... Review *Oh, Those Amazing Feats* Reading Discussion Questions................. Read *The Trouble with the Elephant* Reading.. Review *The Trouble with the Elephant* Reading Discussion Questions................. Turn in **Philosophy Paragraph** Rough Draft [Assignment Due on Day 13].....................	72 73 74 77 ---	
9	Read *How to Be Your Own Selfish Pig* Reading (Ch. 3).............................	---	
10	Review *How to Be Your Own Selfish Pig* Reading Discussion Questions (Ch. 3)...........	78	
11	Turn in & Share **Christian Scientists** Presentation Assignment.....................	---	
12	Turn in & Share **Christian Scientists** Presentation Assignment.....................	---	
13	Turn in **Philosophy Paragraph** Assignment.. Take **Learn to Discern** Quiz.. Prepare **Unit 02** Test..	--- --- ---	
14	Take **Unit 02** Test...	---	
15			

A World of Ideas:
What about Truth and Reality?

Objects on this page are no smaller than they appear. If you can read this, you are too close to your workbook.

KEYS TO UNDERSTANDING

Key Questions: What is true and how do we know?

Key Idea: The nature of reality is foundational to every worldview.

Key Terms: philosophy, truth, epistemology, science, empiricism, metaphysics, materialism, spiritualism, supernaturalism, miracle.

Key Verses: 2 Corinthians 10:5 and Colossians 2:8

"We demolish arguments and every pretension that sets itself up against the knowledge of God, and we take captive every thought to make it obedient to Christ" (2 Corinthians 10:5, NIV).

"See to it that no one takes you captive through hollow and deceptive philosophy, which depends on human tradition and the basic principles of this world rather than on Christ" (Colossians 2:8, NIV).

The Matrix and the <u>Real</u> World

"Have you learned anything in school about philosophy?" asked Uncle Joel.

Charlie looked up, surprised. What kind of a question was that? This weekend was supposed to be fun…just him and Uncle Joel playing video games and kicking the soccer ball around. Why would he want to spoil the mood with that kind of conversation?

"Are you kidding?" Charlie asked, his mouth full of Uncle Joel's famous slow-grilled bratwurst, smothered with mustard and sauerkraut. "Nobody's interested in that stuff!"

"I bet you're more interested than you think," Joel said, unfazed. He carefully drizzled mustard on his brat, ladled on the raw onions, and took a bite. "Umm," he said, sighing. "Nothing finer."

"But seriously, Charlie, philosophy is pretty exciting."

Charlie turned to grab a sip of his soda, careful not to let his uncle see his eyes rolling. Maybe all that time studying for his Ph.D. was turning Uncle Joel into a boring adult. "I thought we agreed to just have fun while you're here."

"Okay," Uncle Joel said. "Let's talk about movies then. Have you seen *The Matrix*?"

"Oh, yeah," Charlie said, scooting to the edge of his chair. "That's one of my favorites! Neo was stuck in a computer program that looked like real life."

"How did Neo learn about what the real world was like?"

"Well," Charlie said, putting his brat down on the plate and licking mustard off his fingers, "Neo was kidnapped by agents, but Morpheus and his friends helped Neo escape. Then Morpheus gave him a choice between two pills—red and blue—and told him that if he chose the red one, he would know the truth. But if he chose the blue one, he would go back to his old life."

"Which pill would you have chosen, Charlie?"

"The red one, of course!"

"So you're interested in what's real and what's not?"

"You bet!" Charlie picked up his brat again and took a big bite.

"Well, that's all philosophy is—finding out the truth about what is real and what isn't."

Charlie thought about that while he chewed. "Yeah, but that's just a movie. People aren't really stuck in pods of goo, being batteries for evil machines."

"That's true," Uncle Joel said. "Okay, think about this. What if your little brother came to you and said that he'd just seen a leprechaun. What would you do?"

Charlie laughed. "I'd tell him he's crazy…or was just imagining it."

"Why?"

"I wouldn't want my friends to find out that my kid brother believes in leprechauns!"

Uncle Joel chuckled. "Why not?"

"Because leprechauns aren't real!"

"Exactly! Now it may be cute for an eight year old to think he sees little men, but imagine what would happen if he still thought leprechauns were real when he's thirty!"

"Ha! Then I'd know he's crazy!"

"Right. Since leprechauns aren't real, if he still believed in them, he'd be out of touch with…"

"Reality!" finished Charlie triumphantly.

"You got it," said Uncle Joel, smiling.

"So, even if we aren't hooked up to machines living in some fantasy world, we still need to find out what's real and what isn't," Charlie noted.

"Yep," Uncle Joel said. "And that's what philosophy is all about."

Charlie reached for his soda and started to smile. Maybe this weekend wouldn't be dull after all.

Thinking about Thinking

Want to see your friends' eyes roll back in their heads? Ask them this question: "What is the meaning of life?" Many people start rolling their eyes when they are asked to think very deeply about life. Maybe you've even thought that such discussions are impractical. And yet, thinking about your life cannot be avoided. That's because you always live out what you think is real. The ideas that you believe to be true affect how you think about yourself and eventually how you act toward others. In other words, the way you behave begins with the way you think about life—your worldview!

However, if you're like most people, you haven't spent a lot of time considering the foundational ideas about life. This chapter takes you on the second step of your journey into developing a biblical worldview—understanding the difference between what is real and what is not. You'll also explore what we mean by "truth" and then see how these ideas relate to your everyday decisions.

Loving Wisdom

In the last chapter you learned that everyone's worldview begins by answering the theological question *What about God?* In this chapter you'll discuss two other important questions:

What is truth? (instead of what is just someone's opinion)
and
What is reality? (instead of what is purely imaginary)

Whether you recognize it or not, the answers to these questions affect every area of your life. Seeking answers to these questions involves the study of philosophy. **Philosophy** comes from two Greek words—*philo* meaning "love of" and *sophia* meaning "wisdom." It's important to get the correct answers to these questions since the results of not knowing what is true and what is real can be disastrous.

For example, what if you came into your kitchen after playing soccer for several hours and saw a glass of clear liquid on the counter. You start to take a big gulp just as your mom comes in and screams to stop. She explains that what's in the glass is chlorine, not water! You thought the liquid would quench your thirst, but this was not true. In reality, it would have made you very sick. Even this simple example illustrates the importance of knowing the difference between what is real and what is not real.

If you know the right answers to the questions of truth and reality, you will enjoy life with greater confidence. It's really awesome to build your life on well-thought-out answers to these big questions. Are you ready to love learning about wisdom? If so, this chapter will point your thinking in the right direction.

Philosophy: The study of truth, knowledge, and the nature of ultimate reality.

Should Christians Use Their Minds?

Some people contend that things like science and reason are opposed to religion—that philosophy and religion are enemies. Unfortunately, even some Christians think this way. For example, some read Colossians, where the Apostle Paul writes, "See to it that no one takes you captive through hollow and deceptive philosophy" (Colossians 2:8, NIV), and they conclude that God does not want us to meddle in something as vain and deceitful as the study of philosophy.

However, people who point to this passage as a warning against studying philosophy overlook the rest of the verse. Paul describes the kind of philosophy he is warning against: philosophy that depends on "*human tradition and the basic principles of this world rather than on Christ.*" Here Paul is warning us not to be duped by bad "humanistic" philosophy. Rather, Paul wants us to build our philosophy upon the worldview foundation of Christ.

Throughout the Bible Christians are told to use our God-given ability to reason. For example, Isaiah quotes God as pleading with His people, "Come now, let us reason together…" (Isaiah 1:18, NIV). In the New Testament, Peter urges Christians to "[A]lways be prepared to give an answer to everyone who asks you to give the reason for the hope that you have" (1 Peter 3:15, NIV). In fact, God designed our minds to think by using the rules of logic. Jesus is even called "the Word of God" (John 1:1, NIV). The term *Word* is translated from a Greek term, *logos,* meaning "logic" or "reason." So John is telling us that God is expressing Himself to us in a reasonable way through the person of Jesus. Jesus was the best way God could deliver His message of salvation to us!

God does not bypass our minds when it comes to knowing Him. In fact, many people have become Christians by using their minds. A number of years ago, a man by the name of C.E.M. Joad (pronounced "Joe-ad"), who had spent most of his life convinced that God didn't exist, appeared on British radio with a famous atheist philosopher, Bertrand Russell. The two of them attacked Christianity, trying to show that it was unreasonable, that belief in God made no sense. Later in his life, however, he began to reason differently, saying, "It is because…the religious view of the universe seems to me to cover more of the facts of experience than any other that I have been gradually led to embrace it." He concluded his long journey toward Christ by admitting, "I now believe that the balance of reasonable considerations tells heavily in favor of the religious, even of the Christian view of the world."[1] Joad finally determined that Christianity made the most sense of the world, and this reasoning lead him to accept Christ as his Savior.

For another example of an atheist-turned-theist, consider Anthony Flew. Flew, like Joad, is a British philosopher who defended atheism for most of his life. When he reached his eighties, though, he had a change of mind. In an interview in 2005, Flew described his personal odyssey from atheism to theism and the central place the design argument had in his journey. Flew currently believes "…the most impressive arguments for God's existence are those that are supported by recent scientific discoveries." He came to this conclusion because "the findings of more than fifty years of DNA research have provided materials for a new and enormously powerful argument to design."[2]

While Flew hastens to add that his spiritual belief is not in the God of the Bible, but in an impersonal deity (similar to the Deistic conception of God discussed in the previous unit), the fact remains that another world-class philosopher has re-visited the argument from design and found it compelling.

In this chapter, you will look for biblical answers to the two major questions of philosophy: *What is true?* and *How do we know*? Along the way, you'll find answers to other interesting questions, such as…

1. What is the relationship between Christianity and science?
2. Is the study of philosophy practical?
3. What happens when I die?
4. Are miracles possible?

What is Truth?

The first question of philosophy is *What is true?* Most people agree there is a difference between truth and falsehood—between an accurate belief and one that is in error. So when we use the word **truth**, we are referring to a thought, belief, or statement that *correctly reflects the world as it really is.*

For example, if you believe that your wallet contains $40 when, in reality, it contains $4, then your belief does not correspond with reality (and you are in for a rude awakening when you try to buy that $35 shirt!). Whenever a belief does not correspond with reality, it is called *false*. On the other hand, if there is $40 in your wallet, then your belief lines up with reality and is *true*.

This same principal goes for all of your beliefs. Consider this cheesy example: what if someone believed that the moon is made of green cheese? Well, astronauts have traveled to the moon and found it to be made of dust and rocks, not cheese. Therefore it is correct to say, "The belief that the moon is made of green cheese is not true."

Misunderstanding Truth

Now that we've defined what we mean by "true" and given a couple of examples, we need to clear up two misconceptions. The first misconception is that believing something makes it so. A lot of people fall for this one!

Think again about the idea that the moon is made of green cheese. Does believing the moon is made of green cheese somehow magically change the composition of the moon? Obviously not. Remember, "truth" is defined as something that accurately reflects the way things really are. So no matter how sincerely or how firmly you believe something, believing it *simply cannot make it true*.

Here is another example. Have you ever answered a math problem incorrectly? Your teacher told you that it was okay, because "it's your truth," right? Not likely. But why not? Simply put, what is incorrect is not true. It doesn't matter how sincere or passionate you are. If you sincerely think that $2 + 2 = 3$, then you are sincerely wrong. Such a belief, *because it does not match reality*, is false.

These examples help illustrate that believing something does not automatically make it true. You need something more than just a belief—you need to find out if that belief matches up with reality.

There is a second common misconception about truth. Maybe you've heard someone say, "That's just your truth." This is commonly applied to subjects like religion or ethics. However, to say that something is true for one person and false for another is to actually misuse the words *truth* and *opinion*. That's because truth is not just what you personally believe (or prefer). For example, if you were to say to your friend, "Look out, a bus is speeding straight toward you," your friend would never respond, "That's just your truth." Everyone knows that in the real world either a bus is coming down the road or a bus is not coming down the road. And if a bus is coming, a statement to that effect is true for everyone, not just for some people!

When someone says, "That's just your truth," he or she may mean, "That's just your *opinion*." People have different opinions, and all opinions are not equally true. Therefore, you shouldn't say, "That's just your truth." According to our definition, truth is a statement, belief, or idea that correctly reflects the real world. If a particular statement, belief, or idea is true, then it is true for everybody, not just the person making the statement or holding the belief or idea.

So what does all this mean for you? The bottom line is that truth is universal. If a statement is true, then it's true for everyone, no matter who they are, where they live, or even when they lived. Thus, either

---

Truth: A thought, statement, or belief that correctly reflects the real world.

Jesus rose from the dead or He didn't; either reality is merely matter or it is not; either Buddhism is the path to enlightenment or it isn't. As you can see, understanding the idea of truth has significant implications for your life and everyone else's, too.

How Do We Know?

Now that you have a definition of truth, let's explore the idea of how we *know* what we know (the ten dollar word for this pursuit is **epistemology**). There are many methods for knowing what is true in addition to revelation. For example, you can appeal to *authority*. None of us saw Abraham Lincoln assassinated, yet we are confident this happened because we have it on good authority that this event occurred, mostly from eyewitness accounts and other historical sources.

Another way of gaining knowledge is through our *intuition*. Somehow every human being who has ever lived has known that it is wrong to kill the innocent. For example, Cain knew it was wrong to kill his brother, Abel, even though he lived before God gave the Ten Commandments to Moses. Our God-given human conscience, which is part of us created in God's image, provides this innate understanding about right and wrong.

We can also know truth through *reason*. For instance, Can a man be a married bachelor? Of course we know this is not logical. Common sense tells us that one thing and its opposite cannot both be true at the same time and in the same way.

Another way of knowing things is through *personal experience*. Have you ever tried to put a square peg in a round hole? If you have, than you know through practical experience something about how shapes fit together. This way of knowing is important for science to work.

Epistemology: The study of how we know what we know.

Christianity and Science

The scientific method involves observation, experimentation, and, of course, the use of our five senses (what you hear, see, feel, touch, or smell) to learn what the physical world is really like. For instance, science tells us that "what goes up must come down." Through observation (i.e., seeing) and experimentation (i.e., testing), we have figured out something about our world—we call it "gravity." Simply put, **science** is a means of investigating the world through empirical observation, experimentation, and hypothesizing. Science can and does deliver knowledge when it comes to understanding our physical/material universe, but it is not the only means for learning about the totality of reality, i.e., the supernatural realm.

However, in recent years a false idea about science and knowledge has become increasingly popular. **Empiricism** is the belief that science is the *only* reliable method for gaining knowledge. This belief claims that science and Christianity don't mix—that science is actually opposed to Christianity because science is based on *fact* gained from the five senses, while religion is based only on *belief* (defined as a subjective conviction not based on any evidence). This is why public schools today refuse to teach about the Creator in biology classes, claiming that God is a religious concept but that evolution is based on science. (We'll explore this idea more in Unit 04.)

What should be your answer to this belief? First of all, in contrast to the current trend separating religion and science, Christians have every reason to be engaged in scientific study. After all, only those who believe in God expect the world to be the way it is. Christians reason that if the Creator of the world is intelligent and we are created in His image, then we can use our minds to know more about Him and how He made the universe.

In addition, Christians believe that God designed our senses, and that they are reliable for telling us what is really there. For example, if we see a tree, there is really a tree before us, not just an illusion made up by our imaginations. Therefore, we can have confidence that our observations of nature are true. Even though we may not completely comprehend everything we observe (e.g., seeing a magic trick but not knowing how it's done) or though our senses may sometimes be misled (e.g., a desert mirage), we can generally trust our observations to give us accurate knowledge about the world.

Science: A means of investigating the world through empirical observation, experimentation, and hypothesizing.

In contrast, someone who does not believe in God must assume there is no plan or purpose to the universe because there is no one to do the planning. Further, this person assumes that the universe came about through a random process. For the atheist, studying the world is no different than studying the accidental shapes that clouds make.

How would you respond to someone who believes this way? You may recall from the last chapter our discussion about the "mind argument." This argument demonstrated why it makes good sense to believe in God. We can use this line of reasoning to show why atheistic beliefs do not stand up to reason or experience, and cannot account for the scientific method.

To revisit the mind argument one more time, imagine for a moment that everything came about by chance, without God (i.e., an Intelligent Designer) and without any purpose or ultimate reason for it to exist. This means that your mind exists purely because of blind accidental processes in the natural universe.

Empiricism: The belief that science is the only reliable method for gaining knowledge.

In that case, how can you trust your thoughts? Suppose, for example, that while playing Scrabble, your tiles spelled out the words "Call Mom." Would you assume that this random occurrence was actually a message? Would you grab your phone and call your mother? Probably not, but why? Because, this random arrangement of letters was merely accidental. It was a mindless, random event with no real purpose behind it.

Similarly, if only matter exists and if we are just the accidental occurrence of random collision of atoms, then why would we assume that anything we think is true? Of course, on the other hand, if there is a God, then the universe is more than merely matter, and we have reason to believe in our ability to know what is true and what is false. In this case, it seems perfectly reasonable to trust our thoughts.

The Foundation of Modern Science

There's another difficulty with the atheist's view, though. The fact is that the scientific method has revealed an abundance of orderly processes at work throughout the universe. We even refer to the discovery of this order in terms of physical laws, such as the "law of gravity." But how would a universe of molecules randomly bumping into each other arrange themselves into consistent laws?

If the universe displays orderly, law-like activity, and laws don't come about by themselves, then there must be something more than the material universe of molecules in motion. This leads us to infer that a Super-Intelligent Being must exist who created the law-like behavior of the cosmos—the logical source of all the orderly processes we see. Therefore, to make sense of the laws of nature, we must assume that God is real. And this is the starting place for scientific research.

Not only does our mind tell us that the existence of God is necessary to make sense of our world, the story of the development of modern science demonstrates how the modern scientific enterprise actually grew out of ideas found in the Christian religion. And here you see how practical a Christian worldview can be.

A study of the history of science shows that the Christian worldview provided the foundation for modern science. The pioneers of modern science were all working from the foundation of a Christian worldview. Take, for example, Roger Bacon, who pioneered the experimental method, or Johannes Kepler, who discovered the laws of planetary motion, or Sir Isaac Newton, co-inventor of calculus and discoverer of the law of gravity and the three laws of motion. Because of their belief in a Creator, these scientists expected nature to be understandable, orderly, and predictable. In addition, they believed that humans could understand nature and discover its order.

C.S. Lewis explains that humans became scientific because they expected to find laws in nature, and "they expected Law in Nature because they believed in a Legislator"[3]—that is, an Intelligent Lawgiver. The first modern scientists understood the connection between what they believed about God and how they thought about the natural universe. For instance, Newton wrote, "This most beautiful system of the sun, planets, and comets could only proceed from the counsel and dominion of an intelligent Being."[4]

All of this makes perfect sense from the perspective of a Christian worldview. Francis Schaeffer writes, "Since the world had been created by a reasonable God, [scientists] were not surprised to find a correlation between themselves as observers and the thing observed…Without this foundation, modern Western science would not have been born."[5]

Think again about that last statement. What would it mean for your life today if modern science had never been born? You would not have cars, air conditioned houses, or MP3 players. No computers, lights, or even refrigerators. All of these things, and so much more, are the direct result of the technology that developed as a result of modern Western science. So if you like the high-tech society in which you live, you have Christianity to thank for it.

Contrary to what you hear through the media and in much of public education today, history reveals that mankind's greatest minds—scholars, mathematicians, doctors, lawyers, historians, and, yes, scientists and inventors—have been and continue to be Christians. There is no conflict between the Christian worldview and the study of science.

> "The most beautiful system of the sun, planets, and comets could only proceed from the counsel and dominion of an intelligent Being."
> — Sir Isaac Newton

But how does all of this tie together? First, early scientists had the idea that God exists and that He is a rational Being. They also believed that God created the universe to behave in certain ways. Furthermore, they believed that man is made in God's image and can use reason to understand things about God's creation. As a result of these beliefs, it made sense to use their five senses and their rational minds to investigate the natural world and find out what God was thinking when He put it all together. In essence, Christianity was "the mother of modern science."[6] Therefore, you cannot separate the religious ideas found in Christianity and our modern understanding of science. It is ultimately futile to try.

Now that you have a better understanding of what we mean by truth and how to know it, it's time to move on to what we mean by "reality."

What Is Reality?

The study of what is really real is called **metaphysics**. Metaphysics seeks to answer the question *What is real?* There are three main ways to answer this question.

Those people who do not believe in God answer this question by saying that reality is composed *only* of the material or physical universe. This is called **materialism**. If nature is all there is, then what we consider supernatural—God, angels, or the spirit realm—is simply an overactive imagination at work. God is not real, merely a man-made invention.

> **Metaphysics**: The study of the nature of reality.

Others, who are convinced that God is an impersonal force, believe reality is composed *only* of the spiritual. This is called **spiritualism**, the belief that ultimate reality is completely spiritual or immaterial and that what seems like physical stuff is actually just an illusion.

Christians (and Muslims) propose a third alternative between these two extremes.[7] **Supernaturalism** is the belief that reality is composed of the physical universe *and* a supernatural realm. In other words, the physical universe, which is known through our five senses, is only part of what exists. Reality also includes God, a non-physical being, who created the universe and who continues to interact with it, sometimes in miraculous ways.

Also, supernaturalism holds that human beings are more than just physical beings, and yet are also more than mere spiritual beings with no physical parts. It is the belief that a human being is a wonderfully designed combination of spiritual and physical reality (Genesis 1:27 and Psalm 139:14). This important aspect of what makes us human will be explored further in unit five.

> **Materialism**: The belief that reality is composed of only the material or physical.
>
> **Spiritualism**: The belief that reality is completely spiritual or immaterial.
>
> **Supernaturalism**: The belief that reality is composed of both the physical and non-physical.

Miracles

Another aspect related to reality is the issue of whether miracles are possible. Some people say that miracles are not possible because they go against science. Yet we find many examples of miracles in the Bible. How should we explain this? Exactly what is a miracle and what are some objections to believing in miracles?

Simply put, a **miracle** occurs when God *supernaturally* intervenes in the natural course of history. In other words, if things were left to carry on as they normally would, given the laws of nature, then no miracles would occur. Yet when God decides to accomplish something particular in the midst of our world, He intervenes, causing nature to act in a way it normally would not have.

There are many examples of miracles in the Bible. Some of the more prominent miracles of the Bible have to do with creation, judgment, and redemption. For example, in the beginning God created the universe from nothing (Genesis 1), the first man from dust (Genesis 2:7), and the first woman from the rib of the first man (Genesis 2:21–23). None of these would have occurred naturally.

In judgment God brought the great flood (Genesis 6:17), confused human language at the Tower of Babel (Genesis 11:7), destroyed Sodom and Gomorrah with burning sulfur from heaven (Genesis 19:24), and brought ten stunning plagues upon the Egyptians so they would know that the Lord is God and there is no other (Exodus 7:5; 8:10; 9:14).

In deliverance and redemption God brought the Hebrews through the parted waters of the Red Sea and destroyed the Egyptian army in the very same waters (Exodus 14:21–28). The ultimate act of redemption took place when Jesus died on the cross for our sins and conquered death through His resurrection (1 Corinthians 12:22–23, 57). All of these events could not have happened according to the natural laws of the universe. They all require miraculous (i.e., supernatural) intervention.

As you might have guessed, not everyone is impressed with the biblical accounts of such miracles. There are a few common objections to miracles. Some people claim that miracles cannot happen since a miracle is a violation of the laws of nature, which cannot be broken. But this is usually based on the *assumption* that God does not exist. If you simply assume that God does not exist, then of course you will conclude that miracles are not possible.

However, if God does exist and created the natural world, who is to say that God could not intervene in the natural course of events? For someone to successfully argue that miracles cannot occur, he or she would need to successfully argue that God does not exist. However, we have already seen in the last chapter that we have solid reasons to believe God does exist. Therefore, God *can* intervene in His world in whatever miraculous ways He chooses.

Other people say that since human beings have a tendency to believe in the fabulous and fantastic, we cannot trust stories about miracles. However, though it is true that some humans are gullible and others may tell tall tales, it does not follow that miracles cannot or have not occurred. All this objection can claim is that you should not believe everything you hear, and that you should examine the evidence on a case-by-case basis.

Still others have argued that since miracles occur in all different religions and these religions argue against each other, then we have no reason to believe that one religion is true and the others false. But this objection assumes that all the miracle stories are equally true. The Bible tells us, though, that even false teachers can perform miraculous signs. Again this raises the issue of carefully examining each instance of a reported miracle to determine if it is true before believing it. Therefore, this objection does not stand.

But there is one miracle that distinguishes Christianity from all other religions: the resurrection

Miracle: God's supernatural intervention in the natural course of history.

of Jesus. Not only is this the crowning miracle of our faith, it is also essential to our understanding of what it means to be a Christian. If the miracle of the resurrection is true, than it means that Jesus is who He claimed to be, the Son of God and the Forgiver of sins.

What Happens When I Die?

While exploring the topic of what is real, there is another question that everybody is interested in—*What happens when I die?* Worldviews that deny the existence of God, such as materialism, also deny that humans live beyond the grave. On the other hand, a predominant feature of Christian supernaturalism is the reality of life after death.

Many of the reasons that Christians believe in life after death are found in the authority of the Bible. First, Jesus promised the thief on the cross that he would be in paradise with Jesus on the day of his death (Luke 23:43). Paul also noted that, for a Christian, to be apart from the body (a way of describing death) is to be with Jesus (2 Corinthians 5:8; Philippians 1:23–24). John not only described the souls of the slain calling out to God, but also the reassuring answer given to them by God (Revelation 6:9–11). John also spoke of the dead as those who are blessed (Revelation 14:13), which means they must still exist in some way in order to be blessed. Added to these illustrations of life after death is the account of the transfiguration of Jesus, where Moses, along with Elijah, appeared and talked to Him (Matthew 17:3).

But the major reason Christians believe in an afterlife is the physical resurrection of Jesus. While some people deny that Jesus was resurrected from the dead, the historical evidence supporting this incredible event is very convincing. (There will be much more on this subject in unit ten of this study.)

In addition to the reasons for believing that Jesus' resurrection is true historically and biblically, the Bible explains the theological significance of His rising from the dead. Without the resurrection of Jesus, no one could be saved from his or her sins (Romans 10:9; 1 Corinthians 15:1–7). As the Apostle Paul states, "If there is no resurrection of the dead, then not even Christ has been raised. And if Christ has not been raised, our preaching is useless and so is your faith. More than that, we are then found to be false witnesses about God, for we have testified about God that he raised Christ from the dead...If only for this life we have hope in Christ, we are to be pitied more than all men. But Christ has indeed been raised from the dead, the first fruits of those who have fallen asleep" (1 Corinthians 15:13–20).

Conclusion

Throughout this chapter you have seen that the Bible teaches that reality is made up of both the physical and spiritual aspects of the universe. This philosophy is called supernaturalism. Christians believe that there is a physical universe and that non-physical entities exist, such as God, angels, demons, thoughts, and souls.

Christianity also affirms that truth is what conforms to reality as it really is. This means that truth is not simply someone's opinion or belief, as though you could create reality by merely wishing that something is true. Christianity holds that reality is consistent, tangible, and designed by God so that it can be scientifically investigated and understood.

Christians note that it is reasonable, even necessary, for there to be a distinction between our brains (which are physical) and our minds (which are spiritual). Thus our thoughts are not simply physical events (the result of chemical reactions in our brains), but mental events (dependent on our supernatural souls to be initiated). Moreover, our thoughts, ideas, and the things we say are either true or false depending on how they fit with reality—the way things actually are.

Endnotes

[1] C. E. M. Joad, *Recovery of Belief* (London, UK: Faber and Faber, 1955), 16, 22.

[2] Taken from an interview at http://www.biola.edu/antonyflew/.

[3] C. S. Lewis, as quoted in *A Mind Awake*, ed. Clyde S. Kilby (New York, NY: Harcourt, Brace & World, 1968), 234.

[4] *Principia*, Book III; cited in *Newton's Philosophy of Nature: Selections from his writings*, ed. H.S. Thayer (New York, NY: Hafner Library of Classics, 1953), 42.

[5] Francis A. Schaeffer, *How Should We Then Live?* (Old Tappan, NJ: Fleming J. Revell, 1976), 134–133.

[6] C. S. Lewis, *Broadcast Talks* (London, UK: 1946), 37–38.

[7] Although Jews and Muslims also believe in aspects of supernaturalism, we won't discuss them in this text. See "The Compact Guide to World Religions," edited by Dean Halverson, for more information.

A World of Ideas
Reading Discussion Questions

1. What is philosophy? What key questions does philosophy seek to answer? What is the key idea of Christian philosophy?

2. Should Christians use their minds? Why or why not?

3. Define "truth," and explain the two misconceptions people often have concerning truth.

4. How do we "know" what is real?

5. What is science? Is it the only way to learn about reality?

6. Are science and Christianity opposed to each other? Why or why not?

7. How did Christian beliefs lead to the development and flourishing of Western science?

8. What is a miracle? What are three common objections to miracles and how do they fail?

9. How would you define the following terms: epistemology, empiricism, metaphysics, materialism, spiritualism, and supernaturalism?

Philosophy Paragraph
Assignment

*As you continue your study, write your own paragraph titled **My Christian Worldview of Philosophy**. You will be able to correct it, add to it, put it into your Lightbearers Journal, and memorize it. Below is a checklist to help you with this assignment.*

- ☐ The paragraph begins with a definition of philosophy.
- ☐ It includes why we should use our minds.
- ☐ It includes how to know what is true.
- ☐ It includes the nature of reality.
- ☐ It includes why miracles are possible.
- ☐ It includes what happens after we die.

Wisdom
Exercise

The wonderful philosophy books of Proverbs and Ecclesiastes in our Scriptures are the foundational study of philosophy. Work through the first six chapters of Proverbs in class. The section on Ecclesiastes will be optional extra credit.

Proverbs
Chapter 1

1. What is the main theme of this chapter?

2. How is this to be understood and applied in today's world?

3. What will I do with what I have learned from this chapter of Proverbs?

Chapter 2

4. What is the main theme of this chapter?

5. How is this to be understood and applied in today's world?

6. What will I do with what I have learned from this chapter of Proverbs?

Chapter 3

7. What is the main theme of this chapter?

8. How is this to be understood and applied in today's world?

9. What will I do with what I have learned from this chapter of Proverbs?

Chapter 4

10. What is the main theme of this chapter?

11. How is this to be understood and applied in today's world?

12. What will I do with what I have learned from this chapter of Proverbs?

Chapter 5

13. What is the main theme of this chapter?

14. How is this to be understood and applied in today's world?

15. What will I do with what I have learned from this chapter of Proverbs?

Chapter 6

16. What is the main theme of this chapter?

17. How is this to be understood and applied in today's world?

18. What will I do with what I have learned from this chapter of Proverbs?

Ecclesiastes

19. What things did Solomon pursue to try to find meaning in life?

20. What is the value of knowing this now in my life?

21. What is Solomon's final conclusion about the truly meaningful earthly life?

re:View: Seen
Video Discussion Questions

Synopsis: The grand curtain opens, and a wonderful story begins to play out before a packed house. Laughter, anger, sadness, and joy are felt by all—except the person whose life it is about. As the play continues, Darren realizes he is seeing his own life and, unfortunately, everyone is watching.

1. When does Darren realize it is his life on stage? What about Deborah?

2. How do the people in the audience respond throughout the play?

3. What is the pivotal point of the play? What caused it? How was it resolved? How did the audience respond?

4. If you had a similar opportunity to change something about your life, what would it be? How would this change affect those who are watching?

5. What do you think the guy at the end of the play meant when he said, "Will you be the changed or the change?"

The Christian Influence on Science
Presentation Assignment

In this assignment, you will have the opportunity to research an influential scientist who was also a Christian. The class as a whole will create a bulletin board displaying the various fields of study developed by these Christian scientists. Write one paragraph on your assigned scientist (or one of your own choosing, with the teacher's approval) from the list below, showing his or her contribution to a particular area of the development of modern science.

In addition, bring one or two typed sentences summarizing the scientific field and contribution your scientist made, suitable for pinning on the bulletin board, and a picture (if available). Give these to the group in charge of putting up the display.

Be prepared to discuss the benefits that have resulted from applying a biblical worldview of reality to our human condition. How have the research and discoveries of these men and women contributed to the betterment of mankind?

1. Robert Grosseteste
2. Roger Bacon
3. Leonardo da Vinci
4. Sir Francis Bacon
5. Johannes Kepler
6. Galileo Galilei
7. William Harvey
8. Blaise Pascal
9. Robert Boyle
10. Sir Isaac Newton
11. Antony van Leeuwenhoek
12. Carolus Linnaeus
13. William Herschel

14. John Herschel
15. Samuel F. B. Morse
16. Michael Faraday
17. Charles Babbage
18. James Prescott Joule
19. Lord Kelvin
20. James Clerk Maxwell
21. Gregor Mendel
22. Louis Pasteur
23. Joseph Lister
24. Henrietta Swan Leavitt
25. George Washington Carver
26. Wernher von Braun

re:View: Response to Culture A
Video Discussion Questions

Synopsis: We can isolate ourselves from culture, be assimilated by it, or engage it with the heart and mind of Jesus Christ. What would the latter look like in our day?

1. What are the three responses we can have to culture?

2. What are the three actions these responses lead to?

3. Why do many Christians choose to withdraw from culture?

4. Why do many Christians choose to assimilate into culture?

5. What are some ways we can become aware of what's going on in culture without becoming a part of it?

6. Nine Inch Nails (Trent Reznor) sings, "Your God is dead and no one cares / If there's a hell, I'll see you there." Give an example of how Christians could respond to this by being offended, by assimilating, and by engaging the culture.

re:View: Response to Culture B
Video Discussion Questions

Synopsis: Paul "makes himself a slave" to everyone in order that he may win them. The passages that follow describe how he tries to get into the hearts and minds of people so he can build a bridge to Jesus Christ for them. How can we do this on a practical level?

Oh, Those Amazing Feats
Reading

Experiences are tricky things. They come without interpretations—we supply those ourselves, or we allow others to supply them for us. *Why did that happen? What does it mean?* These questions show our desire for immediate understanding and significant meaning in life. If we are not careful, we can be deceived by false interpretations.

The popular human potential speaker Anthony (Tony) Robbins says you have a special mental power. He even claims that you can awaken this "giant within" through such amazing acts as walking barefoot across a bed of hot coals. So, at his conferences, the conferees line-up to try their hands—or rather their feet, as the case may be—at fire-walking. Tony claims that if you focus your inherent mental powers, you will be enabled to trek the bed of hot coals without burn or blister.

And what could be more wondrous? Well, perhaps a lesson in physics.

Imagine. The scene is set. The temperature gauge rises to blistering-hot temperatures. The conferees are focusing their mental energies intently. Some are nevertheless nervous; others are quietly confident. But...off they go, traversing the bed of hot coals in their bare feet. In a flash it's all over. They did it! Look Ma, no burns, no blisters...and no wonder.

Certainly, the coals are very hot indeed, there is no debating that. But the questions begin to arise when we find out that coals don't conduct heat very quickly. What I mean is that a bed of hot coals may be blisteringly hot (according to the temperature gauge), but unlike other substances that could be just as hot, coals don't immediately transfer their heat. So if you hurriedly scoot your feet across those coals (no standing around, of course), you won't get burned. No wonder.

Now, think about your oven. Let's say you want to bake some cookies. You pre-heat the oven to around 375°. After the oven is pre-heated, you can stick your hand into the oven for a few moments. But the air in that oven is about 375°! So, why don't you get burned? Simply because air (like coals) is not a good conductor of heat. But, what if you were to touch the preheated rack? Maybe you know what would happen. Maybe you have touched it before, by accident. Without a hot-pad, we are at the mercy of searing hot metal. Wow, what a burn!

Where is all this leading us? Patience, patience, we'll get to the punch line soon enough. Just focus your mental energies a little longer.

So, I claim that hot coals are not as dangerous as one might think at first blush. I have also claimed that when compared to a 375° oven rack, hot coals are not so hot (at least not at first touch, and especially not if they have a layer of ash on top of them and your feet are sweaty). So, where's my proof? I have no statistics. No pictures. No video. But I do recommend that you *not* try this at home!

All I ask is this. For those who think that fire-walking is such an awesome exercise, line up a row of skillets set to about 375°, and scoot those amazing tootsies across as fast as you can. But remember...the skillets better have a non-stick surface, since the skillets will conduct the heat much more efficiently than the ash-covered coals! But, then again, don't forget my previous plea: *Please don't try this at home!*

Spiritual powers? Supernatural phenomena? Certainly they exist. But the common feat of fire-walking is not in that category. Rather, those who claim that fire-walking is the result of their spiritual powers are peddling the merely mysterious, or basic physics, as being magnificently wondrous. These people are simply deceivers (and they make a lot of money at it).

The power of the mind indeed...to see what we believe. Or, rather, to be deceived by what we believe.

Until next time, don't be taken captive through fine sounding arguments and empty deceit (Colossians 2:8). And may our great and gracious heavenly Father richly bless you as you seek to bring every thought captive to the obedience of Christ Jesus our Lord (2 Corinthians 10:5).*

---

* Used by permission. Copyright © 2003, Kevin Bywater. All rights reserved.

Oh, Those Amazing Feats
Reading Discussion Questions

1. Why must we be careful when interpreting our experiences?

2. According to Tony Robbins, we must awaken the "giant within." What is this giant and what is a way it can be awakened?

3. Why is the act of walking across hot coals not quite as amazing as we may first think?

4. Why do you not get burned when you reach into a 375° oven?

5. What experiment could you conduct to prove the author's point? Is it recommended?

6. What are those who promote fire-walking relying upon?

Unit Two

The Trouble with the Elephant
Reading

The ancient fable of the blind men and the elephant is often used to illustrate the fact that every faith represents just one part of the larger truth about God. However, the attempt is doomed before it gets started. Here's why.

In the children's book *The Blind Men and the Elephant*, Lillian Quigley retells the ancient fable of six blind men who visit the palace of the Rajah and encounter an elephant for the first time. As each touches the animal with his hands, he announces his discoveries.

The first blind man put out his hand and touched the side of the elephant. "How smooth! An elephant is like a wall." The second blind man put out his hand and touched the trunk of the elephant. "How round! An elephant is like a snake." The third blind man put out his hand and touched the tusk of the elephant. "How sharp! An elephant is like a spear." The fourth blind man put out his hand and touched the leg of the elephant. "How tall! An elephant is like a tree." The fifth blind man reached out his hand and touched the ear of the elephant. "How wide! An elephant is like a fan." The sixth blind man put out his hand and touched the tail of the elephant. "How thin! An elephant is like a rope."[1] An argument ensued, each blind man thinking his own perception of the elephant was the correct one. The Rajah, awakened by the commotion, called out from the balcony. "The elephant is a big animal," he said. "Each man touched only one part. You must put all the parts together to find out what an elephant is like." Enlightened by the Rajah's wisdom, the blind men reached agreement. "Each one of us knows only a part. To find out the whole truth we must put all the parts together."

This fable is often used to illustrate one of two points. The religious application holds that every faith represents just one part of a larger truth about God. Each has only a piece of the truth, ultimately leading to God by different routes. Advocates of Eastern religions are fond of using the parable in this way.

The second application is used by skeptics who hold that cultural biases have so seriously blinded us that we can never know the true nature of things. This view, *de rigueur* in the university, is called post-modernism.

This skepticism holds for all areas of truth, including the rational, the religious, and the moral. In *Folkways*, a classic presentation of cultural relativism, anthropologist William Graham Sumner argues that morality is not objective in any sense. "Every attempt to win an outside standpoint from which to reduce the whole to an absolute philosophy of truth and right, based on an unalterable principle, is delusion," he states.[2]

Sumner is making a very strong assertion about knowledge. He says that all claims to know objective truth are false because each of us is imprisoned in his or her own culture, incapable of seeing beyond the limits of personal bias. Sumner concludes, therefore, that truth is relative to culture and that no objective standard exists. There are three serious problems with the elephant, but first a procedural concern.

Pictures Don't Prove

There is a difference between an assertion and an argument. An assertion is just a point of view, an opinion. An argument is a point of view supported by reasons that demonstrate the view is a good one.

The parable of the blind men and the elephant is a clear and powerful illustration, but an illustration is a mere point of view in more vivid terms. It is not an argument, but a well-articulated assertion. It doesn't prove anything in itself. It doesn't make the point *valid*—it only makes it *clear*.

Proving the point is another matter. It requires evidence and justification. Given the illustration of the blind men and the elephant, why should anyone believe this parable actually describes the way things really are?

Here are three reasons why the illustration fails at what it attempts.

PROBLEM #1: EXTERNAL INFORMATION

The first serious limitation is that even though the men are blind, the elephant isn't necessarily mute. This is a factor the illustration doesn't allow for. *What if the elephant speaks?*

The claim of Christianity is that man doesn't learn about God by groping around in the dark. Instead, discovery is through God's own self-disclosure. He is not passive and silent, leaving us to guess about His nature. God tells us what He is like and what He wants.

If God speaks, this changes everything. All contrary opinions are silenced, all conjectures are put to rest. God has made Himself known, giving us a standard by which to measure all other religious claims. The parable of the blind men does not take this possibility into account. Yet three of the world's great religions—Christianity, Judaism, and Islam—make this claim.

PROBLEM #2: DEDUCTIVE, NOT INDUCTIVE

There is a second problem with the parable. It presumes that Christians reject pluralism because they lack exposure to other beliefs, much as the blind men erred because each explored only a part of the elephant. Had they searched more completely, they would have seen their error. Christians are just uninformed.

This is not the case, though. Christians reject pluralism, in part, because defining elements of different religions contradict each other. It's not an inductive problem of discovery; it's a problem of coherence.

Judaism teaches that Jesus is not the Messiah. Christianity teaches that He is. Jesus is either the Messiah or He's not. Both groups can't be right. The notion that Christianity and Judaism are somehow equally true is contradictory, like square circles.

What if the elephant in the parable was a miniature, so small the blind man could close his hand and completely encompass the elephant? If another then claimed, "The elephant is bigger than a house," the first would be correct to disagree. Why? Because an elephant can't be small enough to fit into one's hand and also be as big as a house at the same time.

No possible future discovery is going to change the fact that religious claims cannot be harmonized. Rather, exploration complicates the issue. The more someone knows about the core beliefs of various faiths, the more complex the problem of harmonizing becomes.

Appealing to the ubiquity of something like the "golden rule" is no help. It is a moral action guide that says almost nothing about any religion's fundamental understanding of the shape of the world. Profound contradictions between foundational beliefs are not removed by pointing out shared moral proverbs.

Contradictory claims can't be simultaneously true. This has nothing to do with further discovery. Religious pluralism is false on deductive grounds, not inductive.

PROBLEM #3: CONTRADICTING FOUNDATION

The third objection is the most serious. The application of this parable to issues of truth is doomed before it gets started. The view commits suicide; it is self-refuting. Here's how.

There's only one way to know that our cultural or religious biases blind us to the larger truth that all religions lead to God—someone who sees clearly without bias must tell us so. This parable, though, teaches that such objectivity is impossible.

For example, in order for William Graham Sumner to conclude that all moral claims are an illusion, he must first escape the illusion himself. He must have a full and accurate view of the entire picture—just as the king had of the blind men and the elephant from his balcony. The Rajah was in a position of privileged access to the truth. Because he could see clearly, he was able to correct those who were blind.

Such a privileged view, though, is precisely what advocates of both religious pluralism and the radical skepticism of post-modernism deny. Completely objective assessments are illusions, they claim. The truth lies in some combination of opinions, or, for the more skeptical, is out of reach for any of us. However, this is precisely the kind of thing the parable does not allow you to say.

The skeptical view itself is a claim meant to be understood as an objective and true assessment of the world. It's as if someone said, "Each of us is blind," and then added, "but I'll tell you what the world really looks like." This is a clear contradiction.

The problem becomes obvious by offering this challenge. Ask the person offering the parable, "Where would *you* be in the illustration? When you apply this parable to the issue of truth, are you like one of the blind men, or are you like the king?"

This dilemma is unsolvable. If the story-teller is like one of the six who can't see—if he is one of the blind men groping around—how does he know everyone else is blind and has only a portion of the truth? On the other hand, if he fancies himself in the position of the king, how is it that he alone escapes the illusion that blinds the rest of us? The postmodernist finds himself in the position of offering the insight of the Rajah while simultaneously claiming he is one of the blind men.

At best, this parable—if it were accurate—might justify agnosticism, not religious pluralism. All we could really say is that it *may* be the case we're all groping about with no one in full possession of the truth—but this can't be known for sure.

The King Sees

If everyone truly is blind, then no one can know if he or anyone else is mistaken. Only someone who knows the whole truth can identify another on the fringes of it. In this story, only the king can do that—no one else.

The most ironic turn of all is that the parable of the six blind men and the elephant, to a great degree, is an accurate picture of reality. It's just been misapplied.

We are like blind men, fumbling around in the world searching for answers to life's deepest questions. From time to time, we seem to stumble upon some things that are true, but we're often confused and mistaken, just as the blind men were.

How do I know this? Because the King has spoken. He is above, instructing us, advising us of our mistakes, and correcting our error. The real question is: *Will we listen?*[*]

Endnotes

[1] Lillian Quigley, *The Blind Men and the Elephant* (New York: Charles Scribner's Sons, 1959). Possible original sources of the story are the *Jataka Tales*, a collection of Buddhist birth stories, and the *Pancatantra Stories*, Hindu religious instruction fables.

[2] William Graham Sumner, *Folkways* (Chicago: Ginn and Company, 1906), excerpted in Louis B. Pojman, ed., *Ethical Theory— Classical and Contemporary Readings* (Belmont, CA: Wadsworth, 1995), 27.

---

[*] This excerpt was used with the permission of Gregory Koukl and was taken from "The Trouble with the Elephant," *Clear Thinking* Vol. 3 (No. 1), 7–10.

The Trouble with the Elephant
Reading Discussion Questions

1. What two applications are taken from this fable?

2. Is the fable an assertion or an argument? Why?

3. What three reasons prove that this illustration of the elephant fails?

Chapter 3: Let's All Meditate on Our Navels

1. Name some of the beliefs Joe had.

2. Does the claim that people do not have separate selves match reality?

3. What human needs contradicted Joe's belief that the physical world is an illusion?

4. Does the claim that religious truth lies beyond common sense match reality?

5. Why were Joe's beliefs false?

6. How does real truth deal with the world around you?

7. What major issue of truth does the story about the Hindu and the teakettle illustrate?

8. Reflection Question: Since real truth is practical and sensible, what is your view and can you live that way? Does your worldview make sense with what you observe of the world?

9. Reflection Question: Did you use a certain logical "process" to reach your view of reality and truth? How do you know you can trust that process?

10. Reflection Question: Does having faith mean you have to choose between what you believe and what you observe? Why or why not?

LIGHTBEARERS

Unit Three

A Summit Ministries Curriculum

Day	UNIT 03: syllabus & outline	SW	✓
1	Read *A World of Ideas* Reading..	81	
2	Read *A World of Ideas* Reading..	Ditto	
3	Review *A World of Ideas* Reading Discussion Questions....................................	88	
4	Review *A World of Ideas* Reading Discussion Questions....................................	Ditto	
	Complete **Moral Relativism and Tolerance** Exercise..	89	
	Assign **Ethics Paragraph** [Rough Draft Due on Day 8]......................................	91	
5	Watch **"Mind Over Media"** Video..	---	
6	Review **"Mind Over Media"** Video Discussion Questions..................................	92	
	Complete **Ethical Evaluation** Exercise..	93	
	Assign **Electronic Media Fast** [Assignment Due on Day 11 or 12].....................	94	
7	Watch **"My Truth, Your Truth, Whose Truth?"** Video..	---	
8	Review **"My Truth, Your Truth, Whose Truth?"** Video Discussion Questions..............	95	
	Complete **Biblical Foundation for Ethics** Exercise..	96	
	Turn in **Ethics Paragraph** Rough Draft [Assignment Due on Day 13].................	---	
9	Read *How to Be Your Own Selfish Pig* Reading (Ch. 6)......................................	---	
10	Review *How to Be Your Own Selfish Pig* Reading Discussion Questions (Ch. 6).........	97	
11	Turn in & Share **Electronic Media Fast** Presentation Assignment.....................	---	
12	Turn in & Share **Electronic Media Fast** Presentation Assignment.....................	---	
13	Turn in **Ethics Paragraph** Assignment..	---	
	Take **Learn to Discern** Quiz...	---	
	Prepare **Unit 03** Test...	---	
14	Take **Unit 03** Test..	---	
15			

A World of Ideas:
How Should We Behave?

KEYS TO UNDERSTANDING

Key Question: How should we behave?

Key Idea: God is concerned about our inner attitudes as well as our outward actions. We discover what is moral by learning about God's character and how He has made us and the world.

Key Terms: ethics, individual moral relativism, cultural moral relativism, moral absolutes

Key Verses: Matthew 22:37–39 and Colossians 3:17

"Love the LORD your God . . . Love your neighbor as yourself" (Matthew 22:37–39, NIV).

"And whatever you do, in word or in deed, do everything in the name of the Lord Jesus, giving thanks to God the Father through him" (Colossians 3:17, HCSB).

Unit Three

Is There Any Real Right or Wrong?

You were probably brought up to believe that certain things are morally right and other things are wrong. But have you ever stopped to consider where these ideas of right and wrong come from?

Some people believe that society decides what is acceptable behavior. If this is true, then morality is simply whatever you have been raised to believe. But are the moral ideas you learned from your culture also true for someone living in a different culture halfway around the globe? Or how about someone living five hundred years ago? Or five hundred years in the future? Is morality something that changes according to time or location? Or how about from person to person? Who's to say what's right, anyway? Doesn't it all depend on the situation? In case you're confused, this chapter will help you sort out the truth about right and wrong.

As you've learned in earlier chapters, what someone believes in one area of life will affect what he or she believes in other areas of life. The "worldview tree" illustrates how all beliefs begin by answering questions about God (theology). Once you understand that God exists and learn what He is like, that knowledge becomes the root system that nourishes the rest of your worldview tree. The sap (theology) flows up the trunk and out the branch of philosophy to produce fruitful answers about what is real and how you arrive at true knowledge.

Now let's talk about another limb on the branch of someone's worldview tree—ethics. **Ethics** is the study of right and wrong, or how and why we make moral choices. Practically, though, it seeks to answer the question *How should we behave?*

In this chapter you will find out:

Ethics: The study of why and how we make moral choices.

. . . The true source of what is right and what is wrong.

. . . The difference between moral relativism and moral absolutes.

. . . How to maintain a close personal relationship with the God of the universe

Who's to Say What's Right?

Here's a little thought experiment to get you started thinking about your moral values. In the sentences below, circle the word that you feel best completes the sentence according to your ethical worldview:

1. Pushing a child down a staircase is.............................	a) spiteful	b) gratifying
2. Helping out with chores around the house is.............	a) evil	b) rewarding
3. Poking a stick into someone's eye is..........................	a) cruel	b) comical

Now, why did you make the choices you did? It may seem obvious that some behavior is right, and other behavior is wrong. You wouldn't think of pushing a child down the stairs, and it seems repulsive to poke a stick in someone's eye. But why are these actions wrong? Where do we get our ideas of "right" and "wrong" anyway? Or, in other words, *Who says what's right or wrong?*

There are basically three ways to answer this question. The first way of determining right and wrong is to base ethical decisions on personal preferences. In other words, "I say what is right for me." This position is called **individual moral relativism**. It means that morality is up to each person to decide. Moral decisions are thus *subjective,* or based upon our own personal feelings. In the end, morality is "relative" to each individual. This viewpoint also means that there are no moral mandates that are true for everyone.

> **Individual Moral Relativism:** The belief that right and wrong change from person to person (i.e., are relative to each individual).

Maybe you've heard someone say "You shouldn't force your morality on someone else." This idea is an expression of individual moral relativism.

A second position many people hold is called **cultural moral relativism**. This view is similar to individual moral relativism because it also assumes there is no set of moral standards that is true for everyone. Although, according to this position, morality is still "relative," the difference is the source. Instead of each individual determining right and wrong, it is the culture that determines what is right and what is wrong. This means that each culture determines what is right for everyone who lives in that culture. For example, there was once a primitive tribe that held betrayal as a supreme act of courage.

> **Cultural Moral Relativism:** The belief that right and wrong change from culture to culture (i.e., are relative to each individual culture).

Imagine the first missionary's shock when he presented the story of Jesus' last supper with His disciples and the tribe thought Judas was the hero because he betrayed Jesus! (This true event is told in the book *Peace Child* by Don Richardson.)

Where Moral Relativism Leads

Both naturalists and transcendentalists usually believe in some form of moral relativism described above. But there are at least two problems with this approach to ethics.

First, since the human heart is deceitfully wicked (Jeremiah 17:9), looking within *ourselves* for a standard of good and evil is to search in the wrong place. C.S. Lewis explained, "Those who stand outside all judgments of value cannot have any ground for preferring one of their own impulses to another except the emotional strength of that impulse."[1] If there is no standard outside of us (like the Bible), then we can only base our ethical decisions on what we *feel* is right. What if it *feels* right to hurt someone else? Does this make it right? Because our feelings are unstable and sometimes lack perspective, using them as our moral standard will only lead to confusion and chaos.

The second problem is that if morality changes with each individual (or each culture), then every moral argument boils down to just one preference against another preference. As Francis Schaeffer once observed, "If there is no absolute beyond man's ideas, then there is no final appeal to judge between individuals and groups whose moral judgments conflict. We are merely left with conflicting opinions."[2] If there is no God to judge between right and wrong, then we are left to judge each other. But who gets to say that my view of right and wrong is better than your view? What happens when people or cultures disagree over right and wrong? To whom do they appeal to settle such disagreements? In the end, those who have the most power will ultimately determine right and wrong through force. And no matter how you look at it, this just seems wrong!

Sooner or later, we must come back to the question of God in order to figure out what is good and what is evil. If we do not, then we will have no definitive authority to decide who is right when our views of ethics conflict. In the end, those who have the most power will ultimately determine right and wrong through force. In other words, this would mean that might makes right. So, if the Nazis had won the war, then they would have been right in killing over 9 million people, including 6 million Jews. But, there is no way that the cruelty of killing can ever be right.

Moral Absolutism

In contrast to these two views, **moral absolutism** states that there is a standard of right and wrong that applies to each of us regardless of time, location, personal preference, or culture. This is the position of the Christian worldview, with right and wrong being grounded in God's nature, His character, and the way He designed the world. Since God is righteous and since He has created us in His image, He expects us to reflect holiness. Moreover, since God's character is eternal and unchanging, His moral laws share these same attributes. According to the Christian worldview, morals do not change, but remain absolute regardless of your preferences or culture. In other words, a moral absolute is true for all people, at all times, in all situations. It is wrong to push a child down the stairs for the sheer fun of it. It was wrong yesterday, it is wrong today, and it will be wrong tomorrow. And even if there were a strange culture somewhere that thought that it is not wrong to push a child down the stairs for the sheer fun of it; it would still be wrong.

> **Moral Absolutes:** The belief that moral rules exist that are true for all people, at all times, in all situations.

Right and Wrong, and the Character of God

A Christian view of ethics is rooted in the character of God. "One of the distinctions of the Judeo-Christian God," says Francis Schaeffer, "is that not all things are the same to Him. That at first may sound rather trivial, but in reality it is one of the most profound things one can say about the Judeo-Christian God. He exists; He has a character; and not all things are the same to Him. Some things conform to His character, and some are opposed to His character."[3] The task of Christian ethics is to determine what conforms to God's character and what does not.

Ultimate ethical principles are revealed to us through special revelation in the Bible. While it is impossible for the Bible to address every situation, Christians are given enough specific values, guidelines, commands, and laws to have a clear sense of what is right or wrong in all situations. Some of the more obvious biblical principles are contained in the Ten Commandments, but these commandments are not the only ethical statements in the Bible.

God's Law Written on our Hearts

Not only does God reveal His moral precepts through His word, God has made us in such a way that deep down everyone knows His moral righteousness. You learned this earlier in our discussion of God's general revelation. The Apostle Paul wrote that all people have God's laws "written on their hearts" (Romans 2:15).

When it comes to the idea that all people are aware of God's moral laws, you might be thinking, "But doesn't every culture have different ideas about what is right and wrong? How can it be true that everyone is aware of God's moral truth?" These are good questions. Christian writer and philosopher C.S. Lewis responds this way: "Think of a country where people were admired for running away from battle, or where a man felt proud of double-crossing all the people who had been kindest to him. You might just as well try to imagine a country where two and two make five... Men have differed as to whether you should have one wife or four. But they have always agreed that you must not simply have any woman you liked."[4]

English sociologist David Martin agrees, citing results from the International Values survey. "We are mostly agreed about good and bad. People are, it seems, adamantly opposed to lying, stealing, cheating, coveting, killing, and dishonoring their parents."[5]

Based on these two quotes, what can you conclude about moral ideas? Are they subjective (depending on each individual's preferences), cultural (depending on how your society has taught you to behave), or absolute (universal standards that are true for all people at all times)?

The bottom line is that the Bible teaches that God has established moral absolutes. These are standards that do not change with location, situation, culture, or time. When we talk about an absolute standard, we mean a standard that does not change for any reason. Think about a ruler or tape measure. An inch is the same no matter where you live or in what circumstances you may find yourself. It is a standard by which you can measure whether something is five inches or ten inches. In a similar way, God's moral laws help us determine if our behavior "measures up" to His standards.

Law and Love

Sometimes it's easy to assume that the Old Testament only talks about God's law, while the New Testament just talks about God's love. In reality, though, this perspective is mistaken. Both the Old and the New Testaments agree on what is right and wrong. For example, nine of the Ten Commandments, as found in Exodus 20 and Deuteronomy 5, are repeated in one form or another in the New Testament as commandments for Christians.

- No other gods (Matthew 4:10; 1 Corinthians 8:4–6)
- No idols (1 Corinthians 5:10–11; 10:14)
- Misuse of God's name (Matthew 5:33); false oaths (6:9); honor His name (Colossians 3:17)
- Honor your parents (Mark 7:10; Ephesians 6:2)
- Do not murder (Mark 10:19; James 2:11)
- Do not commit adultery (Matthew 5:27; Romans 13:9)
- Do not steal (Matthew 19:18; Ephesians 4:28)
- Do not bear false testimony (Luke 3:14); false accusations (Roman 3:8)
- Do not covet (Luke 12:15); greed, love of money (Ephesians 5:3)

The majority of Jesus' teachings reflect moral principles for how Christians should act. This is especially true of the Sermon on the Mount (Matthew 5–7). The reason the ethical teachings recorded here are so radical is because Jesus emphasized that true ethics include the heart or character of a person, and not just his or her outward actions. This is why Jesus could make hatred equal to murder and lust equal to adultery. The fact is, to live unlawfully toward other people is to fail to love them, which points out who we really are on the inside. Love and law are not opposed to each other. Rather, the command to love others summarizes the law of God and fulfills it from the inside out (Romans 13:10–11; Matthew 7:12).

Jesus summed up His entire teaching ministry when He was asked about the greatest commandment:

Then one of the scribes came, and having heard them reasoning together, perceiving that He had answered them well, asked Him, "Which is the first commandment of all?" Jesus answered him, "The first of all the commandments is: 'Hear, O Israel, the LORD our God, the LORD is one. And you shall love the LORD your God with all your heart, with all your soul, with all your mind, and with all your strength.' This is the first commandment. And the second, like it, is this: 'You shall love your neighbor as yourself.' There is no other commandment greater than these" (Mark 12:28–31, NKJV).

These are not *new* commandments—both of them come from the Old Testament (Deuteronomy 6:5 and Leviticus 19:18). In light of the greatest commandment, it should be no surprise that Christ's "Great Commission" includes "*teaching* [the nations] to observe all things that I have *commanded* you" (Matthew 28:20, NKJV; emphasis added).

As a result of the special revelation given in the Bible, we can never justify wrong actions by claiming that God has not been clear about what He expects of us. Not only does God's Word present a series of ethical principles, those principles are also stamped into the hearts and minds of everyone made in His image.

Responsibility and the Christian Faith

As a Christian, you are called to "love the Lord your God with all your heart, with all your soul, and with all your mind" and to "love your neighbor as yourself" (Matthew 22:37–39, HCSB). Woven into these commands is a responsibility toward God and toward others.

Some people confuse responsibility with duty. Duty implies that only your outward behavior matters. But in the Christian view, everything falls into the context of a love relationship with God. Imagine a husband who decides to buy a beautiful bouquet of flowers for his wife. When he presents his gift to her, she is overwhelmed with the love expressed in his actions. Now imagine he responds to her gratitude with, "That's okay, I was just doing my duty." The flowers suddenly lose all their meaning. She does not just want the flowers—she wants his heart, his unconditional love. In the same way, God wants our hearts and actions to act in unison. We need God to create in us an undivided heart (Psalm 86:11, Ezekiel 11:19).

This responsibility to love others requires you to not only be willing to speak the gospel, but also to care for people in need with basic necessities such as food, clothing, and shelter. "[M]an is more than a soul destined for another world," says Norman Geisler, "he is also a body living in this world. And as a resident of this time-space continuum, man has physical and social needs which cannot be isolated from spiritual needs. Hence, in order to love man as he is—the whole man—one must exercise a concern about his social needs as well as his spiritual needs."[6] In other words, people not only need Jesus Christ in order to fulfill their spiritual needs, they need food, water, shelter, and clothing to maintain their physical needs. This is one way that you can show by your actions that Jesus has changed your life.

In examining the Christian responsibility to love our neighbors, we encounter an even more fundamental obligation: to love God. Our love for God is much more than a feeling—it is an *attitude* that results in *actions*. As Jesus said, "If anyone loves me, he will keep My word; and My Father will love him, and We will come to him and make Our home with him. He who does not love Me does not keep My words…" (John 14:23–24, NKJV).

As you think about the commands of God and how we are called to obey them, it is important to remember that it is not our good deeds that somehow persuade God to accept us or make Him love us more. It is the righteousness of Jesus applied to us by God's mercy that makes us acceptable in His eyes.

For we ourselves were also once foolish, disobedient, deceived, serving various lusts and pleasures, living in malice and envy, hateful and hating one another. But when the kindness and the love of God our Savior toward man appeared, not by works of righteousness which we have done, but according to His mercy He saved us, through the washing of regeneration and renewing of the Holy Spirit, whom He poured out on us abundantly through Jesus Christ our Savior, that having been justified by His grace we should become heirs according to the hope of eternal life (Titus 3:3–7, NKJV).

The Apostle Paul balances our free gift of salvation with our responsibility to live for Jesus as he continues in verse 8. "This is a faithful saying, and these things I want you to affirm constantly, that those who have believed in God should be careful to maintain good works. These things are good and profitable to men."

For Your Own Good

It may seem that rules are simply a way for someone else to control you or force you to live a certain way. This may be the case when humans make the rules, but not with God. Since God is our Creator and Designer, He knows what is good for us, and we should expect that His commandments, rules, and principles for living would be useful and good for our well being. God gives us commands because He wants to protect us and provide for us.

Consider five-year-old Rachel. Her parents love her and want to protect her from being hurt in any way. They know that the street in front of their home is a dangerous place, so they make some rules:

"Rachel, you may play in the yard as much as you like, but don't go into the street. Even if your ball bounces into the street, don't go after it. Instead, come and tell us and we'll get it for you." But Rachel gets frustrated by her parents' rules. Her ball bounces better in the street than on the grass, and the sidewalk leading up to the front door is too narrow. She thinks that her parents are just being mean, trying to keep her from having fun. But Rachel is wrong, and if she decides to break her parents' rules and play in the street, it could be painful or even fatal for Rachel.

Just like Rachel's parents, God wants the best for you. He wants you to experience what is best in life, to enjoy what He has provided for you. But He also knows that unless you keep His commandments, you won't be able to experience the best He desires for your life. So God has given His commandments for your own good (Deuteronomy 10:13).

Some people claim that the Christian view of ethics is restricting, that it removes our true freedom. But the truth is that you don't need to choose between liberty and obedience to the law. In fact, these two things go together very well. As one Christian thinker writes:

> [I]t is only when man walks along the path delineated (set out) by God's commandments that he can realize true fulfillment of his personality. The law is not a tyrannical imposition, confining man and cramping his opportunity to enjoy life: on the contrary, it is God's gracious revelation of the structure of the spiritual universe, which teaches man to move along the cosmos' lines of force rather than at cross-purpose with his true destiny.[7]

Just like traffic laws exist to keep everyone safe on the road, God's laws aren't intended to make you into an obedient but mindless robot. In fact, true liberty comes when you choose to follow the right, rather than letting your sinful nature control you and lead you into the wrong. The Psalmist says, "I will run the course of Your commandments, for You shall enlarge my heart" (Psalm 119:32, NKJV). When you follow (run the course of) God's commandments, you are staying in line with His purposes and are able to grow spiritually.

Staying in a Right Relationship with God

In order to maintain our relationship with God, we cannot simply rely on Jesus Christ to save us and then continue in our sinful ways. God did not save us just so we could have a free ticket to heaven. He saved us so that we could enter into a loving relationship with Him that will span eternity. When we understand the love behind the ultimate sacrifice God made for us, we cannot help but respond with a grateful desire to please God by adhering to His moral order.

Even though we became His children by faith, and even though we recognize all that He has done for us, at times we still disobey His moral commands because we are fallen. God takes this disobedience seriously. It damages who you are on the inside and your relationship with Him.

Fortunately, once you realize you have sinned, there is a way to restore your character and fellowship with God. The process is based on 1 John 1:9, which says, "If we confess our sins, He is faithful and righteous to forgive us our sins and cleanse us from all unrighteousness" (HCSB). This verse offers some principles that allow you to maintain a close walk with God.

To help remember these principles, we'll use the "ABCs" of walking with God.

A: The A reminds you to Agree with God about your sin and repent of it. Don't try to make excuses for what you have done. Because of who God is (holy and sovereign), we must agree with His assessment of our sin and agree with the way He says we should go. So, we must confess our sin (admit it), and we must repent from our sin (turn away from it)

B: The "B" reminds you to *Believe* God's promise. 1 John 1:9 states that God will cleanse you of your unrighteous behavior. Did you notice that God's forgiveness is linked to His character? God will forgive you because Jesus paid the penalty for your sin. God took the punishment that you deserve and placed it on Jesus when He died on the cross. In that way, God's justice has been met.

C: The "C" for *Control* reminds you to allow Christ to control and direct your life—every part of it.

Let's use Ephesians 5 as an example:

Do not get drunk on wine, which leads to debauchery. Instead, be filled with the Spirit. Speak to one another with psalms, hymns and spiritual songs. Sing and make music in your heart to the Lord, always giving thanks to God the Father for everything, in the name of our Lord Jesus Christ. Submit to one another out of reverence for Christ (Ephesians 5:18–21, NIV).

This verse contrasts getting drunk with being filled with the Holy Spirit. Instead of allowing alcohol to influence or control your thoughts and actions, you should be filled up (controlled) by the Holy Spirit. Being "filled" with the Spirit means allowing the Holy Spirit to influence and direct your life.

Now read Colossians 3 and look for what the Apostle Paul says should fill your life:

Let the word of Christ dwell in you richly as you teach and admonish one another with all wisdom, and as you sing psalms, hymns and spiritual songs with gratitude in your hearts to God. And whatever you do, whether in word or deed, do it all in the name of the Lord Jesus, giving thanks to God the Father through him (Colossians 3:16–17, NIV).

Now compare the results between the Spirit's filling in Ephesians 5:18–21 and God's Word dwelling in you in Colossians 3:16–17. Do you notice similarities? Are these the characteristics you would like to define who you are? If so, then ask God to fill you with His Spirit as you make time to study and meditate on His Word!

Conclusion

Christian ethics is grounded in the character of God. God's moral nature is absolute and unchanging—God always hates evil and loves good. The Bible guides us in knowing the difference between right and wrong behavior, and is the unchanging foundation for building a system of ethics. Christianity maintains that a specific moral order has been revealed to man not only through the special revelation of the Bible, but also through the person of Jesus Christ and the general revelation in creation.

Endnotes

[1] C.S. Lewis, *The Abolition of Man* (New York, NY: Macmillan, 1973), 78.
[2] Francis Schaeffer, *How Shall We Then Live?* (Old Tappan, NJ: Fleming H. Revell, 1976), 145.
[3] Francis Schaeffer, "Christian Faith and Human Rights," *Simon Greenleaf Law Review*, 2 (1982–3), 5. Cited in John Montgomery, *Human Rights and Human Dignity* (Dallas, TX: Probe Books, 1986), 113.
[4] Lewis, *Abolition*, 78.
[5] Quoted in "Not So Christian America," Thomas C. Reeves, *First Things* (October 1996), 18.
[6] Norman L. Geisler, *Ethics: Alternatives and Issues* (Grand Rapids, MI: Zondervan, 1979), 179.
[7] Roger R. Nicole, "Authority," in *Baker's Dictionary of Christian Ethics*, ed. Carl F. H. Henry (Grand Rapids, MI: Baker, 1973), 47.

A World of Ideas
Reading Discussion Questions

1. What is ethics? What key question does ethics seek to answer? What is the key idea of Christian ethics?

2. What are the two primary ways that people answer the question *How should we behave?*

3. What problems does moral relativism create?

4. Why do non-Christians, from all times and all nations, know right from wrong?

5. According to the Christian worldview, what are the two basic principles of ethics?

6. Why did Jesus equate hatred to murder and lust to adultery?

7. Does God have good reasons for His commands and rules? Where does true liberty come from?

8. Why do Christians sometimes disobey God? How do we restore our relationship with Him when we sin?

9. Reflection Question: Does the Bible spell out how we are to act in all situations?

10. Reflection Question: Is God more pleased when His children serve Him out of a sense of duty or love? Are you living for Him out of duty (because it's what you are supposed to do) or because you sincerely love Him?

Moral Relativism & Tolerance
Exercise

There are two ethical viewpoints that must be called to your attention here. The first idea about ethical choices popular in the world today is that *the situation dictates what is right*. In other words, the moral choice is "relative" to the circumstances. This kind of thinking says that in some situations a certain choice or action is right, and in other situations it is wrong. This viewpoint is called *moral relativism*.

However, Christians need to beware of this kind of thinking, since it directly contradicts the Bible. God's absolutes do not allow for moral relativism, which puts man in God's place as the creator of law and order. According to moral relativism, humans write their own rules using life experience and "the scientific method" as their guide, when in reality the moral order precedes both. The result of moral relativism is chaos, and anyone who follows it is lost because there is no stability in this changeable moral base.

There is a second ethical issue presently active in our culture—the issue of *tolerance*. Normally, tolerance would be defined as sympathy or indulgence for beliefs or practices differing from your own. In other words, tolerance is supposed to mean that those holding different views can disagree and discuss their differences civilly, but neither party is obligated to accept the other opinion as valid.

However, in our current politically correct culture, that definition has been greatly altered. Now when tolerance is promoted, it means that *all individual beliefs, lifestyles, and truth claims are of equal value*. This kind of tolerance condemns discernment and says you need to accept all truth claims and lifestyles as if they were your own. This kind of tolerance is asking you to make your worldview one that accepts every kind of thinking and all other worldviews.

Yet this "positive tolerance" goes beyond just respecting other worldviews. It also demands that you not impose your worldview on anyone else. It means that you will be labeled intolerant for attempting to share Christ with others.

This is the kind of tolerance you must be keenly aware of as you listen to the worldviews being advertised in the world. In this kind of thinking, you must abandon your worldview as a Christian because it is socially offensive (although Buddhists, Hindus, New Agers, etc., do not have to, because their faiths are already all-inclusive). In the past, a person studied opposing truth claims to *evaluate* them. Now, according to this thinking, you study to understand and *appreciate* them.

In order to properly comprehend and confront this ideology, you need to consider four things:

- Pursue the truth (1 Peter 3:15; John 8:32; Deuteronomy 10:6). Embrace all people, but not all beliefs. Embrace the speaker, but not the message. Listen and learn from all people, but do not agree with all people.
- Study and affirm your beliefs so they become your *convictions*.
- Identify with justice (Micah 6:8; Jeremiah 4:1–24).
- Act in love. You are not called to be tolerant, but to love. Love is defined in Ephesians 5:28–29 as protecting, providing, nurturing, and cherishing (but love also never overshadows truth). Tolerance is indifference, but love is involvement.

Moral Relativism & Tolerance
Exercise Discussion Questions

1. What is moral relativism?

2. What did "tolerance" mean in the past?

3. What does it mean now?

4. How does the present use of tolerance affect you as a follower of Jesus Christ?

5. What can you do about this idea of tolerance as a Christian?

Ethics Paragraph
Assignment

As you continue your study, write your own paragraph titled **My Christian Worldview of Ethics**. *You will be able to correct it, add to it, put it into your Lightbearers Journal, and memorize it. Below is a checklist to help you with this assignment.*

☐ The paragraph states that a Christian worldview of ethics is based on moral absolutes.

☐ It states that these moral absolutes reflect the character of God and are therefore perfect and unchanging.

☐ It clarifies that these moral absolutes are outlined in the Ten Commandments, (Exodus 20:1–17), the Sermon on the Mount (Matthew 5–7), and the "greatest commandment" passage (Matthew 22:37–39).

☐ It includes a statement about what a Christian can do to restore fellowship with God when he or she sins.

Mind Over Media
Video Discussion Questions

1. What is "media?" How prominent a role does media play in our lives?

2. Can media influence how we think?

3. Is there a link between violence in the media and an increase in aggressive behavior? What are some of the more extreme examples?

4. Reflection Question: Why is it that movies, TV, music, and comedy have gotten darker, more profane, and more sexual over the years?

5. Reflection Question: Is your culture, your movies and music, part of who you are?

Ethical Evaluation
Exercise

Circle your response to each statement and be prepared to discuss your answers in class.

1. **What's true for you may not be true for me.**

   Strongly Agree   Agree   Don't Know   Disagree   Strongly Disagree

2. **It's okay to do what you want as long as you don't hurt anybody.**

   Strongly Agree   Agree   Don't Know   Disagree   Strongly Disagree

3. **It's narrow-minded to believe that there is one moral "truth" for everybody.**

   Strongly Agree   Agree   Don't Know   Disagree   Strongly Disagree

4. **Any religion is fine as long as it works for you or helps you be a better person.**

   Strongly Agree   Agree   Don't Know   Disagree   Strongly Disagree

5. **What is right or wrong depends on the situation.**

   Strongly Agree   Agree   Don't Know   Disagree   Strongly Disagree

6. **It's prejudiced to say that other people's beliefs are wrong.**

   Strongly Agree   Agree   Don't Know   Disagree   Strongly Disagree

7. **It's intolerant to say that other people's actions are wrong.**

   Strongly Agree   Agree   Don't Know   Disagree   Strongly Disagree

8. **We need to figure out what is right for ourselves; we don't need God to tell us.**

   Strongly Agree   Agree   Don't Know   Disagree   Strongly Disagree

9. **If the Bible says something is right, then it is right for everyone.**

   Strongly Agree   Agree   Don't Know   Disagree   Strongly Disagree

10. **My beliefs about what is right or wrong affect my everyday life.**

    Strongly Agree   Agree   Don't Know   Disagree   Strongly Disagree

Electronic Media Fast
Presentation Assignment

Many of us are addicted to media and don't even realize it. One of the best ways to examine any addiction is to remove the source and analyze our responses. This assignment should show you how addicted you are to electronic media—TV, movies, radio/music, and internet. This will probably not be an easy assignment, but often you learn the best lessons from the hardest processes. Follow the instructions below. You will turn in a one-page paper and share your thoughts on your electronic media fast on day 11 or 12.

Step One: Between now and the next class, refrain from electronic media of any kind for 72 consecutive hours. Please do not cheat—it will hamper the honesty of your results and weaken the strength of your analysis. (Note: recording your favorite TV shows and watching them after the fast is cheating, because it misses the point. The point is to actually refrain from watching what you are used to. This will be a major test of how addicted you are to certain shows.)

Step Two: Take notes in your Journal during your 72–hour e-media fast. Answer the following questions to help you get started.

1. What are your assumptions about this experiment?
2. How hard or easy do you anticipate this experiment will be for you?
3. How do you plan to spend your media-free time?

Be vigilant to continue noting your reaction throughout the 72–hour period, especially when the urge strikes to check your email, look something up online, or watch your favorite show. How does it feel? And most importantly, *why* do you think you are having that particular reaction?

Step Three: Use your notes to write a one-page essay relating your thoughts and feelings during this experiment. Answer the following questions in your essay:

1. Which electronic medium (TV, music, internet, etc.) did you miss the most and why?
2. What obstacles did you encounter (i.e., your family wanting you to watch a program, your friends teasing you or not understanding, etc.)
3. How close were your initial assumptions to the actual experience of going without electronic media for 72 hours?
4. Was this experiment hard or easy for you? Why?
5. How did you spend your time? Why did you choose to spend it that way?
6. What did you learn from this experiment?
7. What habits will you change in the future after this experiment?

Hint: Dig deep—go beneath the surface when asking and answering "why." This is hard to do and requires time, concentration, and effort, but your discoveries will likely be eye-opening and rewarding.[*]

* Ideas for this exercise were taken from the following blog: http://nomorethneeds.blogspot.com/2008/03/cr-6-media-fast.html

My Truth, Your Truth...
Video Discussion Questions

1. Is basing ethics on consequences a good system?

2. Is basing ethics on instinct a good system?

3. What are some mistaken ways that tolerance is often defined? Ultimately, what is tolerance? And are there some actions that should not be tolerated?

4. What is moral relativism? What are some problems with this ethical position?

5. What is truth? Can truth change? Is truth worth pursuing?

Biblical Foundation for Ethics
Exercise

There are three very important points we must remember about biblical ethics. The **first** and most important feature of biblical ethics is the fact that it is grounded in the character of God. When God gave laws to His people, He was setting up principles that would, if followed heart, mind, and soul, shape His people according to His character. If we follow God's commandments, we will become godly.

Take a few minutes to write down some of God's attributes that are reflected in His commandments:

You probably came up with several attributes, but hopefully one of the most important ones was love. The importance of love in relation to God's law is the **second** important point. This may or may not surprise you, but both God the Father and God the Son said that the *whole* law can be summed up in one command: "Love...." This means that if you are loving the Lord and your neighbor, then you are keeping the whole law. Likewise, if you are keeping the whole law, then you are loving the Lord and your neighbor. You see, the law was never supposed to be merely a set of rules that you just acted out. They are, first and foremost, supposed to be internalized in our hearts and minds. If we do this, our obedience will become visible through our actions, too.

This might be different from the way you typically think of love. When you go to a movie, or listen to popular songs, the type of love that is described is a passionate feeling toward someone or something. In the Bible, however, we find out that "love is a verb." In other words, when God calls us to love Him, He is not asking us only to have a certain feeling toward Him. He is asking for both passion *and* obedience. As Jesus explains, "If anyone loves Me, he will keep My word" (John 14:23). He is asking for our heart, mind, soul, and strength—everything that makes us who we are.

The **third** point to keep in mind is that the law of Christ, which is what Christians are to follow, is not a new law. If you read through the Sermon on the Mount (Matthew 5–7), you will see that the ethics Jesus describes for those who follow Him are very similar to the ones that Moses received in the Old Testament. Because God's holiness hasn't changed throughout history, the way He asks us to behave hasn't changed either. We are simply invited into a new relationship with Him that the Hebrews hadn't heard about yet.

Chapter 6: If it Feels Good, Do It!

1. What is a common idea today about morality?

2. What idea did the Marquis de Sade present to the world?

3. If there were no right and no wrong, what would we say instead of "be good" or "be nice"?

4. According to C. S. Lewis, what ideas do people generally agree about?

5. After hearing Sally describe how her decisions affected her life, do you believe there is an inner morality in every person? If so, where does it come from?

6. What is Fritz's response to the "right and wrong" question?

7. Because right and wrong are real, our _____ matter.

8. What does C. S. Lewis say about Moral Law (page 55)?

9. Reflection Question: Look inside yourself. Do you feel some direction about right and wrong in your own mind? If so, where do you think it came from?

10. Reflection Question: What defines what is "good"?

LIGHTBEARERS

Unit Four

A Summit Ministries Curriculum

DAY	UNIT 04: syllabus & outline	SW	✓
1	Read *A World of Ideas* Reading..	101	
2	Read *A World of Ideas* Reading..	DITTO	
3	Review *A World of Ideas* Reading Discussion Questions.........................	109	
4	Review *A World of Ideas* Reading Discussion Questions......................... Assign **Biology Paragraph** [Rough Draft Due on Day 8].........................	DITTO 110	
5	Watch **"Incredible Creatures That Defy Evolution"** Video........................	---	
6	Review **"Incredible Creatures That Defy Evolution"** Video Discussion Questions...... Assign **God's Incredible Creatures** [Assignment Due on Day 11 or 12]........	111 112	
7	Research **God's Incredible Creatures** Presentation Assignment..................	---	
8	Research **God's Incredible Creatures** Presentation Assignment.................. Turn in **Biology Paragraph** Rough Draft [Assignment Due on Day 13]........	--- ---	
9	Read *How to Be Your Own Selfish Pig* Reading (Ch. 4).........................	---	
10	Review *How to Be Your Own Selfish Pig* Reading Discussion Questions (Ch. 4)........	113	
11	Turn in & Share **God's Incredible Creatures** Presentation Assignment.........	---	
12	Turn in & Share **God's Incredible Creatures** Presentation Assignment.........	---	
13	Turn in **Biology Paragraph** Assignment.. Take **Learn to Discern** Quiz.. Prepare **Unit 04** Test..	--- --- ---	
14	Take **Unit 04** Test..	---	
15			

Objects on this page are no smaller than they appear. | If you can read this, you are too close to your workbook.

A World of Ideas:
What is the Origin of Life?

KEYS TO UNDERSTANDING

Key Question: What is the origin of life?
Key Idea: Life's origin and design display the work of an Intelligent Designer.
Key Terms: biology, Darwinism, design theory, abiogenesis, Law of Biogenesis, spontaneous generation, macro-evolution, adaptation, micro-evolution, information theory
Key Verses: Genesis 1:21–27 and John 1:3

"God created the great creatures of the sea and every living and moving thing with which the water teems, according to their kinds, and every winged bird according to its kind… God made the wild animals according to their kinds, the livestock according to their kinds, and all the creatures that move along the ground according to their kinds…God created man in his own image, in the image of God he created him; male and female he created them" (Genesis 1:21–27, NIV).

"All things were made through Him, and without Him nothing was made that was made" (John 1:3, NIV).

What's the Big Fuss?

It's in the daily papers and all over the nightly news broadcasts: another lawsuit over whether to teach "intelligent design" in public school biology classes. Your friend Mike brings up the subject by saying:

"Who cares what is taught in public school biology class? I don't see the big problem. Can't we just teach about plants and animals and not worry about how they got here? What difference does it make if God created life or if it started in some 'primordial soup' billions of years ago? The fact is we're here, so let's just get on with life!"

How would you respond? Does it really matter what you believe about the origin of life? Let's think about that for a minute. The theory of evolution states that starting over 3.5 billion years ago life developed from non-living chemicals acted upon by random, natural processes, producing all the plants and animals that have ever lived. If evolution is an accurate description of how life arrived on our planet, what difference does this make to our lives? What difference does it make to our view of God, ourselves, others, creation, and, most importantly, the choices we make?

What a Difference it Makes!

The root question is not really about how life got here—it's about whether God exists. If the naturalistic theory of evolution is true, then God is not necessary to bring about human life or all the plants and animals. Therefore, God might as well not exist. "God" becomes nothing more than a concept that primitive man developed in an attempt to understand the mysteries of life.

Evolution describes mankind as the highest form of life and assumes that we are basically good and getting better all the time. There is no sin problem marring our basic makeup and instincts since we are simply evolved matter.

In terms of the choices we make (i.e., ethics), evolution implies that concepts of right and wrong are simply what societies have developed over time, and are constantly changing to fit the evolutionary progress of the human species. Morals are therefore relative or invented by us.

But let's paint a different picture. What if there is scientific evidence that all life forms display unmistakable elements of incredibly complex design far exceeding anything nature can accomplish? Based on this, what can we conclude about God, human nature, and ethics? This observation would indicate that a Supernatural Designer is necessary for life to exist. Further, there would be the possibility that human beings were created for a purpose and that morals come from a higher source than us.

Since Charles Darwin published his book describing his theory about the evolution of species in 1859, the issue of how life arose on earth has been hotly debated, from science labs to biology classrooms to the courts. How are we supposed to sort through the conflicting viewpoints, especially as Christians? Some Christians want to argue the point every time the subject of evolution comes up. Others accept the idea of evolution and, consequently, began doubting the accuracy of the biblical account of creation. Still others try to reconcile evolution with the Bible. And then there are those who just back away from the subject altogether.

Should you care about how life arrived on earth? The answer is a resounding "Yes!" That's because what you believe about the origin of life directly effects how you think about other areas of life, such as who we are as *homo sapiens*. Are we a little "higher" than the apes (according to evolutionary theory) or a little "lower" than the angels (according to the biblical view—see Psalm 8:5)?

Your journey in this chapter takes you into the middle of the creation/evolution debate. You will discover…

. . . The difference between the evolutionary theory and the theory of intelligent design.
. . . Why the two main principles of evolution—mutation and natural selection—do not lead to greater complexity.
. . . Why an Intelligent Designer (God) is the only scientifically confirmed answer to the question of how life originated on earth.

Evolved or Designed?

The study of **biology** includes many different things. For our purposes, this chapter will focus primarily on the questions surrounding the origins and development of life. Also, keep in mind that biology is not studied in isolation from other worldview categories. Biology, like every subject you study in school, grows out of foundational beliefs rooted in the questions about God, the nature of reality, and how we gain knowledge.

For example, if someone rejects the existence of God, then he or she is driven to believe that the existence, diversity, and wonder of life are the result of purely natural laws. Consider well-known British atheist Richard Dawkins, who said, "Biology is the study of complicated things that give the appearance of having been designed for a purpose."[1] Here Dawkins admits there is abundant evidence pointing toward design in living things. But he also knows that if life was designed, then, by implication, a Designer (God) must also exist. As an atheist, though, he cannot tolerate this idea. Therefore, Dawkins tries to get around that logical train of thought by assuming that life only has the *appearance* of design. He then has to postulate an alternative theory to account for such complex things as eyes and wings.

Biology: The study of living things and their origins.

Dawkins brings out the main issue when it comes to the question of the origin of life. It is obvious to any observer that all living organisms have characteristics of purposeful design. For example, the human eye is a very complex organ with a multitude of specialized cells organized for the purpose of seeing. So the question is *how can we best explain this kind of design*? In this unit we will discuss two hotly debated competing views—Darwinism and Design Theory.

The theory of evolution was first formulated by Charles Darwin in his 1859 book *On the Origin of Species by Means of Natural Selection, or the Preservation of Favoured Races in the Struggle for Life*. Darwin's original theory has been modified over the years and is commonly referred to simply as evolution. But because evolution can mean different things, we will use the more generic name of Darwinism. **Darwinism** is the theory that species evolve through time through random *genetic mutations* and *natural selection*.

Darwinism: The theory that species evolve over time by random genetic mutations and natural selection.

The word "evolve" simply refers to any change. A *mutation* occurs when there is a change in the genetic code of the offspring of an organism. *Natural selection* takes place when those genetically mutated offspring are "selected" by nature because they are better able to survive and reproduce. In this way, nature "selects" the fittest animals and "eliminates" the unfit.

In addition, Darwinism proposes that life began as a single-celled organism and changed over time into all the different plants and animals that have ever lived. This also means that all the species that have developed on earth, including mankind, could turn out differently if the process started again from scratch.

> **Design Theory:** The theory that holds that certain features of the universe and of living things are best explained by an intelligent cause.

Design Theory

The theory of design stands in black and white contrast to Darwinism. **Design Theory** holds that certain features of the universe and of living things are best explained by assuming an intelligent cause. While scientists who support Design Theory may or may not be Christians, the idea of an intelligent designer is a key part of a biblical worldview.

The Christian understands that life is the result of intentional design, which implies a Designer. The Bible declares that this Designer is God, who created all living things. The first chapter of Genesis summarizes the events leading to the creation of life (Genesis 1:21–22, 25, 27).[2] The Bible is also clear that all living things were designed with a purpose, and that mankind is God's crowning achievement. Our purpose is to glorify God through an intimate relationship with our Creator.

As you learned in Unit Two, a biblical worldview includes the idea that God is the Master Designer of the universe. So, with this foundation, when it comes to the study of biology we would expect to find examples of design in all living things. In contrast to Richard Dawkins's assertion that the design we find is only apparent, the Christian finds the design in nature to be real because God is real.

But while the Bible states that God created life, it does not explain in detail *how* organisms are made. To find this out, you must think like a scientist by studying the biological world around you. What do you actually observe in nature? Is there evidence for design in nature, leading to the conclusion of the reality of an intelligent cause? Or do your observations support the idea that natural laws and random processes can account for the origin and diversity of life? What conclusions can you draw from experiments in the laboratory, observations from breeding plants and animals, and excavations of the layers of the earth to uncover what remains of ancient life? Let's put on our lab coats and start exploring the wonders of life. Along the way we'll discover that the biblical worldview is the true representation of what we observe in the world of living creatures.

The Origin of Life

> *"Okay, so there are a few scientists today who believe that God has something to do with science and the origin of life," Mike acknowledges. "But I learned in biology class that most scientists think life arose on earth from some kind of chemical 'soup.' And our textbook showed an experiment by Stanley Miller demonstrating how the building blocks of life could have formed spontaneously. It seems that scientific experiments prove that life could come about without the help of some supernatural being."*

Is Mike correct? Has science proven that the origin of life did not need God's intervention? In your quest to understand the nature of living things, you need to take a closer look at two competing theories for the origin of life.

The first theory is called **abiogenesis**. This is the belief that life originally came from non-living matter. Scientists who do not believe in God must instead believe that basic chemicals have the ability to combine themselves into living organisms. The problem is that, contrary to what most biology textbooks lead you to think, no one has been able to produce an experiment that demonstrates this is even possible.

> **Abiogenesis:** The belief that life originally came from non-living matter.

Imagine If. . .

But, you might ask, what if scientists were able to produce life in a laboratory? What if they were working along, combining just the right chemicals, just the right amount of electrical inputs, just the right atmosphere, and—*poof!*—there was life? Wouldn't that show that life could be created "all by itself" without an intelligent designer? Obviously not, because it took *intelligent* scientists to create the perfect conditions in the first place!

In addition, even if life were somehow produced in a lab, this does not mean that life *originally* came about that way. It simply means that we are able to produce life now in a certain way. But more than that, when it comes to the origin of life on earth, there are a number of known properties of chemistry and biology that would keep life from being produced by random molecules in a chemical soup.

To begin with, scientists who attempt "origin of life" experiments must start with pure ingredients in order to get the results they want. In a natural setting there would be all sorts of impurities leading to unpredictable chemical reactions. No pure ingredients means there is no way to start down the road to life.

Next in their experiments, scientists filter out certain wavelengths of light. In a natural setting, light from the sun would destroy the required amino acids (the building blocks of life) and kill any developing life. If the sun was shining, you could be sure no life would be forthcoming.

Then, scientists build a trap into their apparatus. This trap removes the amino acids that are being formed to protect them from disintegration. How, in the natural setting of the early earth, would a "trap" form to separate out the right amino acid compounds to keep them from breaking down into their original chemicals? Only in the apparatus of the laboratory is such a trap found! No trap for evolving compounds means no evolving life.

We've just covered three obstacles natural evolution would face, but there are actually additional roadblocks that would keep any so-called evolving molecule from becoming a living, reproducing organism. These roadblocks are well-known laws of chemistry understood by all chemists. But Darwinists must get life from non-living matter or concede the possibility of a Creator. In fact, even a prominent Darwinist such as Richard Dawkins admits that the origin of the first life form from natural processes was so unlikely that the only way he can account for it was an "initial stroke of luck."[3] This is an incredible admission from an Oxford professor and one of today's most vocal proponents of evolution.

But the question remains—*how can non-living matter morph into the first living, reproducing cell?* Dawkins attempts to answer that question by appealing to a lucky break and, further, by assuming "a very large number of planetary opportunities."[4] As it turns out, proposing multiple earth-like planets sprinkled throughout the universe is another unfounded assumption on his part. The actual chances that other life-supporting planets exist has been investigated and found absurdly improbable. With both assumptions, Dawkins fails to be persuasive in any scientific sense.

In their book *The Privileged Planet,* authors Guillermo Gonzalez[5] and Jay Richards describe ground breaking research into how the earth is uniquely situated to sustain complex life. These "just right" conditions include being an optimal distance from the right kind of star, having a moon perfectly sized to stabilize the planet's axis, relying on the shielding presence of larger planets nearby, having the right amount of oxygen and water, and the planet's system of plate tectonics... just to name a few. Mathematically speaking, Gonzalez and Richards estimate that the probability of a planet having all of the necessary conditions to sustain complex life is ten to the negative fifteenth power, or one thousandth of a trillionth.

No wonder Dawkins's last stronghold of hope for a naturalistic explanation of all earth's ideal factors requires a major infusion of luck!

Lots of Luck vs. the Law of Biogenesis

Dawkins wants you to believe that, given innumerable opportunities and a whole universe full of luck, anything can happen. Well, only if the "anything" is in the realm of possibility. On the other hand, some things will never happen no matter how many times you try or how much luck you have. That's because some things are simply impossible.

For example, drawing a square circle is not logically possible, because by definition a square has four sides of equal length and a circle has no sides. That is one kind of impossibility. Another type of impossibility is based on well-established science, like the principle that it is impossible for an unaided living organism to survive in the vacuum of space.

It is this second kind of impossibility that Dawkins fails to fully appreciate. Dawkins' origin-of-life scenario turns a blind eye to the well-established law of biogenesis. The **Law of Biogenesis** states that life only comes from pre-existing life. In other words, it is impossible for life to generate itself. But people have not always believed this.

It may seem strange to you, but for most of human history people believed in **spontaneous generation**. This is the idea that living organisms sprouted directly from such things as mud and rotting food. For example, they thought that if you left food outside, maggots and flies would emerge directly from the decaying meat. However, this idea was shown to be false in 1668, when scientist Francesco Redi experimented with rotting meat. Covering meat

> **Law of Biogenesis:** The scientific law that states that life only comes from pre-existing life.

with a screen, he found that swarming flies deposited eggs on the screen, rather than springing to life from the meat itself. This helped prove that large organisms, like flies, did not arise spontaneously.

In 1860, French scientist Louis Pasteur followed this up with some experiments showing that even microscopic organisms like bacteria do not arise spontaneously. He was able to determine that some bacterial spores floated in the air, landed in various laboratory mixtures, and then grew into noticeable life forms. When these mixtures were properly cleaned and kept protected from bacterial spores in the air, no bacteria was found growing in the mixtures. Following Pasteur, scientists rejected spontaneous generation as an explanation for the sudden appearance of organisms.

Biogenesis has since been firmly established as a scientific law. Therefore, the idea of *abiogenesis*—that life *does not* arise from pre-existing life—has been scientifically proven to be false for nearly one hundred fifty years. If this is the case, why do Darwinists continue to believe such a theory? It is because their dogmatic belief in atheism forces them to hold onto their theories in spite of the evidence.

To summarize our investigations up to this point, we find that the foundational basis for Darwinism, abiogenesis, fails as a scientific theory. In contrast to Darwinism, the Christian worldview explains that God, an eternally living being, gave life to all other living things. This is what science has confirmed—

life only comes from life! As the Bible states, "In the beginning was the Word, and the Word was with God, and the Word was God. He was with God in the beginning. Through him all things were made; without him nothing was made that has been made. In him was life…" (John 1:1–4, NIV).

> **Spontaneous Generation:** The idea that living organisms sprouted directly from such things as mud and rotting food.

In Genesis 1:1, we find the most scientifically accurate statement regarding the origin of life: "In the beginning, God created…"

Bird's Beaks and Natural Selection

Even after talking with your friend Mike about the problems with origin-of-life experiments, he is still convinced evolution is true. He says:

> *"But look at all of the evidence for evolution. I mean, take natural selection for example. Scientists have conducted breeding experiments to produce sweeter corn, cows that give more milk, and cats with fluffier fur. If a breeder can select for certain traits, then nature can select changes for the better. So natural selection proves evolution!"*

How should you respond to Mike's argument that natural selection creates new species? Let's take a look at what Charles Darwin actually discovered over 150 years ago. In 1835, Darwin made a now-famous voyage that included a visit to the Galapagos Islands just off the coast of Ecuador. While there, he discovered finches on the various islands with different beak sizes. He thought he had discovered evolution in action. But had he really?

Darwin's theory of evolution assumes that all the diversity of life came from simpler, less complex forms of life. You might call it the "amoeba to man" theory, or **macro-evolution**. This theory poses that large scale changes in biological traits result in different species. For this "amoeba to man" idea to actually work, new complex structures must emerge, like eyes, fingernails, and hair. After all, we are much more complex than an amoeba! For evolution to occur, you have to add "new stuff" to simpler organisms.

Macro-evolution: Large scale changes in biological traits resulting in different species.

So did Darwin observe any "new stuff" being added to the finches? No. Darwin only observed small changes in the size of the finches' beaks, not the addition of new features. Their beaks did not change, for example, into an elephant's trunk. The birds began as finches with beaks and ended up as finches with beaks. The only change was that their beaks were of slightly different sizes.

In fact, studies of these birds during the 1970s showed that during a time of drought, the average size of their beaks increased slightly. However, when the rains returned, the beaks reverted back to their original smaller size. This demonstrates that there was no overall net gain that became permanent in the population. It also shows that any changes can be reversed. So this can't be used to prove any progression to "higher" organisms.

Adaptation: When certain organisms become better suited to survive.

What Darwin called "natural selection" is actually **adaptation**, when certain organisms become better suited to survive in their environment. We find an example of adaptation when bacteria develop resistance to certain chemicals. When a population of millions of bacteria are exposed to an antibiotic that kills the majority, there will be a few within that population that have mutated slightly in just the right way and will not be affected by that particular drug. These survivors live and reproduce, and the new offspring will inherit that same trait of resistance to that chemical. But these small adaptive changes within a species' gene pool, or **micro-evolution**, have never been observed to lead to whole new structures. No "new stuff" has been added to the species.

Therefore, the idea of macro-evolution—changes that add "new stuff" to a species—has never been directly observed. Instead, it is *inferred* from the instances of micro-evolution that are observed. Darwin's concept of natural selection is better understood as small adaptive changes that do not lead to wholly different organisms. Since we never see "new stuff" being added, Darwin's concept of "amoeba to man" evolution has no scientific basis.

Micro-evolution: Small adaptive changes within a species' gene pool.

Creator to the Rescue

If the theory of evolution does not provide a compelling answer to the question of the origin of life, then we need to consider a different idea. Look at Genesis 1:12, 21, 25. You will notice that God created various plants and animals to reproduce "according to their kinds." The phrase "according to their kinds" suggests that the boundary between kinds is defined by reproduction: a "kind" is an inter-breeding group. For example, the entire cat family—from domestic cats to leopards and tigers—forms a breeding chain and thus constitutes a single "kind." So does the dog family, from friendly beagles to wolves and jackals. Even though there is variety within a kind, these animals are considered an inter-breeding group.

The point here is that the Bible describes what we actually observe in the natural world. First, we find fossil remains of fully developed creatures, not animals that are half one thing and half another. Second, after hundreds of years of breeding various kinds of plants and animals, we observe small adaptive changes, but these changes never accumulate to create bigger changes leading to entirely new structures. For example, we can breed cows to produce more milk or flowers with certain colors of petals, but we cannot breed pigs with wings! Our scientific observations confirm the Law of Biogenesis and the biblical statement that all living things reproduce after their own kind. These two fundamental laws of biology contradict the basic tenets of Darwinism and confirm a Christian worldview.

The Design Inference

There is one final idea we need to discuss—the idea of design. We all know that if something is designed, then it provides positive evidence of an intelligent source behind it all. For example, if you walk along the beach and see ripples in the sand, you would assume that the waves or wind produced them. But if you saw the words "John loves Mary" written in the sand, you would conclude that someone with intelligence must have written that message. In other words, from the specific design of those markings, you'd infer they must have an intelligent source.

Searching for design is not new to science. The entire government-funded SETI Project (Search for Extra-Terrestrial Intelligence) is based on the notion that we can detect an intelligent agent beyond earth by searching for coded, specified messages from space.[6] Using this same logic, scientists seek to uncover evidences of coded "messages" inherent in biological systems. This science is called **information theory**, which is the idea that a biological system, like the inner workings of every living cell, contains a very specific sequence, or a coded message.

The clearest example of a coded message found in biology is DNA, the genetic code that is foundational for all living things. Scientists compare our genetic code to language—different letters are assembled to make words, which are strung together into sentences to convey meaning. In a similar way, protein bases (like letters of the alphabet) combine to make genes that provide a meaningful sentence structure for living things. Some scientists suggest that a single cell contains more coded information in its DNA than all thirty volumes of the *Encyclopedia Britannica*. If it takes human intelligence to produce the massive information found in the encyclopedia, then, by analogy, the information found in DNA must also have an intelligent cause.

> **Information Theory:** The search for coded "messages" inherent in biological systems.

Designer Eyes

Evidence for design is found everywhere in the biological world. For example, there is incredible design found in the human eye. Charles Darwin used the eye to illustrate how a complex organ could have evolved. But then, instead of providing a scientific explanation by showing actual evidence, Darwin proceeded to tell a highly imaginative story, stringing together several "intermediate" stages to explain how the process from "simple" light sensitive spots to "complex" eyes may have transpired. That makes for a good story, but not good science.

As it turns out, Darwin was totally ignorant of the inner workings of the cell and the actual chemical pathways required for sight. For images to be registered in the brain, it takes a complex arrangement of photo-chemical receptors, nerve cells, electrical signals to and within the brain, muscles, tear ducts, and skeletal structures.

An absurdly complicated arrangement of molecules makes up the eye itself. Just to give one example, the retina is a very thin and complex tissue lining the back of the eye. According to Dr. Geoffrey Simmons, the retina contains 7 million cone cells for color assessment, 125 million rod cells for adaptation to the dark, and 1.2 million nerve cells that collect billions of bits of information.[7] But what good would 125 million rod cells be if there weren't also 1.2 million nerve cells to make the connections? Put simply, the entire arrangement needs each part it has or it doesn't work!

The bottom line is that Darwin's explanation of the origin of sight was totally inadequate to explain the complexity of the eye. In fact, after 150 years of research, today's evolutionary scientists have not produced any better explanation. While we observe various kinds of eyes throughout the animal kingdom today, there is no clear fossil evidence of any kind to support Darwin's story of gradual, step-by-step evolution from simple to complex chemical pathways needed for sight.

Complex Inboard Engines

Another area that demonstrates complex design is the molecular machinery found in every living cell. You know what an inboard engine on a boat is like—the engine has rotors, bushings, propellers, and all kinds of moving parts that produce motion for the boat. But did you know that in a similar way some micro-organisms have "engines" that are made from molecules that run on chemical charges?

One example of such an engine is found in bacteria, which have a flagellum—a long tail-like structure that acts like a propeller. The bacteria swim by rotating this flagellum. While scientists do not yet understand exactly how everything works, what they have discovered so far is that it takes over forty different proteins to make this engine go. This means that each of these factors must be coordinated in the making of the motor to the exact detail and set of specifications or the motor will fail to function and the bacteria will not be able to move in its watery environment.

All these examples point out that the various organs and machinery in living things are too complex 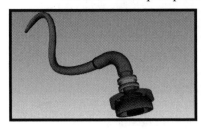 to have come about through some random, unguided progression. In fact, there are no natural processes (biological, chemical, or mechanical) that can produce coordinated, specific instructions and build complex biological machines to do what every living organism does to survive and reproduce. In order to produce that level of complexity, life must have come from an Intelligent Creator. Design Theory is the only explanation that fits our observations of the real world.

Conclusion

When it comes to the origin of living systems and the great diversity of life, the Christian worldview maintains that the only adequate explanation for the design observed in every level of nature is the existence of an Intelligent Designer. Christianity trusts the authority of Genesis as well as declarations about creation found elsewhere in Scripture, such as Mark 10:6 and Colossians 1:16.

In addition to what the Bible teaches, when we look at the universe surrounding us and all the living organisms on our planet, we find evidence of intricate design and complexity. Christians believe design theory fits the facts of science, whereas Darwinism does not. Thus, our scientific observations of the world and biblical declarations about creation agree. Science and Christianity are demonstrated to be compatible and to declare in unison that God "created all things" (Ephesians 3:9).

Endnotes

[1] Richard Dawkins, *The Blind Watchmaker* (New York, NY: Norton, 1986), 1.

[2] Since this is an introductory level chapter on biology, we have chosen not to discuss the various approaches Christians take to the age of the earth or details concerning the creation account. We assume those areas will be covered in a biology course, and instead will concentrate on the major issues separating the biblical and secular views of biology.

[3] Richard Dawkins, *The God Delusion* (Boston, MA: Houghton Mifflin, 2006), 140.

[4] Ibid., 140.

[5] Guillermo Gonzales and Jay Richards, *The Privileged Planet: How Our Place in the Cosmos is Designed for Discovery* (Washington DC: Regnery Publishing, Inc., 2004).

[6] William Dembski and Michael Behe, *Intelligent Design: The Bridge Between Science and Theology* (Downers Grove, IL: InterVarsity Press, 1999).

[7] Geoffrey Simmons, *What Darwin Didn't Know* (Eugene, OR: Harvest House, 2004), 114.

A World of Ideas
Reading Discussion Questions

1. What is biology? What key question does biology seek to answer? What is the key idea of Christian biology?

2. How does a person's belief in evolution effect his or her view of God, mankind, and ethics?

3. How would you define Darwinism, genetic mutations, and natural selection?

4. What is Design Theory? Why does this theory work well with the Christian worldview?

5. How is the earth uniquely situated for life?

6. What is the theory of abiogenesis? What is the Law of Biogenesis? Which theory better explains the origin of life?

7. What is the difference between micro-evolution and macro-evolution?

8. Why is Darwin's explanation for the origin of the eye inadequate?

9. How would you define the following terms: adaptation and information theory?

10. Reflection Question: Have you ever had doubts about creation and wondered if evolution is true? Has this chapter strengthened your belief in creation?

Biology Paragraph
Assignment

*As you continue your study, write your own paragraph titled **My Christian Worldview of Biology**. You will be able to correct it, add to it, put it into your Lightbearers Journal, and memorize it. Below is a checklist to help you with this assignment.*

- ☐ The paragraph states that the Christian worldview of biology focuses on the scientific evidence of design in nature.
- ☐ It includes how the law of biogenesis supports the need for God.
- ☐ It mentions examples of design in living things which evidence the need for a Designer.

Incredible Creatures
Video Discussion Questions

1. How does the bombardier beetle defy evolution?

2. How does the bull giraffe defy evolution?

3. How does the woodpecker defy evolution?

4. How does the Australian incubator bird defy evolution?

5. How does the chicken egg defy evolution?

6. How does the beaver defy evolution?

7. How does the duck-billed platypus defy evolution?

8. How does the black and yellow garden spider defy evolution?

9. How does the gecko lizard defy evolution?

10. How does the chuckwalla lizard defy evolution?

God's Incredible Creatures
Presentation Assignment

Today you will be going to the library to research animals that display examples of design. You are to write at least a half-page paper citing two or more specific evidences for design found in the animal you choose. You will present and turn in your paper on day 11 or 12.

How to Be Your Own Selfish Pig
Reading Discussion Questions

Chapter 4: I Bet You Believe in the Tooth Fairy, Too

1. What two questions did Richard need to separate during his discussion of suffering?

2. Is the sin and suffering we see in the world God's fault?

3. What do some people say they need to witness in order to believe that God exists? What evidence are they overlooking?

4. In the L'Abri dinner discussion, the question of proving God's existence is brought up. How does Kit, a biologist, explain his view of God in the world?

5. How do Ranald and Susan respond to the comment that "everything evolved"?

6. What are the three choices about the existence of God?

7. John R.W. Stott said: "There is a hunger in the heart of man which none but _____ can satisfy, a vacuum which only _____ can fill."

8. Reflection Question: Did the complicated human being, with all his hopes, desires, and experiences, as well as his ability to make choices, merely happen?

9. Reflection Question: Do you think that by laying out your homework assignment one night with a piece of paper and a pencil, you could wake the next morning to find it completed? If even this couldn't happen, why do people say that the universe happened by random chance?

10. Reflection Question: What do your actions say about what you believe? Are you acting like there is order in the universe? Do your actions match what you say?

LIGHTBEARERS

Unit Five

A Summit Ministries Curriculum

DAY	UNIT 05: syllabus & outline	SW	✓
1	Read *A World of Ideas* Reading...	**117**	
2	Read *A World of Ideas* Reading...	DITTO	
3	Review *A World of Ideas* Reading Discussion Questions...................................	**124**	
4	Review *A World of Ideas* Reading Discussion Questions................................... Assign **Psychology Paragraph** [Rough Draft Due on Day 8]..............................	DITTO **125**	
5	Assign **What's Your Worldview?** [Assignment Due on Day 11 or 12]................... Watch **"The Case against Abortion"** Video Outline..	**126** **127**	
6	Watch **"The Case against Abortion"** Video Outline..	DITTO	
7	Watch **"The Case against Abortion"** Video Outline..	DITTO	
8	Review **"The Case against Abortion"** Video Discussion Questions.................... Complete **Who Are We?** Exercise.. Turn in **Psychology Paragraph** Rough Draft [Assignment Due on Day 13]........	**133** **134** ---	
9	Read *How to Be Your Own Selfish Pig* Reading (Ch. 9).....................................	---	
10	Review *How to Be Your Own Selfish Pig* Reading Discussion Questions (Ch. 9).......	**135**	
11	Turn in & Share **What's Your Worldview?** Presentation Assignment..................	---	
12	Turn in & Share **What's Your Worldview?** Presentation Assignment..................	---	
13	Turn in **Psychology Paragraph** Assignment.. Take **Learn to Discern** Quiz.. Prepare **Unit 05** Test...	--- --- ---	
14	Take **Unit 05** Test..	---	
15			

A World of Ideas:
What Does it Mean to be Human?

Objects on this page are no smaller than they appear.

If you can read this, you are too close to your workbook.

KEYS TO UNDERSTANDING

Key Question: What is human nature?

Key Ideas: Humans have a dual nature—a physical body made from the dust of the earth, and a spiritual self created in God's image. We also have a sin nature. Sin causes problems in our relationships with God, other humans, our world, and ourselves.

Key Terms: psychology, psychological monism, naturalistic monism, transcendental monism, psychological dualism, category fallacy, unity of identity

Key Verses: Genesis 1:27, Genesis 3:6, and 1 Peter 3:18

"So God created man in His own image, in the image of God He created him; male and female He created them" (Genesis 1:27, NKJV).

"When the woman saw that the fruit of the tree was good for food and pleasing to the eye, and also desirable for gaining wisdom, she took some and ate it. She also gave some to her husband, who was with her, and he ate it" (Genesis 3:6, NIV).

"For Christ also suffered once for sins, the just for the unjust, that He might bring us to God, being put to death in the flesh but made alive by the Spirit" (1 Peter 3:18, NKJV).

How to Live with Yourself and Like It

Your attitude often determines how much you enjoy life. Are you happy and satisfied? It's likely because you think that way. Are you sad or depressed? Sometimes those feelings stem from the way you think about yourself.[1]

So what is the source of your thoughts and ideas? In order to answer this question, it is crucial to first answer another: who are you? The root of both of these questions is in the definition of human nature. When you ask the question what is human nature, you are entering into the study of Psychology— knowledge of the "psyche" or soul. Psychology seeks to understand what you are like on the inside, the place where you do all of your real living.

So to enjoy life to its full potential, you need to clear your mind of certain ideas that are wrong and build a new set of ideas from a proper understanding of Biblical Christian psychology! As you're about to find out, God has a lot to say about who you really are.

In this chapter you will...

    . . . Identify ways that popular culture distorts the image of who you are

    . . . Develop a biblical view of YOU

    . . . Understand your "royal heritage" as a Christian

Kathy's World

"It really shattered my life when my parents' marriage broke up," [Kathy] began. "I was thirteen, and I couldn't get it out of my head that somehow I was responsible for the breakup. Everybody had been so grouchy and disapproving of me for so long, that I figured it all must be my fault. . .

"As I went through school, I was very mixed up. I felt unsure of myself, so I tried to do anything that I thought would get other kids to accept me. If they were smoking, I'd smoke. If a boy wanted something sexual from me, I'd give in. When drugs were passed out, I'd try them. All the time I was really crying, 'Am I worth anything to anybody?'"[2]

No one would have guessed Kathy felt that way. On the outside she was full of fun, but beneath the joy and energy was a deep-seated despair. Do you know someone like Kathy? Have you ever had similar feelings?

Kathy's real problem wasn't her parents' divorce. Deep in her heart, she felt that no one cared about her as a person. Maybe even she didn't believe she mattered, that she was really just another human animal taking up space on the planet for a few years; just a thinking, talking, medium-sized biped. Kathy was depressed because she believed a lie.

True Self-Esteem

Many of us have a one-dimensional perspective of the universe. All we can see is the physical world, and so we fail to realize who we really are. But reality is not just physical (like naturalism teaches) nor is it just spiritual (like transcendentalism teaches). Kathy failed to realize that she was created in God's image, and therefore her value as a human being was securely established by God. We can paint the true picture of who Kathy is (and who we are) if we look through the lens of creation, fall and redemption.

You learned in the chapter on philosophy that reality is not one-dimensional, but two-dimensional—consisting of the natural and the supernatural. The same is true of human beings. While our physical bodies are real, we are not just flesh and bones. God created humans as physical and spiritual beings. If we ignore either aspect of who we are, we cannot hope to deal with the deepest, most profound problems we experience.

What makes you so special in the world is that God has made you in His image (Genesis 1:27). God's image is reflected in your physical body, and in your mental, moral, and spiritual capabilities. So if you base your self-image just on the physical side, you'll be let down.

Self-esteem is not produced by just drumming up warm fuzzy thoughts about yourself or telling yourself things like, "I am me and I am enough."[3] True self-esteem comes when you understand who you really are. And the truest thing about you is what God says about you, like the fact that you are "fearfully and wonderfully made" (Psalm 139:14).

But there is another part of your nature that must not be overlooked. Although humans were created in God's image, we have fallen. By yourself you cannot live up to God's moral standards. Romans 3:23 reminds us that we all "fall short of the glory of God." This means that we often respond to situations in life in selfish, sinful ways. This can also lead to feelings of guilt, discouragement, or even depression, since the fellowship we once shared with God has been broken.

However, there is a third thing that also is true about you. It is the good news that God has redeemed you from your sin. The Gospel message is that we are forgiven of our sins through Jesus' death on our behalf, and we can have new life, joy, and peace in our new relationship with Him. All you have to do to take advantage of this forgiveness is accept Jesus as your savior, putting Him in control of your life.

A Biblical Christian view of psychology involves our creation in God's image, our fall into sin, and our redemption in Jesus Christ. These form the core for answering the question with which we began this chapter: *What does it mean to be human?*

Foundations for Psychology

It should not surprise you to find out that someone's theological and philosophical perspective will determine his or her view of human nature. For example, if someone believes in naturalism—claiming that only physical or material things exist—then he or she will logically conclude that our mental actions are nothing more than purely physical activities in the brain. The next logical step based on this is to believe that human beings are basically physical machines that respond to physical stimuli either inside our brains or outside our bodies.

In contrast, a Biblical Christian worldview approaches psychology by acknowledging both the physical and spiritual dimensions of human beings. For that reason, only Christianity can truly address the innermost concerns of the individual. Christian psychology helps people get in touch with their real selves because it allows them to recognize their true design in the image of God, their own sinfulness and, their need for a Savior. Our greatest psychological need is not self-esteem; rather, it is the realization of how we were created, that we are sinners in rebellion against our Creator, and that we are in need of His forgiveness and redemption.

Only after being made right with God through Jesus Christ can we begin to understand our value as creatures made in God's image. Only then can we truly live triumphant, whole, and rewarding lives. Rather than telling people to ignore or block out their guilty consciences or to dwell in their shame, Christianity calls for people to recognize that this guilt is real, and that true redemption is possible if they will face their guilt with confession and repentance. Thus, Christian psychology teaches moral responsibility.

The discipline of **psychology** is the study of the human mind. In particular, it is the study of how the mind works and how we can fix our mental problems. In the following discussion you will see some radically different views of human psychology. In the process, you will discover reasons for why a biblical view of mankind makes the most sense. Let's first focus on the make-up of the human mind.

> **Psychology:** The study of the human mind.

Monism: The Mind as One Essence

There are two fundamentally different views about the human mind: monism and dualism. **Psychological monism** states that the human mind is just composed of one substance. This means there is no difference between the thoughts inside our heads and the chemical reactions going on inside our skulls. But there are two different ways to apply monism, based on your beliefs about philosophy.

> **Psychological Monism:** The belief that human beings are made of only one substance.

Those who believe in a naturalistic worldview hold to monism because they believe that humans do not have spiritual attributes, only physical ones. Since this assertion is based on their belief in naturalism—that only the physical world exists—this belief is called **naturalistic monism**.

In contrast with naturalism, transcendentalism affirms that everything is god, or divine. Thus, everything, including humans, is made up entirely of a non-natural essence. This is a kind of monism as well. Since nothing is physical, only spiritual, the human brain is merely the tool used to think thoughts, and will eventually disappear like everything else labeled physical. The psychological view of transcendentalism can therefore be called **transcendental monism**.

> **Naturalistic monism:** The belief that the human mind is just physical, like the rest of the body.
>
> **Transcendental monism:** The belief that the human mind is just spiritual, like the rest of the body.

Regardless of how it is applied, both naturalistic monism and transcendental monism state that our minds and our brains are ultimately one essence.

Psychological Dualism

The Christian view of psychology stands in sharp contrast to these types of monism. Biblical Christianity states that human beings are both physical and spiritual. We are neither simply matter (as Secular Humanists believe), nor are we simply spiritual (the claim of the New Age movement). Rather, we are "living souls", physical and spiritual, created in the image of God. The Bible describes it this way in Genesis 2:7: "then the Lord God formed man of dust from the ground (physical) and breathed into his nostrils the breath of life (spiritual), and the man became a living creature." In affirming both the physical and spiritual aspects of human nature, a Christian's view of psychology can be classified as psychological dualism.

Psychological dualism is the belief that the human mind is not the same thing as the human brain. *Mind* refers to the non-physical mental activities you experience, whereas *brain* refers to the physical gray matter that is actually inside your head. So, if you were to look inside someone's head, you could see his or her brain, but you could not see his or her mind.

God created human beings as spirits with bodies. The future hope of all Christians is not that we will be spirits in heaven, but that, like our Lord Jesus, we will be reunited with God in our resurrected, glorified bodies (see 1 Corinthians 15:35–44). Thus, Christians acknowledge that human nature is not just spirit or just body, but spirit *and* body together. When the Bible talks about things like body, mind, spirit, and soul, it teaches that human nature consists of two kinds of reality: physical and non-physical (spiritual). This distinction is illustrated by Jesus' statement about fearing the one who could put "both soul and body" in hell (Matthew 10:28), and Paul's statement regarding body, soul, and spirit (1 Thessalonians 5:23). We are more than mere bodies, but we are also more than mere spirits.

In addition to these biblical indications, there are several other reasons supporting the belief that humans have supernatural minds. Let's look at four of these reasons.

Psychological Dualism: The belief that the human mind is not the same thing as the human brain. It affirms both the spiritual and physical aspects of human nature.

REASON #1: MINDING YOUR BRAIN

Is it possible to demonstrate that dualism is true? In other words, can you show that your mind (non-physical) and your brain (physical) are not the same thing?

To see the difference, consider this: the events in your mind are things like feelings and ideas, both of which are non-physical. An idea is not something that can be seen, weighed, or measured. It has no color, taste, texture, or other physical property. For this reason, mental events (like your thoughts) are not the same as physical events, like the chemical and electrical events that a doctor can measure in your brain. We can study the number of electrical firings between the synapses of the nerves in our brains. We can even measure the weight and size of our brains. But ideas cannot be weighed or measured.

Try this. Imagine a pink elephant in your mind. Close your eyes and look at the image. You can see the color pink. You can see the elephant's shape. But is there really a pink elephant in your brain? Nope. If a brain surgeon opened your head, he or she wouldn't find a tiny pink elephant hiding in your brain tissue.

The point is that mental events have properties that the physical events of the brain cannot have, such as thinking of pink elephants. This is because there is a difference between your mind and your brain: one is non-physical (your mind) and the other is physical (your brain).

Okay, one more thought experiment. Pick up a rock or a leaf and try to figure out whether it is true or false, good or evil. Is the rock you are thinking about false? Is the leaf morally good? Even though this may seem silly—after all, rocks don't have any innate morality—the point is that if you were to take any physical object and wonder if it was true or false, good or bad, you would be thinking about it in the wrong way. It doesn't make sense to think of rocks as being false or good. If we do, we have committed what is called a category fallacy.

A **category fallacy** occurs when you mistakenly apply a category to an object or event. For example, what if someone asked you what the number 43 smelled like? Or how much red weighs? This would be nonsensical, because numbers do not have fragrances and colors do not have mass. Both numbers and colors are in the category of non-physical things. Only a physical object, like a rose, is in the category of things that have fragrance and mass.

Can you see now why mental events cannot be physical objects? A rock by definition cannot be false or morally wrong, but our *thoughts* about rocks can be false or morally wrong. For example, we

---

Category Fallacy: This occurs when you mistakenly apply a category to an object or event when the category does not apply.

---

might think some rock is granite when it is actually sandstone. Or, we might want to injure someone with a rock because we don't like them. Either way, the bottom line is that our thoughts are not physical events in our brains. They are actually non-physical, mental events in our minds.[4]

REASON #2: UNITY OF IDENTITY

A second reason that dualism makes more sense than monism is that dualism is the only explanation for our experience of consciousness. We have what could be called a **unity of identity**. What this means is that even though all the cells and molecules of your body are constantly changing, including the cells of your brain, your personal identity does not change. You are the same person you were as a toddler—sure, you are bigger and smarter now, but you are the same *you* today as you were back then. No matter how much you grow or experience, your consciousness—your personal identity—will remain the same throughout the entire course of your life. You will always think of yourself as the same person. This is significant because it implies that our identity is not tied to our *physical bodies* but rather resides in our *spiritual selves*.

Unity of Identity: Although all the cells of your body are constantly changing, your personal identity does not change.

REASON #3: REMEMBERING

A third point supporting dualism is that human memory upholds the existence of a supernatural mind. "What research has shown us thus far," writes Arthur Custance, "is that there is no precise one-to-one relationship between any fragment of memory and the nerve cells in which it is supposed to be encoded."[5] This illustrates the fact that our personal identities and memories cannot simply be located in our physical brains. In other words, our personalities are not things that we can see, hear, taste, touch, or smell. Therefore, they are not things contained in our brains.

REASON #4: FREE TO CHOOSE

Finally, without allowing for the mind to be supernatural, there is no explanation for the reality of our freedom to choose. Let's suppose that our thoughts are nothing more than the effects of physical causes in our brains. This means that our physical environment produces our thoughts, and that our sense of making mental choices is merely an illusion.

If this is true, then we are like balls on a pool table. One ball gets hit into the others and they move according to the laws of physics. So it would be with our thoughts, ideas, beliefs, and even actions. One physical incident starts the process rolling, and our actions are simply the end result. We have no choice. We can only say, "My synapses made me do it!"

Another example is a rock thrown across a room. Since the rock is purely physical, it must obey the laws of physics and continue traveling until something stops it. It cannot choose to change direction or even stop. It is just responding to its physical environment.

Ironically, this means that if naturalism is true we have no good reason to *choose* to believe it, because our belief is not really a belief, it is just a response. If the necessary physical causes are present, then our beliefs will necessarily follow in response to our environment. If you eat lunch or dinner, you are not choosing to eat, but merely reacting to your empty stomach.

But this end result is absurd, and doesn't match reality as we know it, because people live and talk as if they actually have free will. We make choices every day, like choosing to sit or stand, talk or remain silent, read a book or take a nap. In order to account for our free will, we must assume that we have a mind that is separate from our material brain. An immaterial mind would break the physical chain of cause/effect events and allow for personal choice.

Human Sinfulness and Responsibility

The Christian worldview affirms that the only way to adequately account for our thoughts and actions—both good and bad—is to acknowledge our changed nature in the wake of Adam and Eve's fall. Although originally created without sin, humanity has been inherently sinful since the Fall (Genesis 6:5; 8:21; Psalm 51:5; Romans 3:23; 5:12–13). The original revolt against God caused a dramatic, reality-shattering change in man's relationship with the rest of existence. In fact, our sinful nature—our desire to rebel against God—is the ultimate source of most psychological problems.

In order to properly understand human nature, we must understand that humans have a tendency since the fall to revolt against God and His laws. This is the essence of sin, the willful rebellion against God. And, the fracture in our relationship with God leads to a fracture in all of our other relationships—with ourselves, others, and the creation. This is the effect of sin, a struggle with who we are and how we should relate to others.

But if humans are basically physical machines, as naturalism would have us believe, then sin would be simple mechanical failure. Without the ability to choose, humans are not responsible for their actions. For example, if your computer stops working, you don't hold it responsible and punish it by making it sit in the corner for an hour until it starts behaving. So naturalism would have us believe that humans, like computers, cannot be held responsible for their actions.

"But if [the human being] is something more than merely a mechanism," writes Arthur Custance, "then his failure must be judged as something worse than the breakdown of a machine."[6] Deep in our souls, we know that the actions of wicked people—like the slaughter of the innocent or the abuse of women and children—cannot be excused simply as the actions of physical machines without moral choice.

Acknowledging the reality of human sin leads us to the reality of human responsibility. "The great benefit of the doctrine of sin," says Paul Vitz, "is that it reintroduces responsibility for our own behavior, responsibility for changing as well as giving meaning to our condition."[7]

The Influence of Society

There is something about our sin nature that we need to clarify. When the Bible states that we are all sinners (Romans 3:23), it is not saying that we always act out the worst that is in us. All people are capable of doing good deeds, even if they have not accepted Jesus as their savior—anyone can help an elderly person across the street, donate money to the homeless, or give up his seat on a bus to a pregnant woman. However, we rarely act out the very best that is in us either. Given the opportunity, we will usually act selfishly, disobey God's moral law, and generally do what we want to do.

The fact is that our culture, including our friendships and even our entertainment choices, has tremendous power to influence us. Based on the choices we make, we can either be encouraged to follow our sin nature and do wrong, or we can be encouraged to follow God's path and do right.

That is why it is so important to be careful about the things we allow into our minds. The Apostle Paul wrote, "Do not be deceived: 'Bad company corrupts good morals' " (1 Corinthians 15:33, HCSB). In other words, our friendships and habits of entertainment can so overwhelm us with temptations that we compromise what we know to be good and right. An old cliché says, "You are what you eat." More appropriate to our discussion would be to say, "You are what you see and hear."

Since, as the Bible states, we are responsible for what we say and do, we must get to the root of the problem: our thought lives. Everything that comes out of our mouths or makes us act a certain way originates from deep inside us. Even though we have many influences around us, *we are responsible for how we react to these influences*. Therefore, we must guard our hearts (Philippians 4:7) and renew our minds, so that we "may discern what is the good, pleasing, and perfect will of God" (Romans 12:1–2, HCSB).

So how do we do this? James teaches us to examine ourselves when we are tempted, because the root of that temptation may be our own hearts. The following passage illustrates the fact that Christians are responsible for their thought lives (internal) as well as for their sins (external).

Let no one say when he is tempted, "I am tempted by God"; for God cannot be tempted by evil, nor does He Himself tempt anyone. But each one is tempted when he is drawn away *by his own desires* and enticed. Then, when desire has conceived, it gives birth to sin; and sin, when it is full-grown, brings forth death (James 1:13–15, NKJV; italics added).

We cannot blame others for our evil thoughts and deeds. In fact, God promises us that He will not allow us to be overwhelmed by temptations.

No temptation has overtaken you except such as is common to man; but God is faithful, who will not allow you to be tempted beyond what you are able, but with the temptation will also make the way of escape, that you may be able to bear it (1 Corinthians 10:13, NKJV).

This means that we can never legitimately say, "I just couldn't help myself" or "He/she made me do it." The responsibility for our thoughts and deeds rests squarely upon us. When you face moments where you are tempted to think or say or do something wrong, remember the promise of God—that there is always a way of escape—and your own responsibility. To encourage you to walk in the right direction, consider these words from the Apostle Paul:

Finally, brethren, whatever things are true, whatever things are noble, whatever things are just, whatever things are pure, whatever things are lovely, whatever things are of good report, if there is any virtue and if there is anything praiseworthy—meditate on these things (Philippians 4:8, NKJV).

Transformed by the Holy Spirit

Our only hope in addressing the evil nature of human sin and avoiding the wrath of God is the redeeming work of Jesus and the indwelling transformation of the Holy Spirit. Paul explains this transforming work in Romans 8. This would be a great passage to memorize and think about often.

Therefore, there is now no condemnation for those who are in Christ Jesus, because through Christ Jesus the law of the Spirit of life set me free from the law of sin and death. For what the law was powerless to do in that it was weakened by the sinful nature, God did by sending his own Son in the likeness of sinful man to be a sin offering. And so he condemned sin in sinful man, in order that the righteous requirements of the law might be fully met in us, who do not live according to the sinful nature but according to the Spirit (Romans 8:1–9, NIV).

Conclusion

Christian psychology deals with the total "you"—body and soul. By trusting Jesus as your Savior, God accepts you as His child. True self-esteem is a result of replacing negative thoughts about yourself with God's perspective. By continuing to focus on God's view of who you are, you will be motivated to submit to the lordship of Christ and live a life that is pleasing to Him.

Those who live according to the sinful nature have their minds set on what that nature desires; but those who live in accordance with the Spirit have their minds set on what the Spirit desires. The mind of sinful man is death, but the mind controlled by the Spirit is life and peace; the sinful mind is hostile to God. It does not submit to God's law, nor can it do so. Those controlled by the sinful nature cannot please God. You, however, are controlled not by the sinful nature but by the Spirit, if the Spirit of God lives in you. And if anyone does not have the Spirit of Christ, he does not belong to Christ (Romans 8:5–9, NIV).

Endnotes

[1] We also acknowledge that depression can sometimes be caused by chemical and/or hormonal imbalances.

[2] Susan Schaeffer Macaulay, *How To Be Your Own Selfish Pig* (Grand Rapids, MI: Zondervan Corporation, 1982), 84–85.

[3] This is an actual quote from a "self-esteem" curriculum used in public schools beginning in the early 1990s called *Pumsy: In Pursuit of Excellence*.

[4] For more information on the differences between minds and brains, see the discussion in Gary R. Habermas and J. P. Moreland, *Beyond Death: Exploring the Evidence for Immortality* (Wheaton, IL: Crossway, 1998), chapter 2, "Body and Soul," 37–66.

[5] Arthur C. Custance, *Man in Adam and in Christ* (Grand Rapids, MI: Zondervan, 1975), 256.

[6] Ibid., 268.

[7] Paul Vitz, *Psychology as Religion: The Cult of Self-Worship* (Grand Rapids, MI: Eerdmans, 1985), 43.

Unit Five

A World of Ideas
Reading Discussion Questions

1. What is psychology? What key question does psychology seek to answer? What are the key ideas of Christian psychology?

2. What is psychological monism? What are two different types of psychological monism?

3. What is psychological dualism? How does this view fit the Christian worldview and the doctrine of sin?

4. If you were to look inside someone's head, would you see their brain or mind? Explain.

5. What are four reasons that support the position that humans have a supernatural mind?

6. How should we properly understand human nature?

7. Are we responsible for our actions if we are nothing more than physical machines? Explain.

8. How would you define the following terms: category fallacy and unity of identity?

9. Reflection Question: What might have influenced Kathy to believe she was just an advanced animal? Kathy wanted to know if she was "worth anything to anybody." If she said that to you, how would you respond?

Psychology Paragraph
Assignment

*As you continue your study, write your own paragraph titled **My Christian Worldview of Psychology**. You will be able to correct it, add to it, put it into your Lightbearers Journal, and memorize it. Below is a checklist to help you with this assignment.*

- ☐ The paragraph states the definition of psychological dualism.
- ☐ It includes four reasons why dualism is the best explanation for who we are.
- ☐ It states that personal psychological health is linked to your beliefs about who you are in Christ.
- ☐ It emphasizes the importance of renewing your mind for overcoming negative thoughts and feelings.

What's Your Worldview?
Presentation Assignment

*Your assignment is to find **three** people outside of your school and ask them the following questions about what they believe. If possible, include at least one person who holds beliefs different than your own. You do not need to reveal the name of the people you interview unless you want to, but they should be relatives, parents, friends, or fellow church members who are willing to respond to your questions. Refrain from sharing your own opinion until they have given you their responses. This will prevent you from influencing their answers.*

Make a record of how each person responded, and be prepared to present your findings to the class. Also, write up these results to hand in to the teacher. Ask the following questions (or similar ones you feel will bring each person's worldview to light):

- ☐ Does God exist? If so, what He is like and how do you know?
- ☐ What is real? Is reality merely matter, an illusion, some combination, or something else?
- ☐ What is the origin of life and the universe?
- ☐ Are human beings special? Are we just animals? Do we have souls? Are we basically good or basically bad or something else?
- ☐ What is right and wrong? How do we know?

The Case Against Abortion
Video Outline

I.   Task #1: Restore Meaning to the Word "Abortion"

A. Our current culture

    1. _____ **culture:** We live in a culture that thinks and learns visually

        i.   We predominantly learn through images

        ii. We no longer learn through books and linear thought

    2. _____ **culture:** Postmodernism, simply stated, says that there is no objective truth

        i.   Debate is no longer over what happens to the fetus, if the fetus feels pain, or if abortion is moral

        ii. Debate is now about the circumstances of individual women and the right to privacy

        iii. Truth has been reduced to personal experience

        iv. Christians have not been a movement of thinkers

    3. _____ **culture:** We live in a culture that wants difficult life problems to "just go away"

"Our generation is the first generation of people [that] having demanded the right to kill its children through abortion is now demanding the right to kill its parents through doctor-assisted suicide." — Greg Cunningham

B. The challenge we face

"How do we communicate truth on abortion to a culture that thinks and learns visually, that wants difficult life problems to 'just go away,' and thinks that truth on abortion is elusive and is nothing more than a personal story or subjective experience? . . . The answer is we have to show the culture abortion; it is not enough to talk about it . . . We don't use images in place of good arguments; rather we use them to support our arguments."

    1. Tell people what they are about to see—don't trick them

    2. Tell them there is no narration, only instrumental music

    3. Stress the fact that our Lord is eager to forgive the sin of abortion

Unit Five

II. **Task #2: Simplify the Abortion Debate**

    A. What is the unborn?

        1. The debate is not over choice and who gets to decide

        2. When someone kills a toddler, everyone agrees that a human was killed

        3. Are fetuses human beings like toddlers?

        4. You cannot answer the question "Can I kill this?" until we ask the question, "What is *it*?"

    B. *Tactic*: _____

"Every time someone gives you an objection to the pro-life view or offers you a justification as to why abortion ought to be allowed, ask yourself if this works as a good argument for killing a toddler."

Note: This tactic is not designed to show that the fetus is a human. It is designed to show that this is the question, and everything else is irrelevant, for example:

        1. Unwanted children

        2. Psychological pain/rape

        3. Back-alley abortions

        "If the unborn aren't human, then no justification for elective abortion is necessary. If they are human, then no justification for elective abortion is adequate." — Gregory Koukl

    C. Showing that the unborn are human

        1. Scientific evidence

            i. _____: Living things reproduce after their own kind

            "How is it possible for human parents to produce an offspring that is not human but later becomes human?"

            ii. Some individuals claim that the unborn are biologically human, but not persons

"What is the difference between being a human and being a person?"

2. Philosophic evidence

   i. _____: large people are not more human than small people

   ii. _____: a four-year-old is not less human than a fourteen-year-old

   iii. _____: a newborn in an incubator is not less human than a child outside the womb

   iv. _____: people on insulin are less viable but no less human

   "[For] any physical change to your body that does not kill you, you remain yourself through that change, because you have a human nature that was present from the moment you were conceived that allows us to say that we are the same person now that was conceived 19 or 20 years ago. The only difference is function—your abilities have changed but your essential nature is the same."

III. **Task #3: Responding to Five Common Objections**

   A. Pro-abortion rhetoric assumes the unborn are not human

      1. _____: When one assumes what they are trying to prove

         "The statement, 'a woman has a right to an abortion,' assumes there is no child in her womb that also has a right to live."

         "The statement, 'a woman has a right to control her own body,' assumes there is only one body involved in the act of abortion."

      2. They are asserting rather than arguing

         i. _____: A claim without evidence

         ii. _____: A claim supported with evidence and/or reasons

      3. *Tactic*:_____

"In order for an argument to be valid it must have walls supporting it. You want to force them to provide walls [justification] for their house [assertion]."

4. *Tactic*:_____

"Sometimes there is an invisible wall in an argument. For example, some assert that 'the Bible is silent on abortion therefore it is fine.' Now the Bible doesn't expressly condemn cutting up your neighbor and feeding him to sharks, or drive-by shootings, or lynching homosexuals, but does that mean we are morally correct if we do those things?"

Ask, "Are you saying that whatever the Bible doesn't expressly condemn, it permits?"

B. Pro-abortion rhetoric often attacks the character of pro-lifers rather than refuting the argument

1. _____ **fallacy:** Attacking the person rather than the argument

    i. You're a man

    "Arguments don't have genders, people do."

    ii. How many unwanted babies have you adopted?

2. *Tactic*:_____

    "How does my alleged unwillingness to adopt a child justify an abortionist killing one? The issue is, 'What is the unborn?' "

C. Pro-abortion rhetoric confuses moral claims with preference claims

1. _____ **claim:** does not address what we like, but what we believe is true or right

2. _____ **claim:** has nothing to do with what is true or right, but with what we personally like

"Here is the problem: we are saying to the culture that abortion is wrong and they are hearing we like chocolate ice cream rather than vanilla. They are taking our truth claim and changing it into a preference claim."

"When we are talking about what is right and wrong, we are not talking about what we like. In fact, there are a lot of things I would like to do, but I do not do because it would be morally wrong. And morality is about not doing some things we would *like* to do. That is why the bumper sticker 'don't like abortion; don't have one' is so off the mark. Imagine me saying 'don't like owning slaves, that's fine don't own one.' "

3. Why relativism fails

    i. It cannot live up to its own standard

      "When someone says 'You shouldn't force your view on me,' they are forcing *their* view on you . . . "When someone says 'You shouldn't force your view on me,' your reply is, 'Why not?' Any answer they give you will be an example of them forcing their view on you."

    ii. You can't say anything is right or wrong, including intolerance

D. Pro-abortion rhetoric confuses functioning as a person with being one

    1. Rights are not based on current capacity, but inherent capacity

    "If our rights are based on functional ability, we are all on a gigantic bell curve. We start off with very little rights of personhood; as we age and mature and reach our physical and intellectual peaks we have maximum rights of personhood and then as we grow old and decline we lose personhood . . . It also results in savage inequality . . . Keep in mind there is a difference between functioning as a person and being a person."

    2. The issue of personal identity

    "Ask, 'Were you ever an unborn child?' If the answer is yes, they have conceded a fundamental point of the pro-life view, that is that human identity is a continuum from conception to death. If they answer that they were never an unborn child, ask them, 'What were you?' "

E. Pro-abortion rhetoric disguises its true position

    1. The case of rape

"Would you be willing to fight with me to end the practice of abortion for every instance except rape?"

"Rape is a tragic thing but should the child be executed for the crime of its father? Or is it fair to demand that the child be killed so that its mother can feel better? . . . Would it be okay to kill a two-year old so its mother can feel better?"

   2. The real issue is not rape, incest, or anything else. It is, "What is the unborn?"

IV. Questions and Answers

   A. How can we respond to those who say that they are personally against abortion but would not make it illegal?

   "You personally oppose abortion because it takes the life of an innocent human baby, but you think it should be legal to kill babies?"

   B. How can we respond to the claim that "Even if we outlaw abortion, people will still get them"?

   "Laws against rape don't stop all rape, but we still have laws against it. Laws against car theft don't stop all cases of car theft but it does stop most of them. The law is a moral teacher."

   C. How should we respond to pregnancies that endanger the life of the mother?

   "It is better to save one person than lose both."

   D. How can we respond to partial-birth abortion?

   "First, these abortions are done for convenience. Second, if the mother's life is in danger why would the doctor use a three-day technique . . . If this is a life or death situation for the mother, you could do a c-section in a matter of minutes."

The Case against Abortion
Video Discussion Questions

1. What three negative characteristics of our current culture complicate the abortion debate?

2. How do we restore meaning to the word "abortion" in our culture?

3. How do we simplify the abortion debate?

4. How do we convey both scientifically and philosophically that the unborn are human beings?

5. What are five common pro-abortion objections to the pro-life position, and how can you best respond?

Unit Five

Who Are We?
Exercise

Understanding our identity in Christ allows us to stand firm in our understanding of who we are in Christ when bombarded by the culture's ideas of what it means to be valuable.

Look up the verses below in your Bible, and fill in the blanks to underscore the significant truths about who you are in Christ.

1. John 1:12: I am a _____ of God.

2. John 15:16: I am chosen and appointed by Christ to bear _____.

3. Romans 8:1: I am free forever from _____.

4. Romans 8:17: I am a joint _____ with Christ, sharing His inheritance with Him.

5. 1 Corinthians 6:17: I am _____ with the Lord and am one in spirit with Him.

6. 1 Corinthians 6:19, 20: I have been _____ with a price; I am not my own; I belong to God.

7. 2 Corinthians 5:17: I am a new _____.

8. 2 Corinthians 5:21: I have become the _____ of God.

9. Galatians 2:20: Christ lives in _____. The life I am now living is Christ's life.

10. Ephesians 1:3: I have been blessed with every _____ blessing.

11. Ephesians 1:4: I was chosen in Christ before the creation of the world to be _____, and I am without blame before Him.

12. Colossians 2:7: I am firmly _____ in Christ and am now being built up in Him.

13. Colossians 2:10: I have been made _____ in Christ.

14. 2 Timothy 1:7: I have been given a spirit of _____, love, and self-discipline.

15. Hebrews 4:16: I have the right to come boldly before the throne of God to receive _____ and find grace to help in time of need.

16. 2 Peter 1:4: I have been given precious and magnificent promises by God, by which I am a partaker of God's _____ nature.

17. 1 John 5:18: I am born of _____, and the evil one cannot touch me.

For the next two weeks, read the above list out loud everyday. Think about what it means to be a child of God. When you are tempted to sin, remember that you have God's mighty power working in you (Ephesians 3:20–21).

How to Be Your Own Selfish Pig
Reading Discussion Questions

Chapter 9: That Does Not Compute

1. What are the two possible answers to the question *what are people?*

2. According to the Bible, what is the source of man's personality?

3. What does "His own image" mean?

4. How does Kathy describe the change she experienced when she accepted her worth as a person created by God?

5. When you accept Christ, what kind of self-knowledge does that give you?

6. As a Christian, how do you view others?

7. Francis Schaeffer said, "The _____ tells us who we are. . . we do not need to be confused, as is much of modern mankind. . ."

8. Reflection Question: Do you believe there is something unique inside you and all other people that cannot be explained by the idea that you are a machine or animal?

9. Reflection Question: Do your ideas of love and beauty and your choices mean anything, or are they illusions?

10. Reflection Question: Do you have value? Why?

LIGHTBEARERS

Unit Six

A Summit Ministries Curriculum

DAY	UNIT 06: syllabus & outline	SW	✓
1	Read *A World of Ideas* Reading...	**139**	
2	Read *A World of Ideas* Reading...	DITTO	
3	Review *A World of Ideas* Reading Discussion Questions..	**146**	
4	Review *A World of Ideas* Reading Discussion Questions..	DITTO	
	Assign **Sociology Paragraph** [Rough Draft Due on Day 8]...	**147**	
5	Watch **"Biblical Christian Worldview: Sociology"** Video Outline.......................................	**148**	
	Complete **Gay Marriage and Broccoli Pizza** Exercise..	**149**	
	Complete **Foundations for Society** Exercise..	**150**	
6	Assign **The Family in Focus** [Assignment Due on Day 11 or 12].....................................	**152**	
	Watch **"Marriage and Family"** Video Outline..	**153**	
7	Watch **"Marriage and Family"** Video Outline..	DITTO	
8	Review **"Marriage and Family"** Video Discussion Questions..	**158**	
	Turn in **Sociology Paragraph** Rough Draft [Assignment Due on Day 13]........................	---	
9	Read *How to Be Your Own Selfish Pig* Reading (Ch. 10)...	---	
10	Review *How to Be Your Own Selfish Pig* Reading Discussion Questions (Ch. 10)........	**159**	
11	Turn in & Share **The Family in Focus** Presentation Assignment......................................	---	
12	Turn in & Share **The Family in Focus** Presentation Assignment......................................	---	
13	Turn in **Sociology Paragraph** Assignment..	---	
	Take **Learn to Discern** Quiz..	---	
	Prepare **Unit 06** Test...	---	
14	Take **Unit 06** Test..	---	
15			

A World of Ideas:
What Makes a Healthy Society

Objects on this page are no smaller than they appear.

If you can read this, you are too close to your workbook.

KEYS TO UNDERSTANDING

Key Question: What makes a healthy society?

Key Idea: God has ordained the social institutions of family, church, and state so that each would foster love, respect, discipline, work, and harmonious community.

Key Terms: sociology, family, church

Key Verse: Hebrews 2:11

"He [Christ] is not ashamed to call them [Christians] brethren..." (Hebrews 2:11, HCSB).

Have you ever noticed how few hermits there are in the world? Most people just naturally want to be around other people. Even when they are alone, people are continually reaching out to others through cell phone calls, text messaging, chat rooms, blogs, and emails. It seems we're made for each other, which, by the way, is what God had designed for us all along. Recall His words to Adam and Eve when God began the human race. He commanded them to build a society:

> So God created man in his own image, in the image of God he created him; male and female he created them. God blessed them and said to them, 'Be fruitful and increase in number; fill the earth and subdue it'... The LORD God said, 'It is not good for the man to be alone. I will make a helper suitable for him'... Then the LORD God made a woman from the rib he had taken out of the man, and he brought her to the man. The man said, 'This is now bone of my bones and flesh of my flesh'... For this reason a man will leave his father and mother and be united to his wife, and they will become one flesh (Gen 1:27–28, 2:18, 22–23, 24, NIV).

Sociology is the study of how we live together in society. As part of an overall worldview, it asks the question "What makes a healthy society?" From the biblical perspective, there are at least three important parts for building a lasting social order—the *family*, the *church*, and the *state*.

Living in a healthy society sounds good, but each level of society has its own benefits and pitfalls. The family can be a place of love and blessing or one of fear and abuse. Churches can fulfill their role of spreading the gospel and serving those in need or they can fall apart into factions. The state can unify people to protect their God-given rights of life and liberty or it can become a bureaucracy that imposes high taxes and takes freedoms away from the people.

This chapter will explore God's design for society as it relates to two of these social institutions: the family and the church (we will cover the state in Unit 8). As you read through these pages, you will learn:

> . . . What it means to be a social creature
> . . . How to change our society for the better
> . . . Why families are the bedrock of all societies
> . . . The importance of the church for maintaining a civilized culture

Sociology: The study of how we live together in society.

Diagnosing the Problem

A medical doctor checks certain physical "vital signs" to determine a patient's health. This might include measuring pulse, blood pressure, or breathing. If these are within a certain range, the patient is considered healthy. But if one or more are outside normal limits, the doctor (and the patient!) has cause for concern.

Like an individual, the society in which we live has certain "vital signs" that indicate its condition. Our culture's vital signs would include things like the crime rate; the number of divorces vs. marriages;

Unit Six

physical, drug, or alcohol abuse; sexual promiscuity; the quality of public education; political ethics and voter turnout; and the success of charities and volunteer organizations.

Let's put on our white coats and try to diagnose our culture. On a scale of 1 to 5, with 1 being "healthy" and 5 being "sick," mark how you would rate the cultural health of our nation:

	Healthy				Sick
Crime rate	1	2	3	4	5
Divorce rate	1	2	3	4	5
Stable families	1	2	3	4	5
Physical abuse	1	2	3	4	5
Drug/alcohol abuse	1	2	3	4	5
Sexual promiscuity	1	2	3	4	5
Racial unity	1	2	3	4	5
Education	1	2	3	4	5
Political ethics	1	2	3	4	5
Voter turnout	1	2	3	4	5
Volunteer organizations	1	2	3	4	5

In Unit 05, you saw that naturalistic beliefs tend to deny human free will. By rejecting God, naturalists reject the image of God in human beings. They believe that our thoughts and actions are determined by a combination of our genetic makeup and our social environment, which includes your family, neighborhood, friends, and the values you've learned from the culture at large. The bottom line, they say, is that individuals are not responsible for their actions, just like computers aren't responsible when they malfunction. If someone does something bad, it's not his or her fault. The blame is most often placed on society, environment, or upbringing.

One of the biggest differences between a secular (or naturalistic) approach to sociology and the Christian approach is the biblical teaching that humans have free will and are therefore responsible for their actions. This means that instead of society shaping the individual, it is the individual who shapes society. Humans must face the consequences of their ideas and actions—their behavior cannot be blamed on society.

William Stanmeyer writes, "If man's behavior were somehow conditioned by genetic code or social externals then no just judge could blame him for the evil he commits. But Scripture teaches unequivocally that God blamed Adam and Eve for succumbing to the temptation to disobedience and punished them accordingly."[1] When Adam and Eve violated God's prohibition regarding the tree of the knowledge of good and evil, they knowingly brought a curse upon the entire human race and all of creation (Genesis 3 and Romans 8:19–22).

The fall of Adam and Eve brought alienation into God's creation. This means that instead of living in harmony, our relationship with God, with ourselves, with others, and even with the natural environment is out of sync. We are separated physically, emotionally, and spiritually from God. The result is that humans tend to consistently break the two greatest commands in the Bible: to love our God with all our heart, soul, mind, and strength; and to love other humans as ourselves. In failing to express authentic love toward God and others, our relationships with God and others is bruised, broken, and in need of healing. This means not only are we individually a mess, but we have a messed up society! This is the impact of the fall on society.

With all this talk about how sinful human beings are, shouldn't Christians have a pretty negative view of society? At first glance you might think so, but in reality this is not the case. In fact, Christians have the most cause to be hopeful about mankind and society because of God's redemption through Jesus Christ. The Christian recognizes that while the power of sin may be great, the power of God is even greater. "For I am not ashamed of the gospel of Christ," declared the Apostle Paul, "for it is the power of God to salvation for everyone who believes, for the Jew first and also for the Greek" (Romans 1:16, NKJV).

The central message of the Bible declares that through God's grace, humans can be made new (2 Corinthians 5:17). Therefore those who have been made new should not only be able to live better lives, but we should also be able to influence society for the better.

In two key passages of Scripture, the Apostle Paul speaks both of our *alienation* (being separated from God) and our *reconciliation* (being brought back together with Him). In Colossians 1:19–22, Paul notes that although we are alienated from God, the work of Jesus reconciles us to the Father. And in Ephesians 2:14–16, Paul comments on how Jesus' work reconciles us to each other in community.

> For it pleased the Father that in Him [Christ] all the fullness should dwell, and by Him to reconcile all things to Himself, by Him, whether things on earth or things in heaven, having made peace through the blood of His cross. And you, who once were alienated and enemies in your mind by wicked works, yet now He has reconciled in the body of His flesh through death, to present you holy, and blameless, and above reproach in His sight… (Colossians 1:19–22, NKJV).

> For He Himself is our peace, who has made both one [that is, Jews and Gentiles], and has broken down the middle wall of separation, having abolished in His flesh the enmity, that is, the law of commandments contained in ordinances, so as to create in Himself one new man from the two, thus making peace, and that He might reconcile them both to God in one body through the cross, thereby putting to death the enmity (Ephesians 2:14–16, NKJV).

Only the Christian approach to sociology has the key to individual and social well being—the cross of Jesus Christ. This is why Christians are so eager to see people come to faith in Him. It is *in Jesus Christ* that we find the only real hope for our social problems.

On the other hand, if we fail to understand the inherent sinfulness of human beings, then we will not be able to properly identify the true causes of social problems and will end up prescribing the wrong solutions. There is a definite connection between someone's view of psychology (who we are) and his or her view of sociology (how society functions).

Focusing on Individuals, Not Just Society

When it comes to society, there are two basic approaches. The approach taken by many who have a naturalistic worldview states that social institutions are more important than individual human beings. This approach is especially true of *Secular Humanists*, who believe that since God does not exist, humans must rely only on their own reason, common sense, and science to advance the human race and save us from our problems. Secular Humanists reason that since individuals live only for seventy or eighty years, while societies last for hundreds of years, then society is more important than individuals. For example, the ancient Roman Empire lasted over 1,000 years, while Chinese culture began over 5,000 years ago.

The second approach comes from Christianity. The Bible presents the overall idea that each human being has worth as an individual, not just as part of a larger society. In fact, each person is created as an eternal being in the image of God. In God's view, societies are here just for a moment, whereas individuals are eternal. Moreover, it is the individual who has been granted authority and responsibility for shaping the larger society.

> Then God said, "Let us make man in our image, in our likeness, and let them rule over the fish of the sea and the birds of the air, over the livestock, over all the earth, and over all the creatures that move along the ground." So God created man in his own image, in the image of God he created him; male and female he created them. God blessed them and said to them, "Be fruitful and increase in number; fill the earth and subdue it. Rule over the fish of the sea and the birds of the air and over every living creature that moves on the ground" (Genesis 1:26–28, NIV).

Although Christians see individuals as having eternal worth and societies as having temporary worth, this does not diminish the importance of sociology for the Christian worldview. This is because humans were created to be social beings. Just as God has perfect relationships within the Trinity, humans as His image bearers were created for relationships. "God created the human being to be a relational creature. Note this point well. Humankind was created to relate to other beings. It was not an accident. It was not the result of sin. It was an intentional, creational given."[2]

A Divine Institution: The Family

Since it is God's original intention that we should live together in society, we find that He provided the best way for society to function. The three primary institutions established by God for the betterment of mankind are the *family*, the *church*, and the *state*. Now let's explore the institutions of family and church, leaving the state for Unit Eight.

When it comes to the family, modern Western society is biased against the traditional view of marriage and family. There is a peculiar disdain for traditional marriage and families. This stems largely from the popularity of the naturalistic worldview and its idea of sexual freedom (after all, we are only animals). Indeed, most naturalists see the traditional family as an outdated, inhibiting institution.

Even as you read this, public school children in sex-education classes are being subjected to lessons about some of the most bizarre concepts and practices imaginable. Homosexuality being taught as a perfectly natural and legitimate lifestyle, students given condoms and advised to use them, and teenage girls are being instructed on how to obtain abortions without the knowledge or consent of their parents. As James Dobson and Gary Bauer note, such sex-ed programs are "a crash course in relativism, in immorality, and in anti-Christian philosophy."[3]

In addition to what is being taught in public schools, many people in popular culture promote for sexual immorality. This is evident in successful TV shows, major motion pictures, and popular songs and music videos. There is even popular support in the media for same-sex marriage. For instance, as far back as 1989, *Chicago Tribune* columnist Stephen Chapman wrote, "Like broccoli pizza, gay marriage isn't for everyone, but that's no reason to keep it off the menu."[4]

It shouldn't be surprising that the attempt to redefine marriage and family is sponsored by proponents of moral relativism and evolution. Their disregard for the existence of the human spirit—a supernatural part of mankind—leads them to assume that non-biblical values are best for the growth and development of individuals and societies.

However, Christians recognize that the covenant of marriage and the institution of the family were ordained by God (Genesis 2:23–25 and 1:28). The family is intended to provide a loving environment that encourages mental, emotional, and spiritual growth. And the basic form of the human family is a husband, a wife, and their children. Although this structure may be altered through death, divorce, or infertility, it does not change the original biblical family structure of husband-wife-children.

Scientific studies agree that this biblically-based view of the family is best for individuals and society. After surveying more than 130 studies, Professor Robert H. Coombs of the UCLA School of Medicine concluded: "Married people live longer and generally are more emotionally and physically healthy than the unmarried."[5] This supports what we know as Christians, that God's design for marriage and the family is the way we function best.

But do these traditional families really have an influence on society? Consider Jonathan Edwards—pastor, scholar, and leader of the First Great Awakening (a time of spiritual renewal in America in the 1700s). Jonathan and his wife Sarah, who raised eleven children, left a remarkable legacy to American society. Two hundred years after their death the family had 1,400 descendants, including:

- 13 college presidents
- 65 professors
- 100 lawyers
- 30 judges
- 66 physicians
- 3 governors
- 3 senators
- and a vice president of the United States![6]

This is one example of what can happen when a spiritually healthy family tradition is passed down from generation to generation. Ultimately it is society that benefits the most.

Education: A Family Responsibility

One of the fundamental responsibilities of the family is the education of children. In Deuteronomy 6:6–7, God assigned parents the task of passing on a spiritual heritage to their children. Even when parents decide to have their children educated at Christian or public schools, the fact remains that parents have the ultimate responsibility and authority for the education of their children.

> These commandments that I give you today are to be upon your hearts. Impress them on your children. Talk about them when you sit at home and when you walk along the road, when you lie down and when you get up (Deuteronomy 6:6–7, NIV).

But in a culture deeply influenced by naturalism, the state often claims greater authority over children than parents. Ray Sutton writes, "Any time you try to argue that someone, or some 'institution,' owns the family, you will end up viewing the family as just a human creation, a mere contract. If that's all it is, then there's no reason for the state not to violate it, just as it violates all sorts of private contracts. What principle is to prevent the State from taking a family's children, re-educating them, or breaking it up whenever it seems socially and politically expedient?"[7]

In such heavily atheistic countries as Russia, China, and Cuba, the mentality of state-sponsored education inevitably leads to brainwashing, where children are taught that God is a myth and religion hurts society. Even in the United States, which was founded on biblical principles, the government has increasingly taken control of education. In fact, the educational system has long been a target of naturalists, who see it as the primary way to influence young people to accept their atheistic belief system. As far back as 1930, Secular Humanist Charles Francis Potter wrote, "Education is the most powerful ally of Humanism, and every American public school is a school of Humanism. What can the theistic Sunday-schools, meeting for an hour once a week, and teaching only a fraction of the children, do to stem the tide of a five-day program of humanistic teaching?"[8]

Because of the atheistic influence over what is taught in American public schools, many Christian parents have chosen to teach their children at home or enroll them in private schools. In this way they are seeking to honor God's command to raise their children under a godly influence.

A Divine Institution: The Church

The church is the primary avenue God has created for making disciples who live and teach His truth throughout the world. Although the state sometimes infringes upon the church by restricting Christians from discussing religious issues in broader society, Christians know that they must obey God rather than men (Acts 5:29), while praying for their civil rulers so that the church may live at peace in society (1 Timothy 2:1–3).

The church is a necessary social institution for several reasons. First, without the church, people would have no teaching about their ultimate need for fellowship with God (Romans 10:14–15). Second, many Christians would be ignorant of their spiritual needs and never come to know God as fully as He intended. Third, Christians would not have an ordered means of worshiping God and enjoying fellowship together. Fourth, Christians would be left to struggle and grow on their own without the help and encouragement of other believers. Fifth, there would be very little change in society. Sixth, in addition to changing individuals, the church also can cause society to turn toward God by providing an example of true community.

If the Christian church shows people that it is possible to "love your neighbor as yourself," then they might be more willing to turn to God and acknowledge Him as the initiator of all relationships. But if Christians retreat from being involved in culture, the light of the gospel flickers and goes out. All that is left is the darkness of man's sinful ideas.

Jesus has called us to spread His light of righteousness. The reason that we go to church and learn more about a relationship with God is so we can be equipped to proclaim His love to others who are still in darkness. 1 Peter notes, "But you are a chosen race, a royal priesthood, a holy nation, a people for

His possession, so that you may proclaim the praises of the One who called you out of darkness into His marvelous light" (1 Peter 2:9, HCSB).

Hope for Civilization

In the parable of the Good Samaritan, Jesus told a story that shows how everyone should be involved in meeting the needs of a hurting neighbor. Christians throughout the ages have taken this teaching of Jesus to heart and sought ways to help their neighbors and their society. A brief survey of history from the beginning of the Christian church will show how this has taken place.

When the church was born, Roman civilization had brought peace and harmony to a large portion of the world. But within four hundred years, Rome fell to the sword of northern barbarians. During the next few centuries, chaos ruled Europe, as warring bands of illiterate Germanic tribes opposed and deposed one another. Cities and cultural centers disappeared. Literacy and law and order crumbled. But one force prevented barbarism from completely taking over—the church.

The medieval church modeled a counter-culture that kept the spark of civilization alive. Monks preserved not only the Bible but classical literature as well. For example, during the seventh century in France, the clergy were the best-educated and least immoral group in Europe. The French monks ran schools and sheltered orphans, widows, paupers, and slaves. They constructed aqueducts, opened hospitals, and gained the respect of a population staggering under the greed and dishonesty of their political leaders.

The same was true in other countries of Western Europe, as well as Ireland and England.[9] Because Christians got involved in society, the barbarous Dark Ages gave way to the light of Christian culture, and civilization was renewed.

What is true in the general sweep of history is equally true in the lives of individual Christians who have sought to make a difference. Abraham Kuyper, a Dutch theologian and pastor in the early 1900s, provides an excellent example. Kuyper worked diligently to influence public life in the Netherlands by founding a Christian university, publishing a newspaper, and even being elected prime minister. The social, political, and educational reforms Kuyper initiated continue to benefit Holland today.[10]

Conclusion

Sociology is the study of how human beings live with each other. You have seen that the naturalistic perspective denies that the institutions of family, church, and state are divinely created and sanctioned institutions. Since naturalists believe in an inherent goodness in human nature, they think that society is what makes individuals do bad things. Thus, if society can be improved, individuals will be improved too.

However, according to the Bible, man is inherently sinful. Therefore, the source of evil in the world is within the human heart. If the human heart can be changed, then the evil that plagues society can also be changed.

The Christian worldview affirms three divinely decreed social institutions—family, church, and state. While Christians do not see these institutions as being untouched by sin, we do see them as important for the spiritual, mental, and moral well being of all humans, individually and socially. And while there is still work to be done to see goodness flourish in society, Christians realize that the "me-centered" focus so popular in contemporary culture is just another expression of human pride and sinfulness.[11]

Sociology, apart from the Bible, is ineffective and destructive. "In the absence of biblical norms to guide the relationship between humanity and God," declares Gaede, "we can expect knowledge of ultimate reality to move in either a fatalistic or humanistic direction."[12] However, neither putting complete responsibility for the way we live on fate nor on mankind is helpful or good.

Christians understand that human beings are not inherently good, and that the remedy for a sick society is to change the individuals in it. Thus, instead of giving up on society, Christians seek to help individuals change for the better through the saving power of God's grace.

Finally, Christians also desire to show everyone that God rules over all social institutions. There is no part of creation over which God does not have authority. The Bible teaches that Christians are God's hands and feet to a needy world—the physical representation of the righteousness taught in the Bible. Therefore, we should seek ways to help our fellow man, such as providing soup kitchens for the hungry, building houses for the homeless, and caring for the physically and emotionally hurting. Throughout history, Christians have always been in the forefront of social activity. History has passed the baton to us, and we can't give up now.

Endnotes

[1] William A. Stanmeyer, *Clear and Present Danger* (Ann Arbor, MI: Servant Books, 1983), 42.

[2] C.D. Gaede, *Where Gods May Dwell* (Grand Rapids, MI: Zondervan, 1985), 78.

[3] James C. Dobson and Gary L. Bauer, *Children at Risk: The Battle for the Hearts and Minds of Our Kids* (Dallas, TX: Word, 1990), 112.

[4] Stephen Chapman, "Tolerance, Social Endorsements and Gay Marriage," Chicago Tribune (Oct 12, 1989), 123.

[5] "Several Studies Link Good Health With Religious Belief, Prayer," *Statesville Record & Landmark* (February 13, 1996), 8–A.

[6] "The Family in America," *Focus on the Family* (June 1991), 2–3.

[7] Ray Sutton, *Who Owns the Family? God or the State?* (Nashville, TN: Dominion Press, 1986), 3.

[8] Charles Francis Potter, *Humanism: A New Religion* (New York, NY: Simon and Schuster, 1930), 128.

[9] Charles Colson, *Against the Night* (Ann Arbor, MI: Servant Books, 1989), 133–4.

[10] Ibid.

[11] Charles Colson, *A Dance with Deception* (Dallas, TX: Word, 1993), 21.

[12] Gaede, *Where Gods May Dwell*.

A World of Ideas
Reading Discussion Questions

1. What is sociology? What key question does sociology seek to answer? What are the key ideas of Christian sociology?

2. What are the biggest differences between a secular (or naturalistic) approach to sociology and a Christian approach?

3. What is God's design for the family? What role does the family play?

4. What are (at least) three of the reasons God ordained the church?

5. Reflection Question: Earlier you read about the remarkable legacy left by Jonathan Edwards. What kind of legacy do you want to leave? Are you living your life and preparing in such a way that will help you pass on a godly legacy to your family? If not, what do you need to change? What practical things can you do to start preparing to leave a godly legacy?

Sociology Paragraph
Assignment

*As you continue your study, write your own paragraph titled **My Christian Worldview of Sociology**. You will be able to correct it, add to it, put it into your Lightbearers Journal, and memorize it. Below is a checklist to help you with this assignment.*

- ☐ The paragraph states the Christian definition of sociology.
- ☐ It talks about the importance of the God-ordained institutions of family, church, and state.
- ☐ It includes the remedy for a sick society.
- ☐ It discusses your personal accountability to God for the direction in which society goes.

Sociology
Video Outline

I. **Biblical Christian Sociology:** _____

    A. Whereas atheistic worldviews see humans as evolving _____, Christians believe that people are created in God's _____.

    "One of the fundamental ways in which Christian sociology differs from Humanistic approaches—whether Marxist, New Age, or simply atheistic—is its affirmation of individual freedom and responsibility. While Humanistic approaches hold that society determines people's consciousness and actions, Christianity believes that, while society does influence people, they have the freedom to choose between right and wrong, and to shape society." — Del Tackett

    B. Biblical Christianity sees every individual as valuable and capable of making an important contribution to society. More than that, Christian sociology recognizes that people were created as social beings.

        1. Biblical Christianity holds that both the individual and society are important.

        2. Biblical Christianity holds that both individuals and societies are accountable to God.

            i. The _____ is not to encroach on family rights or on the church, and neither are the others to overstep their boundaries.

            ii. People must recognize the consequences for the choices they make, both individually and _____.

Gay Marriage and Broccoli Pizza
Exercise

In *A World of Ideas*, you read the following quote from Stephen Chapman: "Like broccoli pizza, gay marriage isn't for everyone, but that's no reason to keep it off the menu." First, notice that this comment was made in 1989. The idea of same-sex marriage has been around for a long time and is not going away anytime soon, if at all.

Discuss this analogy between gay marriage and broccoli pizza. Then answer the following questions as a class.

1. Is equating gay marriage to a person's choice in pizza a good analogy? Why or why not?

2. What does Chapman assume about both your choice of pizza and of your marriage partner?

3. How would you respond to these assertions from a Christian standpoint?

Foundations for Society
Exercise

Read Genesis 1 and scan for the recurring phrase that describes what God thought of His creation (see especially verses 10, 12, 18, 21, 25, 31). Then, discuss the questions with the class. This chapter is taken from the NIV.

Genesis 1

[1]In the beginning God created the heavens and the earth. [2]Now the earth was [a] formless and empty, darkness was over the surface of the deep, and the Spirit of God was hovering over the waters. [3]And God said, "Let there be light," and there was light. [4]God saw that the light was good, and He separated the light from the darkness. [5]God called the light "day," and the darkness he called "night." And there was evening, and there was morning—the first day. [6]And God said, "Let there be an expanse between the waters to separate water from water." [7]So God made the expanse and separated the water under the expanse from the water above it. And it was so. [8]God called the expanse "sky." And there was evening, and there was morning—the second day. [9]And God said, "Let the water under the sky be gathered to one place, and let dry ground appear." And it was so. [10]God called the dry ground "land," and the gathered waters he called "seas." And God saw that it was good. [11]Then God said, "Let the land produce vegetation: seed-bearing plants and trees on the land that bear fruit with seed in it, according to their various kinds." And it was so. [12]The land produced vegetation: plants bearing seed according to their kinds and trees bearing fruit with seed in it according to their kinds. And God saw that it was good. [13]And there was evening, and there was morning—the third day. [14]And God said, "Let there be lights in the expanse of the sky to separate the day from the night, and let them serve as signs to mark seasons and days and years, [15]and let them be lights in the expanse of the sky to give light on the earth." And it was so. [16]God made two great lights—the greater light to govern the day and the lesser light to govern the night. He also made the stars. [17]God set them in the expanse of the sky to give light on the earth, [18]to govern the day and the night, and to separate light from darkness. And God saw that it was good. [19]And there was evening, and there was morning—the fourth day. [20]And God said, "Let the water teem with living creatures, and let birds fly above the earth across the expanse of the sky." [21]So God created the great creatures of the sea and every living and moving thing with which the water teems, according to their kinds, and every winged bird according to its kind. And God saw that it was good. [22]God blessed them and said, "Be fruitful and increase in number and fill the water in the seas, and let the birds increase on the earth." [23]And there was evening, and there was morning—the fifth day. [24]And God said, "Let the land produce living creatures according to their kinds: livestock, creatures that move along the ground, and wild animals, each according to its kind." And it was so. [25]God made the wild animals according to their kinds, the livestock according to their kinds, and all the creatures that move along the ground according to their kinds. And God saw that it was good. [26]Then God said, "Let us make man in our image, in our likeness, and let them rule over the fish of the sea and the birds of the air, over the livestock, over all the earth, [b]and over all the creatures that move along the ground." [27]So God created man in his own image, in the image of God he created him; male and female he created them. [28]God blessed them and said to them, "Be fruitful and increase in number; fill the earth and subdue it. Rule over the fish of the sea and the birds of the air and over every living creature that moves on the ground." [29]Then God said, "I give you every seed-bearing plant on the face of the whole earth and every tree that has fruit with seed in it. They will be yours for food. [30]And to all the beasts of the earth and all the birds of the air and all the creatures that move on the ground—everything that has the breath of life in it—I give every green plant for food." And it was so. [31]God saw all that he had made, and it was very good. And there was evening, and there was morning—the sixth day.

Foundations for Society
Exercise Questions

1. "God saw that it was _____."

2. Read Genesis 2:18. What is one of the first things God said after creating Adam?

   The LORD God said, "It is not good for the man to be alone. I will make a helper suitable for him."

   "It is _____ good for the man to be _____."

3. In Genesis 2:19–20, God knew something about the man He had just created—Adam was not made to be alone. After stating that there was no helper suitable for Adam, God created _____ (Genesis 2:21–22). Why?

   Now the LORD God had formed out of the ground all the beasts of the field and all the birds of the air. He brought them to the man to see what he would name them; and whatever the man called each living creature, that was its name. So the man gave names to all the livestock, the birds of the air and all the beasts of the field.

   But for Adam no suitable helper was found. So the LORD God caused the man to fall into a deep sleep; and while he was sleeping, he took one of the man's ribs and closed up the place with flesh. Then the LORD God made a woman from the rib he had taken out of the man, and he brought her to the man.

4. What is another way to say what Adam felt when he first saw Eve (Genesis 2:23)?

   The man said, "This is now bone of my bones and flesh of my flesh; she shall be called 'woman,' 'for she was taken out of man."

5. In Genesis 2:24, God provides a summation of His creation of Adam and Eve by saying, "For this reason a man will _____ his father and mother and be _____ to his wife, and they will become one flesh."

   For this reason a man will leave his father and mother and be united to his wife, and they will become one flesh.

6. Relating to other people is a part of our inherent nature. It is God's design that we live in _____ with others.

The Family in Focus
Presentation Assignment

For this assignment, you will need to first divide into groups. Then you will need to research and report on the positive effects of living in a traditional family. You will also need to compare these results with the negative effects of less-traditional situations. Each group member will research a different area influenced by marriage, (such as economic prosperity, welfare, abortion, happiness, or child abuse). After doing your individual research, meet with your entire group to report your findings. The group as a whole will then decide which aspects to report to the class and select one person to present the summary. The following resources will help you research your reports. Some of these may be a little challenging, but we believe you can handle the content if you put your minds to it:

- Focus on the Family's website (www.family.org) has numerous articles on this subject.
- A brief article summarizing the research on the importance of fathers is at http://www.tothesource.org/6_11_2008/6_11_2008.htm.
- The Heritage Foundation has brought together under one report a large number of statistics related to marriage and economic prosperity, welfare, abortion, personal happiness, and child abuse. This report is at http://www.heritage.org/Research/Features/Marriage/index.cfm.
- See the article, "Breakdown of the Family," at http://www.leaderu.com/issues/fabric/chap03.html for another summary of the issues.
- The Center for Marriage and the Family has a number of brief reports on a variety of studies related to the family in America: http://center.americanvalues.org/?cat=2.
- The American Values website has a current study on the cost to taxpayers for rising divorce rates and childbearing outside of marriage: http://www.americanvalues.org/html/coff_mediaadvisory.htm.

Marriage and Family
Video Outline

I. Traditional Family

    A. What does the research show?

        1. It is best for _____

            i. Joseph Unwin's study of 16 civilized and 80 uncivilized cultures

- Cultures with strong sexual ethics were more productive and prosperous

- Cultures without strong sexual ethics lacked creative cultural energy

"Those cultures which allowed sexual freedom do not display a high level of social energy—their energy is consumed with meeting their physical appetites. They do not think large thoughts about the physical world…In these cultures, life is for now." — Joseph Unwin

- Cultures which began with, but lost, strong sexual ethics experienced cultural demise within 3 generations (e.g., Romans, Babylonians, and Sumerians)

- There are no exceptions to these findings

            ii. Barbra Defoe Whitehead and the National Marriage Project (Rutgers)

- Best situation for child-rearing

- Produces wealth

- Encourages pro-social behavior

- Generates social capital

        2. It is best for _____

            i. Health

- Mortality rates are 50% higher for unmarried women; 250% higher for unmarried men

- 9 out of 10 married men live to be 65; unmarried only 6 out of 10

ii. Sexual satisfaction

- 43% of married men have sex once per week; unmarried only 6%

- Married men and women find sex more satisfying

iii. Financial benefits

- The average retired married couple has accumulated about $410,000; unmarried only $167,000

iv. Physical security

- Single women are 10x more likely to be victims of rape

- Single women are 3x more likely to be victims of assault

"Married people live longer, are healthier, have few heart attacks and other diseases, have few problems with alcohol, behave in less risky ways, have more sex—and more satisfying sex—and become much more wealthy than single people. There was one exception to this rosy picture: cohabiting couples do have more sex. But they enjoy it less." — Linda Waite

B. Why does the research show this?

1. What did God design marriage for?

   i. God shaped and filled the Earth

   ii. God has asked us to continue shaping and filling the Earth

   iii. Marriage is not about you; it is about God's plan

2. Marriage is for three things:

   i. To show _____

   - **Created:** to bear His image

   - **Redeemed:** to show Christ's love for the Church

   ii. To perpetuate the _____

   - **Created:** to proclaim God's rule

   - **Redeemed:** to grow the Kingdom (have babies!)

iii. To be the Foundation of the _____

- **Created:** Cultural commission (fill and form)

- **Redeemed:** to restrain evil and promote strong commitments (fill and form)

II. Satan's Attack on the Family

A. Culture of _____

1. Choice

2. Convenience

    i. No-fault divorce

    ii. Dating

B. _____ Legacy — Human beings are just animals

1. Sigmund Freud (Psychology) — Sexual ethics are religious oppression

2. Margaret Sanger (Planned Parenthood) — Sexual liberation as religion

"Through sex, mankind may attain the great spiritual illumination which will transform the world, which will light up the only path to earthly paradise." — Margaret Sanger

3. Alfred Kinsey (*The Kinsey Report*) — Sexual norms should be torn down

4. Hugh Hefner — The *Playboy* philosophy

"*Playboy* freed a generation from guilt about sex, changed some laws and helped launch a revolution or two. *Playboy* is the magazine that changed America." — Hugh Hefner

5. Sexuality Information and Education Council of the United States (SEICUS)

    i. Sex education curriculum

"A new stage of evolution is breaking across the horizon and the task of educators is to prepare children to step into that new world. To do this, they must pry children away from old views and values, especially from biblical and other traditional forms of sexual morality—for religious laws or rules about sex were made on the basis of ignorance." — Mary Calderone, SIECUS founder

ii. Funded by Hugh Hefner

6. Pornography

    i. $10 million industry in 1973; $8 billion in 1988

    ii. $3 billion made on child pornography yearly

7. Sexually transmitted diseases (STDs)

    i. 68 million Americans infected

    ii. 15 million new cases yearly

8. Teen pregnancy

9. Violence against women

    i. Increased over 500% since 1960

    ii. States with highest use of pornography also have the highest cases of rape

10. Sexual abuse of children

    i. 1 out 3 girls is sexual molested

    ii. 1 out 7 boys is sexual molested

11. Abortion

12. Sexuality redefined

    i. Homosexuality

    ii. Transgendered dorms and restrooms

13. Destruction of marriage

14. Destruction of the family

III. Implications:

A. For self...

1. Embrace your design as _____ and _____

2. Be the right person

     i. Purity is not a _____, it is a direction towards God's purpose

     ii. Clean up your messes (be reconciled)

     iii. Don't pretend that you can disconnect

  3. Choose wisely

B. For family…

  1. Break generational sin

  2. Start generational legacies (Jeremiah 35)

C. For church…

  1. Family first, church second

  2. Family based youth ministries

  3. Take care of its people

D. For society…

  1. The definition of marriage is worth fighting for

  2. Proceed with caution on emerging technologies (procreation vs. reproduction)

Marriage and Family
Video Discussion Questions

1. How is the traditional family best for society and individuals?

2. Why is the traditional family best for society and individuals?

3. In what ways has the "culture of consumerism" attacked marriage and the traditional family?

4. In what ways has "Darwin's legacy" attacked marriage and the traditional family?

5. How can Christians counter this attack on the traditional family?

How to be Your Own Selfish Pig
Reading Discussion Questions

Chapter 10: Defective Merchandise . . . Please Discard

1. Why do the doctor recommend that Tim and Liz let their baby die?

2. How is the idea of abortion a product of atheistic beliefs?

3. What is the basis for believing each person, each child, is valuable?

4. Can we know at birth what kind of contribution someone might make? How should we handle all life, then?

5. How should we treat the elderly? The handicapped? The terminally ill? What does this say about our beliefs, especially about whether or not God exists?

6. What happens when a society puts a low price tag on some kinds of human life?

7. Francis Schaeffer said, "People are special and human life is _____, whether or not we admit it . . . Each person is worth fighting for . . ."

8. What is the lesson taught by the Martin Niemoller quote on page 99?

9. Reflection Question: Have you ever thought about the fact that God completely "thought you up"? He designed and created you as YOU, just as he did with every other person.

10. Reflection Question: How does that knowledge make you feel? How will it change the way you act or treat others?

Unit Six

LIGHTBEARERS

Unit Seven

A Summit Ministries Curriculum

DAY	UNIT 07: syllabus & outline	SW	✓
1	Read *A World of Ideas* Reading...	163	
2	Read *A World of Ideas* Reading...	DITTO	
3	Review *A World of Ideas* Reading Discussion Questions..	172	
4	Assign **Law Paragraph** [Rough Draft Due on Day 8]..	173	
	Watch **"Biblical Christian Worldview: Law"** Video Outline.......................................	174	
5	Complete **God the Judge** Exercise...	175	
	Complete **Boundaries** Exercise...	177	
6	Complete **Boundaries** Exercise...	DITTO	
	Assign **Making a Difference** [Assignment Due on Day 11 or 12]................................	182	
7	Watch **"Guard Your Heart"** Video Outline...	184	
8	Review **"Guard Your Heart"** Video Discussion Questions..	187	
	Turn in **Law Paragraph** [Assignment Due on Day 13]..	---	
9	Read *How to Be Your Own Selfish Pig* Reading (Ch. 8)..	---	
10	Review *How to Be Your Own Selfish Pig* Reading Discussion Questions (Ch. 8).........	188	
11	Turn in & Share **Making a Difference** Presentation Assignment.................................	---	
12	Turn in & Share **Making a Difference** Presentation Assignment.................................	---	
13	Turn in **Law Paragraph** Assignment...	---	
	Take **Learn to Discern** Quiz...	---	
	Prepare **Unit 07** Test...	---	
14	Take **Unit 07** Test...	---	
15			

A World of Ideas:
What Is the Basis for Law?

KEYS TO UNDERSTANDING

Key Question: What is the basis for law?

Key Ideas: God designed laws that not only run the universe, but also provide the moral framework for human behavior and social interaction. By following God's laws as revealed in the Bible and nature, the institutions of family, church, and state can function together in peace and harmony.

Key Terms: law, just law, biblical law, natural law, positive law

Key Verses: Romans 2:14 and Acts 17:31

"Indeed, when Gentiles, who do not have the law, do by nature things required by the law, they are a law for themselves, even though they do not have the law…" (Romans 2:14, NIV).

"For he [God] has set a day when he will judge the world with justice by the man he has appointed [Jesus Christ]. He has given proof of this to all men by raising him from the dead" (Acts 17:31, NIV).

Laws that Rule our Lives

Do you remember when you were young and you discovered there are rules in life? For most of your childhood, the rules came from your parents, so it appeared that parents were the source of all rules. Then, as you grew older, you realized there was a larger world and there are other sources for the rules that govern your life. Your teacher or principal at school. The policeman on the street. Government leaders. So many people giving you rules to live by!

This leads to a few very basic questions: *How do these people come up with all those rules?* and *What is the ultimate source for the rules that govern life?* When you try to answer questions like this, you are dealing with the worldview category of Law.

It seems there are rules everywhere and no place to hide from them. In the natural world, there are laws of chemistry, biology, and physics. Driving down the highway requires obeying traffic laws. There are laws that require you to pay taxes on the money you earn. Your friends expect you to live by the rule of telling the truth. Even in church there are rules for worshiping God (for example, we do not offer blood sacrifices on an altar, but we do confess our sins to God). Everywhere you go there are laws.

When you think of rules, do you have a positive or negative reaction? Many people would side with the negative! But laws don't have to be bad. Why not? It's simple, really. You'll recall some of the things we learned about the nature of God. God is relational, yes. He is righteous, certainly. But He also is Ruler. God rules over His universe and He designed everything, including us, to work in sync with His holy character.

Everything is designed to operate according to the rules God established—laws of physics (or "constants of nature"), laws of chemistry, laws of ethics, laws of civil government, laws of worship—it's all a package deal. We live in a world of laws. That's the way God designed it—and don't forget, God said that His design is good (Genesis 1:31) Also, read the first three verses of Psalm 1 and you will get a better idea of what's in store for the person who delights in "the law of the Lord."

God saw all that he had made, and it was very good. And there was evening, and there was morning—the sixth day (Genesis 1:31, NIV).

Blessed is the man who does not walk in the counsel of the wicked or stand in the way of sinners or sit in the seat of mockers. But his delight is in the law of the Lord, and on his law he meditates day and night. He is like a tree planted by streams of water, which yields its fruit in season and whose leaf does not wither. Whatever he does prospers (Psalm 1:1–3, NIV).

This chapter will help you:

   . . . Discern why we have laws and why laws are good to have
   . . . Define what is meant by the term "natural law"
   . . . Explore how the freedoms we enjoy have their origin in natural law and the Bible

In Unit 06, we mentioned three basic social institutions God created: *family*, *church*, and *state*. In this chapter, we will see there is a thread that holds these institutions together in peace and harmony—the **law**.

> **Law:** Rules enforced by the State, intended to help those in society live together peacefully.

The key question here is, "What is the basis of law?" Is it the hearts and minds of human beings? Is law the product of an evolved consciousness? Is it something revealed by God? How you answer these questions will determine your understanding of the basis for our nation's laws and fill in another part of your worldview.

Just Laws and Morality

In the spring of 1963 in Birmingham, Alabama, the Reverend Martin Luther King, Jr. led a massive march to bring attention to the widespread segregation and discrimination against African-Americans in the United States. King was arrested for organizing the protest without first obtaining a permit to march in the streets. In jail, King received a letter from a number of Alabama ministers, who questioned why King condoned breaking the law by marching without a permit.

King responded with his now famous "Letter from Birmingham Jail." In it, he wrote, "One may well ask how can you advocate breaking some laws and obeying others?" The answer, he said, "is found in the fact that there are two kinds of laws: just laws... and unjust laws." King continued, "One has not only a legal but a moral responsibility to obey just laws, but conversely, one has a moral responsibility to disobey unjust laws."[1]

Most of us can follow King's reasoning to this point. However, this raises the question *how do you determine whether a law is just or unjust*? A just law, King wrote, "squares with the moral law… An unjust law is a code that is out of harmony with the moral law." According to King, a **just law** is in harmony with the moral law. Further, he supported his view by stating that a just law is rooted in *natural law*.

Now there's a term you don't hear every day. What's natural law, you ask? Natural law is the legal basis for the founding of the United States. King was calling on those principles as the basis for his call to civil rights—equal rights for all people regardless of the color of their skin. But in recent years the idea of natural law has fallen out of favor with lawyers, judges, and politicians and is no longer understood by the general public.

In this chapter, you will discover how natural law came to be the foundation for the United States' concept of law. (Then you will understand why Martin Luther King, Jr. could speak about justice for all people.) More importantly, you will discover why this idea is still needed today if the United States is to continue as a nation based on liberty and justice for all.

> **Just Law:** A law that is in harmony with the moral law.

But first we have to start at the beginning, with the concept of biblical law.

Biblical Law

A biblical worldview centers on the idea that God created the universe and has given humans the authority to rule over the earth (Genesis 1:26–28). But how do we know how to rule? Christians believe that God has provided rules or laws and has given us the means to know and understand these laws. The ultimate Law-giver—God—has revealed His laws in two ways: through biblical law (special revelation) and through natural law (general revelation). Christian theologian Carl F.H. Henry put it this way, "God is the only Legislator. Earthly rulers and legislative bodies are alike accountable to Him from whom stems all obligation—religious, ethical and civil."[2] That means our task is to learn about these laws and apply them to our everyday experience, from our worship of God to our moral behavior and even to the laws we enact through our civil government.

> Then God said, "Let us make man in our image, in our likeness, and let them rule over the fish of the sea and the birds of the air, over the livestock, over all the earth, and over all the creatures that move along the ground." So God created man in his own image, in the image of God he created him; male and female he created them. God blessed them and said to them, "Be fruitful and increase in number; fill the earth and subdue it. Rule over the fish of the sea and the birds of the air and over every living creature that moves on the ground (Genesis 1:26–28, NIV).

Biblical law (revealed in *special revelation*) is the idea that God has given specific instructions in the Bible for rightly ordering society. God continually reminds His people what is right. For example, God warns Moses and the people of Israel not to legally permit the sinful ways of the Gentile nations:

> The Lord said to Moses, 'Speak to the Israelites and say to them: "I am the Lord your God. You must not do as they do in Egypt, where you used to live, and you must not do as they do in the land of Canaan, where I am bringing you. Do not follow their practices. You must obey my laws and be careful to follow my decrees. I am the Lord your God. Keep my decrees and laws, for the man who obeys them will live by them. I am the Lord'" (Leviticus 18:1–5, NIV).

> **Biblical Law:** The idea that God has given specific instructions in the Bible for rightly ordering society.

Throughout Leviticus 18, God tells the Israelites to avoid such sinful practices as incest, adultery, infanticide (i.e., abortion), and homosexuality. Similar commands were repeated in the New Testament. We are told that such practices are contrary to nature (Romans 1:26–27) and result in the destruction of social order (Romans 1:28–31).

> Because of this, God gave them over to shameful lusts. Even their women exchanged natural relations for unnatural ones. In the same way the men also abandoned natural relations with women and were inflamed with lust for one another. Men committed indecent acts with other men, and received in themselves the due penalty for their perversion. Furthermore, since they did not think it worthwhile to retain the knowledge of God, he gave them over to a depraved mind, to do what ought not to be done. They have become filled with every kind of wickedness, evil, greed and depravity. They are full of envy, murder, strife, deceit and malice. They are gossips, slanderers, God-haters, insolent, arrogant and boastful; they invent ways of doing evil; they disobey their parents; they are senseless, faithless, heartless, ruthless (Romans 1:26–31, NIV).

Natural Law

Natural law is God's law as found in nature. It is the physical and moral laws revealed in *general revelation* and built into the structure of the universe (as opposed to the laws invented by human beings). Mankind does not invent this law but discovers it through general revelation—what we can know about God by observing what He has made. This revelation is available to all people, in all places, at all times. Since humans are made in the image of God, have consciences that know right from wrong, and can think about the creation, humans are able to discover this natural law.

William Blackstone, a prominent Christian professor of law in Great Britain during the 1700s, wrote that natural law is grounded in the reality of a personal, all-powerful, and righteous God.

> **Natural Law:** Physical and moral laws revealed in general revelation and built into the structure of the universe.

Man, considered as a creature, must necessarily be subject to the laws of his creator, for he is an entirely dependent being… And consequently as man depends absolutely upon his maker for every thing, it is necessary that he should in all points conform to his maker's will. This will of his maker is called the law of nature.[3]

The theory of natural law begins with the idea that everything has a purpose. We can discern something's purpose by how it is made. For example, the purpose of the internal combustion engine in a car is to give the car motion. Every detail about the engine is designed for that purpose. If you were to carefully investigate how the engine is designed, you would realize that it takes gasoline, among other things, to fulfill this purpose.

You might say there is a rule that describes this reality. We'll call it the law of the internal combustion engine. The law could be expressed like this: "Internal combustion engines run on gasoline." If we cooperate with how the engine is designed by putting gasoline in the tank, the engine performs according to its purpose and everything goes well. But if we refuse to cooperate with the law of the internal combustion engine, say, by putting maple syrup in the tank, the pistons would get gummed up and cease to function according to their design. The engine would fail to live up to its purpose. This would be bad, especially if the engine happens to be in your car. In order for your car to work properly and fulfill its purpose, you need to follow the laws of how it was designed.

Natural law takes this idea of purpose and applies it to humanity. The assumption is that people are made for a purpose. But what is our human purpose? One way to find out is to carefully study how we are made. For instance, it is obvious that males and females are made differently, and that difference has a purpose—continuing our species! Every culture throughout history has acknowledged this male/female difference by placing moral boundaries around the institution of marriage in order to preserve the natural order for producing and raising children. Otherwise the culture wouldn't survive.

This "natural law" of marriage is continually reconfirmed. For example, every study on marriage and the family conducted in recent years affirms that marriage is a better situation for men, women, and children. When society cooperates with our God-ordained sexual design by maintaining marriage only as between a man and a woman, things go better for everyone in the family and society as a whole. On the other hand, when a society departs from that arrangement, individuals, families, and society suffer.[4]

The point is that just as there are physical laws that describe how the world functions, so there are moral laws that describe how we function best in relation to others. As Martin Luther King, Jr. put it, there are "certain universal principles that are inherent in the moral structure of the universe, and these principles are as inescapable as the law of gravitation."[5] In other words, moral laws cannot be denied. They are just as real as gravity!

Just like physical laws are discovered by patient observation (i.e., the scientific method), so moral principles must be discerned through careful thought and study. The moral laws that result are not arbitrary, but are universally applicable and evident to all reasonable people. Natural and moral laws are absolute because they conform to the eternal and unchanging character of God. Natural and moral laws therefore transcend time, culture, and personal preference.

Before we go on, let's do a quick re-cap. We began with the belief that God is real, then established that God created the universe to operate according to fixed laws (gravity being the most obvious in everyday life). Next, we confirmed that humans are part of God's creation, and therefore that God has established the moral laws that operate in our lives. Therefore, we are responsible for discerning what is lawful by observing human nature and social interactions, and carefully studying God's instructions in the Bible. Finally, in order for our society to flourish, the laws that result from our observations should be incorporated into our civil government and upheld by the people.

Civil Law

Since ancient times, the concept of natural law has been the basis for making civil laws. For example, the Greek philosopher Aristotle wrote about this idea over 2,000 years ago. Also, one of the most famous lawyers of ancient times was Cicero, who lived during the century before the birth of Jesus Christ. Cicero wrote in *De Re Publica*, "True law is right reason in agreement with Nature. It is of universal application, unchanging and everlasting."[6]

Christian thinkers, based on their belief in God as creator and designer of the universe, further developed the concept of natural law. Two of the most important thinkers about natural law were the fifth century church father Augustine and the thirteenth century Christian philosopher and theologian Thomas Aquinas.

By the 1700s, natural law was firmly established within Great Britain's legal system, and found its way into the universities of early America through the writing of British legal scholar William Blackstone. Blackstone's *Commentaries* was the primary text for American lawyers and politicians during the earliest years of America's existence. Blackstone stressed that for a civil law to be legitimate, it must rest on natural law. He wrote, "This law of nature... is binding over all the globe, in all countries, and at all times; no human laws are of any validity, if contrary to this... "[7]

This brings us back to the 1960s and Martin Luther King, Jr.. In his "Letter from Birmingham Jail," King echoed Blackstone when he said that a human law is invalid if it contradicts natural law. And the most fundamental law of nature is that the government should treat all people equally, regardless of the color of their skin. Therefore, all civil laws must reflect this fundamental natural law.

By applying natural law and biblical law to society, we can construct a civil law that is truly righteous and concerned about what is best for everyone.

The Legal Heritage of the U.S.

When the founders of the United States sought to establish a free and virtuous society, they appealed to both natural and biblical law. They clearly understood the implications of a biblical worldview (although not all of them affirmed all aspects of it) and sought to incorporate the key elements into our foundational documents and laws. Consider these quotations, which are representative of the majority of the founding fathers:

George Washington (1732–1799), our nation's first president:

> [W]e ought to be no less persuaded that the propitious [favorable] smiles of Heaven can never be expected on a nation that disregards the eternal rules of order and right which Heaven itself has ordained.[8]

Thomas Jefferson (1743–1826), author of the Declaration of Independence and our third president:

> And can the liberties of a nation be thought secure when we have removed their only firm basis, a conviction in the minds of the people that these liberties are the gift of God? That they are not to be violated but with his wrath? Indeed I tremble for my country when I reflect that God is just: that his justice cannot sleep for ever....[9]

Joseph Story (1779–1845), soldier during the War of Independence and the youngest justice appointed to the Supreme Court:

> The promulgation [spread] of the great doctrines of religion, the being, and attributes, and providence of one Almighty God: the responsibility to him for all our actions, founded upon moral freedom and accountability; a future state of rewards and punishments; the cultivation of all the personal, social, and benevolent virtues—these can never be matters of indifference in any well-ordered community. It is, indeed, difficult to conceive how any civilized society can exist without them.[10]

Even one hundred years later, **Harry S. Truman** (1884–1972), our thirty-third president, emphasized the connection between biblical teaching and a government based on liberty for all:

The fundamental basis of this nation's law was given to Moses on the Mount. The fundamental basis of our Bill of Rights comes from the teaching which we get from Exodus and St. Matthew, from Isaiah and St. Paul. I don't think we emphasize that enough these days. If we don't have the proper fundamental moral background, we will finally wind up with a totalitarian government which does not believe in rights for anybody except the state.[11]

Civil Rights and God

There is one more piece to add to the puzzle before we can see the complete picture of human equality before the law—the idea that natural law is rooted in the nature of God. But wait, you might say, aren't we supposed to keep religion separate from politics and law?

As it turns out, trying to separate religious ideas from political ideas is like trying to separate oxygen from hydrogen and still have water. The physical world just doesn't work that way. Neither does the world of ideas. The religious ideas someone has will naturally bear political fruit. As the authors of the Declaration of Independence declared, "We hold these truths to be self-evident, that all men are created equal, that they are endowed by their Creator with certain unalienable Rights, that among these are Life, Liberty and the pursuit of Happiness. [And] that to secure these rights, Governments are instituted among Men."[12]

Beginning with the Creator, there is a direct line from human equality to human rights to the duty of government to secure those rights. And all of this is "self evident." That means that any reasonable person can figure this out by carefully observing nature. Washington, Adams, Jefferson, and the rest understood the link between government and God. As men who were steeped in natural law theory, they believed that there are certain rights that precede civil laws. These rights originate from God and are built into the very fabric of mankind because we are created in God's image. Therefore, the government can only acknowledge them or deny their expression, but it doesn't possess the authority to take them away.

As Jefferson asked, "can the liberties of a nation be thought secure when we have removed their only firm basis: a conviction in the minds of the people that these liberties are the gift of God?"[13] Jefferson wrote these words in the context of decrying slavery, calling on a just God to remedy the inequality of people owning other human beings.[14]

But even though slavery had been abolished in the United States for a hundred years when King wrote his letter in 1963, there was still discrimination directed at black Americans. Later that same year, at a rally in Washington DC, King cited the Declaration of Independence's call for liberty, referring to it as a promise that was made in 1776 and was due the black race. In his "I Have a Dream" speech, King said:

> When the architects of our republic wrote the magnificent words of the Constitution and the Declaration of Independence, they were signing a promissory note to which every American was to fall heir. This note was a promise that all men, yes, black men as well as white men, would be guaranteed the unalienable rights of life, liberty, and the pursuit of happiness. It is obvious today that America has defaulted on this promissory note insofar as her citizens of color are concerned. Instead of honoring this sacred obligation, America has given the Negro people a bad check, a check which has come back marked "insufficient funds." But we refuse to believe that the bank of justice is bankrupt. We refuse to believe that there are insufficient funds in the great vaults of opportunity of this nation. So we have come to cash this check—a check that will give us upon demand the riches of freedom and the security of justice.[15]

> I say to you today, my friends, so even though we face the difficulties of today and tomorrow, I still have a dream. It is a dream deeply rooted in the American dream. I have a dream that one day this nation will rise up and live out the true meaning of its creed: "We hold these truths to be self-evident: that all men are created equal." I have a dream that one day on the red hills of Georgia the sons of former slaves and the sons of former slave owners will be able to sit down together at the table of brotherhood. I have a dream that one day even the state of Mississippi, a state sweltering with the heat of injustice, sweltering with the heat of oppression, will be transformed into an oasis of freedom and justice. I have a dream that my four little children will one day live

in a nation where they will not be judged by the color of their skin but by the content of their character. I have a dream today.[16]

Martin Luther King, Jr. did not live to realize his dream, as he was gunned down on April 4, 1968. But we remember his leadership in making that dream a reality for the next generation—our generation. But even more importantly, we need to remember the catalyst that propelled him to act against injustice: the idea that legitimate laws depend on natural law. The legacy that King left us is not just about civil rights, but the deeper understanding that human rights come from the hand of God.

The Secular Alternative: Positive Law

In contemporary America, the biblical foundations for law have largely been removed, not just in the re-wording of laws, the revisions of our nations' Christian heritage, or the ban of prayer in public schools, but also in the removal of biblical references from public monuments. The ACLU, backed heavily by those with a naturalistic worldview, is trying to remove any public presentation of the Ten Commandments from schools, courts, and other public buildings. This removal of the foundations of God's law is perpetuated in law schools as well. Virginia Armstrong explains:

> Increasingly in modern American, the Western Christian tradition has been replaced by a humanistic system, particularly among America's legal and educational elites. For most of the last 125 years [since the publication of Charles Darwin's On the Origin of Species] the 'rational/secular' form has been in ascendancy [it has been rising in power].[17]

The denial of God and natural law leads the naturalist to a position called positive law. In a strict sense, **positive law** states that the government is the ultimate source for human law. As one atheist has written, "Human beings may, and do, make up their own rules. All existing moralities and all existing laws are human artifacts, products of human society, social conventions."[18]

But if there is no God and humans will not ultimately be held accountable for disobeying divine law, then why should we bother obeying the law? In the final analysis, it seems there is no ultimate reason that laws based merely on human whim should be obeyed.

One flaw, though, is that positive law cannot adequately explain the existence of unjust societies, like, for example, Nazi Germany during the 1930s and 40s. This nation, under Hitler's rule, was determined to exterminate the Jewish race. Since positive law claims that the state decides right and wrong, the logical conclusion is that Nazis were justified in their treatment of the Jews, since they had no higher law to answer to than themselves. Yet, in practice, the rest of the world disagreed with Hitler's viewpoint, and fought and died in defense of freedom. How then can today's atheists justify their foundation of law, based on the very real fact that unjust societies exist? They must scramble to find some kind of foundation for law. "Human beings may, and do, make up their own rules. All existing moralities and all existing laws are human artifacts, products of human society, social conventions."[19]

Ultimately, the atheistic approach to law is hollow. Though they see the need for a law above societies, they deny that God provides it for us. Their belief that it originates solely from human societies leaves them without an objective standard with which to judge. Though they realize that there is such a thing as injustice, they have no way of discerning and retaining justice.

The inherent flaws in any atheistic approach to law have devastating consequences. The historical record of atheistic governments is one of death. Consider communist nations during the twentieth century. From the October Revolution of 1917 in Russia to China's Tiananmen Square, the history of atheistic communism shows that it is one of the most ruthless, efficient killing machines mankind has ever witnessed. According to R.J. Rummel, author of *Death By Government*, the death toll of this seventy-year experiment is over 100 million human beings. "It is as though our species has been devastated by a modern Black Plague."[20]

In the end, the atheistic approach to law boils down to several essential elements. First, since atheists believe human beings are essentially good, they are mystified in trying to figure out why humans do bad things. To place the blame on society is not an effective answer; after all, it is those "essentially good" human beings that make up society.

Second, while atheists are quick to note that we do need a "rule of law" in society, they have no grounding for that law beyond evolution and human agreement. Yet, humans change their minds; thus, law can be changed just as easily. But what if only some humans change their minds while others do not? Which slice of society is right?

Third, the final deciding factor in any atheistic approach to the law is human force—the strongest side gets to choose right and wrong. This position can only mean that might makes right, which leaves us at the mercy of the powerful, the armed, the wealthy, the mob.

In our study of the world of ideas, it must be clear by now that ideas have consequences. You have seen some of the terrible consequences that result from starting with the idea that God does not exist. You have witnessed many wicked ways that intellectuals seek to dull your perception of human sinfulness. You have seen that these are philosophies that have made their way to the common person (after all, what is taught in school in one generation will be believed by the masses in the next). Inhumane teachings lead to inhumane practices, and people die because of some of these teachings.

> **Positive Law:** The idea that the government is the ultimate source for human law.

Conclusion

The Christian concept of law consists of both natural and biblical law originating in the character of God. Divine law is eternal because God is eternal. It is so permanent that someday God will use it to judge the world (Acts 17:31) in a judgment based on natural and revealed law (Romans 2:12). God established human government and the rule of law primarily to keep humanity's sinful nature and passions in check (Romans 13:1–4). Because of the Fall, human history reflects a continuing effort by people to substitute man-made law for God's law.

Christians believe that when God's laws are obeyed, people and societies thrive. The Christian concept of human rights involves the biblical doctrine that all human beings are created in the image of God. These rights, which carry with them specific responsibilities, are unalienable. God's Word and nature's law are sufficient for mankind to establish a legal system that exemplifies man's creative image, but does not minimize our depravity. In the final analysis, the most important concept that we can understand about law is that God has designed it for our protection and prosperity.

Endnotes

[1] http://www.stanford.edu/group/King/popular_requests/frequentdocs/birmingham.pdf.

[2] Quoted in John W. Whitehead, *The Second American Revolution* (Westchester, IL: Crossway Books, 1988), 80.

[3] William Blackstone, "Commentaries on the Laws of England," *Blackstone's Commentaries*, 4 volumes, ed. St. George Tucker (reprint, South Hackensack, NJ: Rothman Reprints, 1969), 1:38–39.

[4] As social science research data and government surveys increasingly show, the decline in marriage since the 1960s has been accompanied by a rise in a number of serious social problems. Children born out of wedlock or whose parents divorce are much more likely to experience poverty, abuse, and behavioral and emotional problems, have lower academic achievement, and use drugs more often. Single mothers are much more likely to be victims of domestic violence. With the rise in these problems comes high program costs to deal with the effects of the breakdown of marriage. For children whose parents remain married, however, the benefits are real. Adolescents from these families have been found to have better health and are less likely to be depressed, are less likely to repeat a grade in school, and have fewer developmental problems. The implications of such mounting evidence for social policy are immense. (For statistical details, see Patrick F. Fagan, et.al., "The Positive Effects of Marriage: A Book of Charts," http://www.heritage.org/Research/Features/Marriage/index.cfm.)

[5] http://www.stanford.edu/group/King/encyclopedia/index.htm

[6] Quoted in Russell Kirk, *The Roots of American Order* (Washington, DC: Regnery Gateway, 1991), 108.

[7] William Blackstone, *Commentaries on the Laws of England*, Introduction, Section 2, http://www.lonang.com/exlibris/blackstone/bla-002.htm.

[8] Quoted in David Barton, *Original Intent* (Aledo, TX: WallBuilder Press, 1996), 114.

[9] Quoted at http://www.monticello.org/reports/quotes/memorial.html (accessed 1/17/2008).

[10] Joseph Story, *Commentaries on the Constitution* 3:§§ 1865–1873 (online at http://press-pubs.uchicago.edu/founders/documents/amendI_religions69.html; accessed 1/20/2008).

[11] Harry S. Truman, Public Papers of the Presidents--January 1 to December 31, 1950 (Washington, D.C.: U. S. Government Printing Office, 1965), 157.

[12] Taken from The Declaration of Independence, online at http://www.ushistory.org/declaration/document/index.htm (accessed 1/20/2008).

[13] Thomas Jefferson, *Notes on the State of Virginia* (Philadelphia: Matthew Carey, 1794), Query XVIII, 236–237.

[14] Some have questioned Jefferson's sincerity over his criticism of slavery since Jefferson owned slaves. This is a multi-layered issue. Some insight can be gained from understanding the context of Jefferson's day. He wrote in 1814, "My opinion has ever been that, until more can be done for them, we should endeavor, with those whom fortune has thrown on our hands, to feed and clothe them well, protect them from ill usage, require such reasonable labor only as is performed voluntarily by freemen, and be led by no repugnancies to abdicate them, and our duties to them." For more on this issue, see http://www.poplarforest.org/tjslavery.html (accessed 1/20/2008).

[15] http://www.usconstitution.net/dream.html.

[16] Ibid.

[17] Virginia Armstrong, "The Flight from America's Foundations: A Panoramic Perspective on American Law," *Restoring the Constitution*, ed. H. Wayne House (Dallas, TX: Probe Books, 1987), 122–123.

[18] Hocutt, "Toward an Ethic of Mutual Accommodation," in *Humanist Ethics*, ed. Morris B. Storer (Buffalo, NY: Prometheus Books, 1980), 137.

[19] Hocutt, 137.

[20] R.J. Rummel, *Death by Government* (New Brunswick, NJ: Transaction Publishers, 1994), 9.

A World of Ideas
Reading Discussion Questions

1. What is law? What key question does law seek to answer? What are the key ideas of Christian law?

2. What are the two ways God has revealed His laws to us? Give a brief description of each.

3. What are just and unjust laws? Why did Martin Luther King, Jr. advocate breaking unjust laws?

4. According to Harry S. Truman, why is it vital that U.S. citizens understand the fundamental basis of American law?

5. What is positive law? What are three essential elements of an atheistic system of law?

Law Paragraph
Assignment

*As you continue your study, write your own paragraph titled **My Christian Worldview of Law**. You will be able to correct it, add to it, put it into your Lightbearers Journal, and memorize it. Below is a checklist to help you with this assignment.*

☐ The paragraph includes the definition of Christian law.
☐ It includes the basis of biblical and natural law.
☐ It includes the basis for human rights.

Unit Seven

Law
Video Outline

I. **Biblical Christian Law:** _____

    A. The foundation of divine law is the nature of God Himself.

        "Law has content in the eternal sense. It has a reference point. Like a ship that is anchored, law cannot stray from its mooring." — John Whitehead

    B. God has revealed much of His law through _____.

    C. Every person has a conscience—some inherent sense of right and wrong.

        "Indeed, when Gentiles, who do not have the law, do by nature things required by the law, they are a law for themselves, even though they do not have the law." — Romans 2:14

    D. Man-made laws are constantly changing because a fallen people will constantly recreate the law to better suit their _____ needs.

    E. God has also made His law known through the _____.

    F. While natural law provides people with a general concept of right and wrong, the Bible clearly outlines God's law.

    G. Together, general and special revelation give people enough information to implement a _____ that does not rest on fallen, fallible human wisdom.

    H. The government is necessary to _____ divine laws, not create them.

God the Judge
Exercise

We are often comfortable with thinking about God as our Father, friend, and helper, one who loves us in spite of our weaknesses and failures. But we don't often like to think of God as Judge. You need to study and understand this part of God's divine character, though, because He *is* your Judge. J.I. Packer has some great insights into this consideration (much of the following is based on his book *Knowing God*).*

Biblical references to God as our Judge abound. For example, look at Genesis 18:25, Psalm 75:7, and Psalm 82:8. God's judgment falls on unbelieving Jews (Matthew 21:43–46, 1 Thessalonians 2:14–16), as well as pagan Gentiles (Romans 1–3), on Ananias and Sapphira for lying to God (Acts 5:1–10), and on Herod for his pride (Acts 12:21–23). All these instances clearly demand that we see God as the final Judge.

The New Testament contains many reminders of the certainty of the coming day of judgment. This causes us to ask "How can we, as sinners, get right with God while there is still time?" The answer is Jesus Christ. Jesus is declared the righteous Judge in the following verses: 2 Timothy 4:8, Acts 10:42, and James 5:9. In John 22:27–29, Jesus proclaims that the Father has entrusted judgment to Him. The same Jesus who is the world's Savior is also its Judge.

Before going further in this discussion, let's look at the characteristics of the Judge:

1. *The judge is a person with authority.* Clearly Jesus is both the Lawgiver and the Judge. He has been given all authority in heaven and on earth. God is your Maker, Owner, and source of reward and punishment. He has complete authority.

2. *The judge is a person identified with what is good and right.* The modern idea of a cold, dispassionate judge has no place in the Bible, which leaves no doubt that God loves righteousness and hates iniquity.

3. *The judge is a person of wisdom who discerns the truth.* When the Bible pictures God as judge, it emphasizes His omniscience and wisdom as the searcher of hearts and the finder of facts. Nothing can escape Him. You may fool men, but you cannot fool God. He knows you and judges you as you really are. God judges according to truth.

4. *The judge is a person with the power to execute a sentence.* In our world, the judge pronounces the sentence and someone else carries it out, but God is His own executioner. As He legislates and sentences, so He punishes. All judicial functions come together in Him.

As Judge, God gives retribution (something administered in payment, such as punishment for wrong-doing). He will give to each person what is deserved. He will reward good with good and evil with evil. Understanding God's retributive nature gives meaning and clarity to your view of life (your worldview). It shows you that the world is meaningful, and gives rightness and direction to your purpose. This view has fearful consequences for godless men, but it is really not meant to "frighten" us as much as to reveal the true nature of God.

God uses the index of your heart as the basis of His judgment. Final judgment will be according to your decisions, your habits, your whole course of life. Your actions do not merit eternal life. They fall too far short of perfection to do that. However, they do provide an index of what is in your heart. Matthew 12:36–37 says: "Men will have to give account on the day of judgment for every careless word they have spoken. For by your words you will be acquitted, and by your words you will be condemned." Your words

* J.I. Packer, *Knowing God* (Downers Grove, IL: Intervarsity Press, 1973), 141–42.

are important because they show what you are inside. "A tree is recognized by its fruit...How can you who are evil say anything good? For out of the overflow of the heart the mouth speaks" (Matthew 12:33–34).

But how does this immovable sense of judgment line up with salvation in Jesus Christ? Well, the scriptures clarify this by telling you that if your name is written in the Book of Life—that is, if Jesus Christ is your Savior—you will not be "thrown into the lake of fire." Does this mean you are entirely off the hook? No. Even as a Christian, your life and habits will one day be assessed by God.

In 1 Corinthians 3:12–15 the Apostle Paul warns about the kind of lifestyle to build your faith on, saying it must be built on Jesus Christ and not the world's values. "If any man builds on this foundation using gold, silver, costly stones, wood, hay or straw, his work shall be shown for what it is, because the Day will bring it to light. It will be revealed with fire, and the fire will test the quality of each man's work. If what he has built survives, he himself will be saved, but only as one escaping through the flames." Although your salvation is not at stake here, since it was accomplished once and for all at the moment you believed on Jesus as your savior, the reward and loss described here signify greater or lesser honor and depth of relationship with God in eternity (though in what ways is beyond our present ability to know).

As you look at your own heart, do you worry that you will not measure up to the heavenly standards of a holy Judge? The fact is that you won't. But if you have accepted that Jesus Christ died on the cross for you, then you are covered by His blood. Your Judge no longer sees your sins, only the death of Jesus that paid the penalty for them. However, you will one day stand before that Judge as He asks what you did with the life He gave you. This should motivate you every day to make decisions that bring honor and glory to God.

However, if you haven't accepted Jesus' death on the cross as being for you and your sins, you will one day stand before your Judge without the covering of Jesus' blood, without "paid" written across your sins. In that case, He will have no choice but to deny you access to eternity with Him, sending you instead to eternal torment in the lake of fire. This is not a scare tactic—this is the truth.

Keep Jesus Christ's role as Judge clearly before you even as you look at His role as Savior. Live each day to honor both your Savior and your Judge.

Boundaries
Exercise

Personal application of biblical principles in your life is the key to growth. God created the Bible to give you intellectual and spiritual insight, but He also wants us to make it practical, to apply it as we learn. The concept of boundaries is a key way to increase the "law of God" in our lives. Please read carefully and discuss this material with the rest of the class.

What is a boundary? In the physical world, boundaries set up limits and define ownership. Let's take a look at this illustration. A new elementary school was built in a small town. To make it easily accessible to parents and children, the school was located on a busy highway. The school was opened in September, but for the first few weeks, due to a delay in construction plans, the playground was left unfenced and open to the busy street. The teachers who supervised the children at recess noticed that the little ones stayed close to the building, using only a small portion of the available playing space. In early October the playground fence was finally constructed. Immediately, within the security of the new protection, the children used the entire playground.

This is an illustration of the benefits of boundaries. You might say that the boundaries you set in your life according to God's law will allow you to conduct your life in freedom and security. Your boundaries are your response to Proverbs 4:23 which says, "Above all else, guard your heart, for it is the well-spring of life." A boundary says, "This is me, and this is not me," and has to do with what you choose to do, and what you choose not to do. It tells you what to own and for what to take responsibility. Boundaries free you to follow God's will for your life.

Here is another illustration of boundaries. A couple who came for counseling had a son who had given them problems for many years. The boy was now having problems staying in school and couldn't seem to make a choice about a career. The couple obviously loved their son very much and were heartbroken over the way he was living. They had tried everything they knew to get him to change and live a responsible life. They had always given him everything he needed and plenty of money so he wouldn't have to work and interrupt his study time and social life. Yet, he flunked out of school and stopped going to classes. When this happened his parents were more than happy to find him another school where it might be better for him. When asking why their son did not come to this meeting with them, the parents replied, "Oh, he didn't come because he doesn't think he has a problem."

The counselor listened carefully to all the parents told him about this boy and finally said, "I believe your son is right, he doesn't have a problem." The couple stared at the counselor in disbelief. "Did we hear you correctly," they replied, "you don't think he has a problem?" "That's right," the counselor answered, "he doesn't have a problem, you do. He can do whatever he wants, no problem. You fret, you pay, you worry, you plan, you exert energy to keep him going. He doesn't have a problem because you have taken it from him. There are things that should be his problem; but as it stands now, they are yours. Would you like me to help him have some problems?"

The couple looked a bit confused, but some lights were beginning to turn on in their heads. "What do you mean, 'help him have some problems'?" the mother asked.

"Well," explained the counselor, "I think that the solution to this problem would be to clarify some boundaries so that his actions cause him problems, not you."

"What do you mean, 'boundaries'?" the father asked.

"Look at it this way. Right now your son doesn't study, plan or work, yet he has a nice place to live, plenty of money, and all the rights of a family member who is doing his part. You need to allow him to feel the consequences of his irresponsible behavior. As it stands now, he is irresponsible and happy and you are responsible and miserable," the counselor explained.

"Isn't that a bit cruel, just to stop helping him like that?" the father asked.

"Has helping him helped?" was the counselor's reply. The father's expression told the counselor he

* The following material is based upon Dr. Henry Cloud's and Dr. John Townsend's book, *Boundaries*.

was beginning to understand.

Boundaries are the personal application of God's law to your life. You are commanded to be responsible for the things that you do. You must deal with what is in your own soul (Proverbs 14:10). In addition to showing you responsibilities, the Bible also shows what you are not responsible for. For example, you're never told that you are responsible to have "other-control," only self-control.

Galatians 6:2–5 states: "Carry each other's burdens, and in this way you will fulfill the law of Christ. If anyone thinks he is something when he is nothing, he deceives himself. Each one should test his own actions. Then he can take pride in himself, without comparing himself to somebody else, for each one should carry his own load." You are responsible *to* others and *for* yourself (but you are not responsible *for* others.) Verses 2–3 explain the responsibility you have to others. However, verse 5 states that "each should carry his own load," meaning there are certain things that others cannot and should not do for you. The Greek meanings of *burden* and *load* give insight into this verse. The Greek word for "burden" means an "excess burden," like a boulder. They crush you. You are not expected to carry these alone. You need help with the "boulders" in your life. In contrast, the word "load" means "cargo." A load is like a knapsack, which each of us can carry on our own. You are expected to carry your own feelings, attitudes and behaviors as well as the responsibilities God has given you, even though it is difficult.

Boundaries help you to distinguish your property so you can take care of it. They guard your treasures (Matthew 7:6). They keep pearls in and pigs out. Our boundaries need "gates" so we can let the good in and the bad out (1 John 1:9, James 5:16, and Mark 7:21–23).

The idea of boundaries comes from the very nature of God. God has a certain moral nature that is expressed in the laws He reveals to us. He defines what is right and wrong, good and bad. These are the types of things that He wants us to understand. He wants us to set boundaries that accord with His laws.

Some examples of boundaries are words (such as "no" and "yes"), truth, physical or emotional distance, time, and other people. People are primary in boundary-setting, since creating boundaries always involves a support network. Your most basic need in life is the establishment and maintainance of your relationships, and you also need others in order to gain new input and learning. Consequences show you the limits of your boundaries and are often the "barbs" in the fences you construct. These tell people your values and what you will fight to guard and protect. Boundaries set limits.

Boundaries support the biblical concept of sowing and reaping. Since behaviors and ideas have consequences, what we sow, we will reap. In other words, you are held accountable for your choices. Our choices need to please God, not men.

In setting limits, or boundaries, you will need to realize that you set boundaries for yourself only, and never for someone else. Our model is God. He does not make your choices. He sets standards, and then allows you to choose what you do about those standards. To those who obey them He extends a welcome; to those who choose otherwise, no fellowship with God is found.

Boundaries help you to set internal limits, as well. You must learn to say "no" to yourself, "no" to your destructive sin nature and even to some good desires that may not be proper at that particular time. Limits on oneself are necessary to pursue God's plan for your life.

Your mind and thoughts are important reflections of the image of God. We are the only creatures on earth called to love God with all our minds. Paul wrote that we are to take "captive every thought to make it obedient to Christ" (2 Corinthians 10:5). To establish thought boundaries you need to do three things: 1) own your own thoughts, 2) grow in knowledge and expand your mind, and 3) clarify your own distorted thinking. Jesus warned us that we do not see clearly because we have "logs" in our eyes (Matthew 7:3–5). Healthy relationships only occur when we are willing to share our thinking with others. If we want others to know our thoughts, we must tell them.

Finally, we are to pursue our desires only after we have checked them out with what God desires for us. Feelings, attitudes and beliefs, behaviors, choices, values, limits, talents, thoughts, desires and love are all boundaries we must examine carefully.

Boundary construction contains three parts. It begins when you have an emotional attachment to others, when you have the ability to say "no" to others without fear of loss, and when you take an appropriate "no" from others without withdrawing emotionally. It's important that you know when to say "yes," when to say "no," and to whom to say "yes" or "no," not only at this crucial time of your life, but for the rest of your life.

Ten Laws of Boundaries

God's world is set up with laws and principles. Even if you have never been taught these rules, you will learn about them by living your life. Let's look at these eight guidelines.

1. THE LAW OF SOWING AND REAPING

Because of the law of sowing and reaping (Galatians 6:7), it is important to understand that to learn to change an irresponsible behavior one must experience the consequences of that behavior. Proverbs 9:8 warns us: "Do not rebuke a mocker [one who is living foolishly] or he will hate you; rebuke a wise man and he will love you." You often need to allow others to experience the results of their errors, and not try to change them. And you also need to set boundaries when you learn from your own experiences.

2. THE LAW OF RESPONSIBILITY

Often people will say that setting boundaries as outlined here is selfish. What they have forgotten is we are to love one another, not *be* one another. I can't grow for you and you can't grow for me. The biblical mandate is to "Continue to work out your salvation with fear and trembling, for it is God who works in you to will and to act according to his good purpose" (Philippians 2:12–13). And remember, it is not wise to rescue people from the consequences of their own sin, because they will only have to do it again in order to learn. You are to give to the needy and put limits on sin. Boundaries help you do that.

3. THE LAW OF POWER

The first part of setting boundaries is admitting our own powerlessness. You don't have power in and of yourself to do some things, but you do have power to agree with the truth of your problems. In other words, confess your sin, acknowledge your inability to God in prayer so He can give you the strength to do what you cannot do on your own, and repent and turn from the evil within you. Then, search and understand what your proper boundaries are. Ask God and others to help you. Seek out those whom you have injured and make amends. When confronting the behavior of others that you cannot change, remember you can still change your behavior toward them so their destructive patterns do not cause you to do wrong.

4. THE LAW OF RESPECT

We all fear that our boundaries will not be accepted and respected. If you want others to respect your boundaries, you must clearly respect the boundaries of others. Jesus said, "So in everything, do to others what you would have them do to you" (Matthew 7:12). When we respect others' boundaries, we feel better about our own.

5. THE LAW OF MOTIVATION

If you are not motivated by love (2 Corinthians 5:14), you will not feel joy. Consider the motive in giving. There is an important truth about motives in the setting of boundaries. If your motives are false, they will keep you from setting boundaries. You may fear loss of love or abandonment, others' anger, loneliness, guilt, payback, loss of approval, or you may over-identify with the pain of the other person so that you won't set boundaries. If your giving is not leading to great joy in your life, examine your motivations. Freedom first, service second.

6. THE LAW OF EVALUATION

When it is necessary to tell someone something that is unpleasant in order to help him or her, you must still do it (Ephesians 4:15). Remember there is a difference between hurt and harm. Hurt often causes growth. Harm is different. It is something that truly causes damage. You need to evaluate the effects of setting boundaries and be responsible to the other person. That's "to," not "for." Jesus refers to this as the "narrow gate." Setting boundaries requires decision making and confrontation. Both are difficult, but bring great freedom. If pain results, we need to evaluate that pain in a positive light.

7. THE LAW OF PRO-ACTIVITY

For every action, there is an equal and opposite reaction. When someone has been victimized, there may be a strong reaction when that person begins to see the truth of what has happened. Think for a minute about the story of the boy whose parents never let him experience the consequences of his irresponsible behavior (the one you read about at the beginning of this "Boundaries" section). Do you think he reacted strongly when his parents withdrew their support to let him experience consequences? This is a reactive phenomena. It is temporary. This phase must pass before boundaries can be set. Boundaries must be pro-active.

8. THE LAW OF ENVY

Envy is probably the most unattractive emotion we have. It defines *good* as "what I do not possess." Envy is the avoidance of personal responsibility for your life. It blames others. Envy should always be a sign to you that you are resentful. When envy rears its ugly head, ask God to show you what you should desire.

9. THE LAW OF ACTIVITY

Remember that being passive never pays off. God will match our effort, but He will never do our work for us (Acts 12:8). He wants us to be active, seeking, knocking on the door of life. Failing to try is no less a sin than failing at all. Our boundaries are to be set by asking, knocking, and seeking (Matthew 7:7–8).

10. THE LAW OF EXPOSURE

Remember that you exist in relationship to God and others. Your boundaries define you in relation to others. Boundaries need to be communicated in relationships. When boundaries are unexpressed, the relationship suffers. The Bible has many warnings about this. Look up Ephesians 4:25–26. Here the mandate is to be honest and in the light. Likewise, there is an admonition in Ephesians 5:13–14. So, do not fear, communicate your boundaries openly.

Boundaries and You

So far, you have read about what boundaries are and how they can help in freeing you to follow God's will in your life. You have looked carefully at the ten laws of boundaries. Now let's conclude this "law" study with a practical look at how you can set boundaries for yourself.

Let's look first at some areas that may need boundaries in your life. Eating habits, money management, time management, task completion, your speech, sexuality, alcohol and substance abuse are all areas of possibility. These are places where boundaries are needed but are often difficult to manage. Now, suppose you have chosen one of these areas to work on in your life. How do you go about setting boundaries?

Three Things to Bring to Your Awareness

First, you are your own worst enemy. External problems are much easier to deal with than internal problems. You must grasp the idea that you are totally responsible for yourself. When someone else steps over a boundary, you can remove yourself from him or her, but what do you do with you? This is often why your "no" may not work. You need more than you. You need God and others.

Second, you often withdraw from relationships when you most need them. This has been true ever since the fall of man. You must decide to connect with others in setting boundaries for yourself. Those others include God, where you go for grace, and other believers who will support you in your boundary construction.

Third, you often try to use willpower to solve your boundary problems. However, if you depend on willpower alone, you will fail. Total dependence on willpower makes it a "worship of will" and you leave out your relationship with Christ. Coupled with the desire to change must be the power of Christ in you, and the helpful support of others.

Five Questions to Help You Set Realistic Boundaries

First, what are the symptoms? What destructive fruit do you see resulting from not being able to say no to yourself? Use the reality of these symptoms to clarify where your boundary problems are.

Second, what are the roots? In other words, what has caused this boundary problem? Consider such possibilities as lack of training, rewarded destructiveness, distorted need, fear of relationships, unmet emotional hungers, being under the law, or covering up some emotional hurt.

Third, what is the boundary conflict? Ask God for insight into what areas of your life are out of control.

Fourth, who needs to take ownership? At this point you make a decision to take responsibility for your out-of-control behavior. Though the cause of the problem may not be your fault, you are still asked to take responsibility for the problem. You do what you can.

Fifth, what do you need? You will need others with whom you can trust and feel safe, people who are grace-filled and caring. Of course, you will need Christ's companionship. These special relationships are God's source of spiritual and emotional fuel for you. They will help you through the difficult times as you struggle to maintain the boundaries you have chosen to set.

Time to Set Boundaries

Now, how do you begin? First, you already may have had boundaries established for you by your parents or others who are in authority over you. Do not change any boundaries already established for you without discussing the matter with them. Once this is done, you must look at your real needs and address those. Often boundaries that are out of control lead you to an understanding of a major need in your life that is not being met. Address this issue. Also, realize that you may fail. And remember that boundary setting is like driving, swimming or typing—you don't learn without error; it takes practice. Failure is a part of gaining maturity. Be sure to listen to empathetic feedback from your supportive friendships and get the permission of your authorities when attempting to set these boundaries.

Finally, surround yourself with people who are loving and supportive. Difficulties are often too much to bear alone. This five-point formula is a cycle. As you deal with real needs, sometimes fail, get plenty of empathetic feedback, suffer consequences, and are restored, you build stronger internal boundaries each time. As you stay with your goal and the right people, you will build a sense of self-restraint that can truly become part of your character for life. God will be your guide and strength in building boundaries in your life.

Making a Difference
Presentation Assignment

Read the following excerpt from "Do Hard Things" by Alex and Brett Harris. Then research a teenager from history who made (or is making—don't forget teenagers who are currently influential) a significant difference in the world, their community, or their family. The purpose of this exercise is to find young people who have done things that our culture would consider out of the "norm" for what is expected of teenagers today. Don't just look for someone who did something impressive, but for a young person who did something that went against the low expectations people have about teenagers. This paper should be one page in length, and will be turned in and presented on day 11 or 12.

Before There Was "My Space"

The word teenager is so common today that most people don't even think about it—and if they do, it's usually not positive. According to the dictionary, a teenager is a person between the ages of thirteen and nineteen years old. There's a good chance you fall in that category. Like most teens, you attend school, have a MySpace or Facebook profile, and are more likely to take a photo with your phone than with a camera.

But would it surprise you to find out that at one time teenagers (in the way we think about them today) didn't even exist? It wasn't until a 1941 issue of *Reader's Digest* that the term *teenager* even appeared.

Prior to the early twentieth century and, really, throughout history, people were either children or adults. Family and work were the primary occupations of the group we now call teenagers. In fact, in 1900 only one out of ten American young people between fourteen and seventeen years old attended high school. One historian, Friedrich Heer, writes about that era, focusing on Europe:

> Around 1800 young people of both sexes could reckon on being considered adults as soon as the outward signs of puberty made their appearance. Girls attained marriageable age at fifteen... Boys could join the Prussian army as officer cadets at the age of fifteen. Among the upper classes entry to university or to a profession was possible at the age of fifteen or sixteen. The school leaving age, and consequently the end of childhood, was *raised* during the nineteenth century to fourteen.

There are many examples of young people who not only worked at this age but who excelled in their areas of responsibility. The question is: what changed? Why is it that young men and women of the past were able to do things (and do them well) at fifteen or sixteen that many of today's twenty-five to thirty-year-olds can't do?

Is it because young people are now called "teenagers"? Not exactly. The answer is that people today view the teen years through the modern lens of adolescence—a social category of age and behavior that would have been completely foreign to men and women not too long ago.

The term adolescence literally means "to grow up." This is true in a biological sense as well as in other aspects of maturity. We have no problem with that, or even with the word itself—you'll notice that we still use the word teenager a lot. The problem we have is with the modern understanding of adolescence that allows, encourages, and even trains young people to remain childish for much longer than necessary. It holds us back from what we *could* do, from what God *made* us to do, and even from what we would *want* to do if we got out from under society's low expectations.

Society doesn't expect much of anything from young people during their teen years—except trouble. But you won't find the words *teenager* or *adolescence* anywhere in Scripture. Instead you'll find the apostle Paul writing in 1 Corinthians 13:11, "When I was a child, I spoke like a child, I thought like a child, I reasoned like a child. When I became a man, I gave up childish ways." In another letter, Paul wrote to a young pastor in training: "Don't let anyone look down on you because you are young, but set an example for the believers in speech, in life, in love, in faith and in purity." (1 Timothy 4:12, NIV). What we find here is clear evidence that God does not hold two standards: one for young adults and one for adults. He has high expectations for both.

Where expectations are high, we tend to rise to meet them. Where expectations are low, we tend to drop to meet them. And yet this is the exact opposite of what we're told to do in 1 Corinthians 14:20: "Brothers, stop thinking like children. In regard to evil be infants, but in your thinking be adults." Our culture says, "Be mature in evil, but in your thinking and behavior be childish."

Of course, sometimes we like being able to do things we know we shouldn't do—or getting away with less than our best. We excuse our choices because that's what teens are supposed to do or by thinking, *Well, I'm not as bad as some people I know*. We go with the crowd. We do what comes easily; we certainly don't do hard things.*

A Few Examples

Craig Kielburger, at age 12, gathered six of his friends to begin fighting child labor around the world. He started *Free The Children*, which is now the world's largest network of children helping children through education, with more than one million youths involved in education and development programs in forty-five countries. The primary goals of the organization are to free children from poverty and exploitation, and free young people from the notion that they are powerless to affect positive change in the world. Through domestic empowerment programs and leadership training, *Free The Children* inspires young people to become socially conscious global citizens and agents of change for their peers around the world. *Free The Children* has built more than five hundred schools around the world and has reached more than one million young people in North America.

Here's another story: on a cold December night in 1983, 11-year-old Trevor Ferrell saw a TV newscast about people living on the streets. Those images stirred compassion deep within Trevor and he pleaded with his parents to take him to downtown Philadelphia so he could give his blanket and pillow to the first homeless person he met. In ensuing weeks, with the help of family, classmates, and neighbors, Trevor made nightly trips into Philadelphia to distribute food, clothing, and blankets to the needy. Through hundreds of generous citizens and businesses, this little campaign soon grew into an entire array of services for the homeless.

* Adapted from *Do Hard Things* © 2008 by Alex Harris and Brett Harris. Used by permission of WaterBrook Multnomah Publishing Group, a division of Random House, Inc.

Guard Your Heart
Video Outline

"Guard your heart above all else, for it is the source of life" — Proverbs 4:23–24 (HCSB)

I. Guard Your Heart

    A. The status of your heart will produce your _____

    B. Guard your heart as if your life depended on it… because it does!

II. What Does "Heart" Mean?

    A. Not _____ or _____

    B. It sets us apart from animals

        1. Our center, our orientation toward life

        2. Our thoughts, feelings, decisions, relationships all connect with our heart

III. Guard, Heart, Keep

    A. Literally, "guard" your heart because it will be _____

    B. Literally, "keep" your heart because it wants to _____ from you

IV. Our Culture's False Worldview

    A. We have an illusion that what we do doesn't really _____

        1. We think we can _____

            i. Seinfeld (everything is random)

            ii. Claiming Christ, but doing whatever we want

            iii. MySpace, Facebook, Second Life

2. We think we are more than one _____

    i. "The Freshmen" by Verve Pipe

      • "I cannot be held responsible"

      • We have removed consequences from actions

         – Sex removed from marriage and pregnancy through condoms and birth control

         – No such thing as sin, only sickness

         – We need therapy, not punishment

    ii. Your decisions will determine your destiny; your _____ will not

B. We have the tendency to be _____ from what ultimately matters

"Let your eyes look forward; fix your gaze straight ahead. Carefully consider the path for your feet, and all your ways will be established. Don't turn to the right or to the left; keep your feet away from evil." — Proverbs 4:25–27 (HCSB)

"I am not afraid to lose; I am afraid to win at something that doesn't matter." — Vince Lombardi

1. A great start does not always equal a great finish

    i. Solomon (1 Kings 11)

      • A life of idolatry, child sacrifice, and sexual perversion

      • Solomon's heart was not complete, like David's had been

2. Watch the _____ that you make because small concessions lead to large concessions

      • No one plans to get AIDS or get involved in sexual perversion

      • No one plans to get divorced, steal, or become a child molester

V. **Characteristics of Those Who Keep Their Hearts**

A. A Biblical Worldview

1. They see the world from _____ perspective

    i. **Note**: You can know the Bible, but not see the world through the lens of Scripture

    ii. Barna studies show little difference between Christians and non-Christians

2. Their worldview is big enough to handle the real issues of life

B. A Mentoring Posture

    1. They seek out significant _____ with others who have a biblical worldview

    2. They are willing to mentor those younger than them

C. Sharpener

    1. They don't hang out with silly putty

    2. They surround themselves with others who share a biblical worldview

Guard Your Heart
Video Discussion Questions

1. Why does Proverbs 4:23–24 warn us to "guard our hearts?" What does this mean?

2. What are two false ideas popular in our culture's worldview today? How does this make guarding our hearts difficult?

3. What are three characteristics that can help us to "keep our hearts?"

4. Reflection Question: Have you allowed yourself to believe that your actions don't really matter or have you allowed yourself to become distracted? If so, how can you change this?

5. Reflection Question: Do you have anyone older in your life who serves as a mentor? Are you mentoring anyone younger than you?

How to Be Your Own Selfish Pig
Reading Discussion Questions

Chapter 8: You Don't Think Anyone's Going to Hell, Do You?

1. What is the question Matthew and Fritz are trying to answer?

2. What do Eastern religions say is the source of evil? Is this a logical way to explain why evil exists in the world today?

3. What is the source of evil, according to the Bible?

4. Why did God give human beings the ability to choose, especially when He knew that they would choose to rebel against Him?

5. Was Adam and Eve's decision to disobey God conscious and worthy of punishment, or were they just tricked and therefore innocent?

6. Why does our sin nature necessitate the existence of hell?

7. According to God's historical plan, how did He bring hope into man's disobedience?

8. What does each person need to do to come back to a right relationship with God?

9. Why is the plan of salvation as found in the Bible unique?

10. Reflection Question: What do you think about evil in the world, and how it came to be? Does it make sense to you that there could be a heaven and a hell? Have you received God's offer to have a relationship with Him?

LIGHTBEARERS

Unit Eight

A Summit Ministries Curriculum

Day	UNIT 08: syllabus & outline	SW	✓
1	Read *A World of Ideas* Reading...	**191**	
2	Read *A World of Ideas* Reading...	Ditto	
3	Review *A World of Ideas* Reading Discussion Questions..............................	**202**	
4	Review *A World of Ideas* Reading Discussion Questions.............................. Assign **Politics Paragraph** [Rough Draft Due on Day 8].............................	Ditto **203**	
5	Watch **"Biblical Christian Worldview: Politics"** Video Outline........................ Read **The American Republic: Can We Keep It?** Reading............................	**204** **205**	
6	Assign **Letter to the Editor** [Assignment Due on Day 11 or 12].................... Watch **Make Mine Freedom** Video... Review **Make Mine Freedom** Video Discussion Questions...........................	**207** --- **208**	
7	Complete **Political Charge** Exercise..	**209**	
8	Turn in **Politics Paragraph** [Assignment Due on Day 13]............................ Watch **Dear Uncle** Video.. Review **Dear Uncle** Video Discussion Questions......................................	--- --- **210**	
9	Read *How to Be Your Own Selfish Pig* Reading (Ch. 11)............................	---	
10	Review *How to Be Your Own Selfish Pig* Reading Discussion Questions (Ch. 11)......	**211**	
11	Turn in & Share **Letter to the Editor** Presentation Assignment......................	---	
12	Turn in & Share **Letter to the Editor** Presentation Assignment......................	---	
13	Turn in **Politics Paragraph** Assignment.. Take **Learn to Discern** Quiz.. Prepare **Unit 08** Test..	--- --- ---	
14	Take **Unit 08** Test..	---	
15			

A World of Ideas:
What is the Purpose of Government?

KEYS TO UNDERSTANDING

Key Question: What is the purpose of government?

Key Ideas: Human governments are instituted by God to provide order and promote justice by protecting the innocent and punishing the guilty. Governments that preserve justice guarantee the rights of all people in spite of the sinful tendencies of others to destroy those rights.

Key Terms: politics, justice, pure democracy, constitutional democracy

Key Verses: Romans 13:1 and Matthew 22:21

"Everyone must submit to the governing authorities, for there is no authority except from God, and those that exist are instituted by God." (Romans 13:1, HCSB)

"But everything must be done decently and in order." (1 Corinthians 14:40, HCSB)

Everybody's Got Rights . . . Right?

- Why do some women abort their pre-born children? Because they claim a legal "right" to do whatever they want to with their own bodies.
- Why do some people try to stop the construction of a new dam? Because they claim that a small fish in one of the creeks has a legal "right" to its own habitat.
- Why do some people take the school district to court if a teacher has a Bible on his desk in the classroom? Because they claim a legal "right" to separate church and state.

You read about them everywhere: women's rights, gay rights, abortion rights, civil rights, animal rights. It seems that everybody and everything has rights. But what happens when someone else's "rights" step on your "rights"? And who's to say which rights are the right rights? And the funny thing is that you hear all this talk about *rights*, but almost none about *responsibilities*.

Only a Biblical Christian worldview, with its proper understanding of the relationships God established in His creation, can sort through the maze of rights and balance them with a correct understanding of our responsibilities. The answer to the rights issue is found in a biblical view of both Law and Politics. There is often confusion about the term politics, but simply put, **politics** is the study of the governing of cities, states, nations, or any other association of people. That is why we have terms such as "family politics" or "church politics." Any time we have a group of people, there must be a way of ordering these people. This is where politics comes in.

As we noticed in the last unit, the United States was founded on the idea that human rights ultimately come from God. We discover those rights through our study of both the Bible (*special revelation*) and the natural world (*general revelation*). But it's not enough to discover what is lawful. We also need to ensure that people obey those laws. This means adding another layer to society. In addition to the family and the church, we also need the state or government.

What is the purpose of government? Is civil government an institution that God ordained? How are rulers to govern? How are citizens to live? These questions are at the heart of politics.

In this chapter, you will add politics as another limb of the worldview tree. Along the way, you will confront some controversial issues. Because

Politics: The study of the governing of cities, states, nations, or any other association of people.

many people are moving away from a biblical understanding of the role of government, some ideas that were agreed to without discussion when our country was founded have become hot topics. But, as always, we will seek God's perspective and principles to guide us toward understanding what it takes to put together the best political system.

This chapter will put you on the right track to understanding what's wrong (and right) with rights as they relate to political ideas. During your reading, look for:

> . . . how God relates to government
> . . . how human nature dictates what type of government is best
> . . . the purpose of government
> . . . why religion and politics *do* mix
> . . . how you should relate to government

Can We Get a Little Order around Here?

Our understanding of biblical sociology revealed that God established the state as one of three central institutions of society, and that He actually designed it for theological reasons. But how does government reflect the nature of God, you ask? The next few pages explore the connection between God and government.

In the first place, God is a God of order. Examples of this are found throughout the Bible. For instance, when God created the universe, He established relationships between Himself and humanity, between humans and other humans, and between humanity and creation. These relationships were the best way to enable humanity to "be fruitful and multiply" and to "fill the earth and subdue it." The order God established in His creation was, as we mentioned earlier, "very good."

In fact, the universe is called the *cosmos*. This is a Greek word that means "order," and it is where we get our English word "cosmetics." The opposite of cosmos is *chaos*, or disorder. So from the very beginning of creation, God was concerned with order. Another example of order is the fact that God gave commandments for how we should live. We call this the moral order. If we try to live outside of the moral order, we find that society itself becomes chaotic. In the New Testament, order was a concern of Paul when he wrote that "everything must be done... in order" (1 Corinthians 14:40, HCSB). God, in the moral and social realms, continues to be concerned with order.

How does God's orderly character relate to government? Before you answer, consider this: what if there were no government, no laws, no police, no courts, no driving restrictions such as speed limits, no civil authority whatsoever?

What word would you use to describe what life would be like then?
- A) Cosmos
- B) Chaos
- C) Confined
- D) Cooperative

Pick one of the following answers to complete this statement: If government is necessary to keep some people from infringing on the rights of others, then government is. . .
- A) a "necessary evil" in the world.
- B) an after-thought of God.
- C) a positive good for mankind.
- D) neither positive nor negative; it just is.

Government, as a reflection of God's nature, is designed to keep order in society so that we can fulfill God's ordained purpose for our lives and for His world. When there is order in society, people are free to enjoy life as God intended, living peaceful and productive lives. But some people choose to act outside of God's moral order, so the state has to step in to try to maintain that order. And this is where a second relationship between God and government comes in.

Seeking Justice

A second connection between God and government is related to God's justice. We can define **justice** as fair and impartial handling, or giving due reward or treatment. The idea of justice, like that of order, also comes from the nature of God. In Unit One, when we asked the question of what is God like, we found that God is, among other things, righteous. Being righteous or just is a central part of God's character. God's justice means that He always judges fairly, and He wants us to reflect His nature by being just with our fellow human beings, too.

Almost everyone believes that furthering justice is an important task of the state, but, because of the fall, Christians see justice as the primary reason for the state's existence. This view of justice can only follow from the idea of unalienable rights. Because our fundamental legal rights come from God, as we established in the last unit, they are unalienable—unable to be taken away. Since the Christian view of the state is based on this foundation, promoting justice becomes more important than any other aspect of government.

In Amos 5:15, the Bible portrays the proper rule of government as administering justice. What does this look like in practice? Among other things, this means that those in authority are to protect the weak from those who are more powerful and the poor from oppression by the rich (Amos 5:12). Government should also work to restrain evil and promote good (Romans 13:3–4) and insure that everyone is treated equally before the law (Exodus 23:6).

> **Justice:** Fair and impartial handling; due reward or treatment.

> Hate evil, love good; maintain justice in the courts. Perhaps the Lord God Almighty will have mercy on the remnant of Joseph (Amos 5:15, NIV).

> For I know how many are your offenses and how great your sins. You oppress the righteous and take bribes and you deprive the poor of justice in the courts (Amos 5:12, NIV).

> For rulers hold no terror for those who do right, but for those who do wrong. Do you want to be free from fear of the one in authority? Then do what is right and he will commend you. For he is God's servant to do you good. But if you do wrong, be afraid, for he does not bear the sword for nothing. He is God's servant, an agent of wrath to bring punishment on the wrongdoer (Romans 13:3–4, NIV).

> Do not deny justice to your poor people in their lawsuits (Exodus 23:6, NIV).

Provide Protection

It is important to know that God designed government to do some things in society but not everything. The family and the church are best able to handle certain things that the government should not interfere with. For example, when it comes to caring for children, God designed the family to be the primary means for nurturing and raising children. More specifically, parents are to take responsibility for their children's education. In Deuteronomy 6, parents are directed to teach their children continuously within day-to-day experiences about the commandments of God. And Jesus' "Great Commission" commands the church to teach the nations all that He taught (Matthew 28:19–20).

> Therefore go and make disciples of all nations, baptizing them in the name of the Father and of the Son and of the Holy Spirit, and teaching them to obey everything I have commanded you. And surely I am with you always, to the very end of the age (Matthew 28:19–20, NIV).

Not only does the Bible place a premium on parents teaching their children, this principle is also obvious from observing natural law (the natural way things work). Since it takes a mom and dad to have children, then it must be their primary responsibility to raise them. Therefore, we can conclude that raising children (feeding, clothing, educating, etc.) is the responsibility of parents, not the government.

> These commandments that I give you today are to be upon your hearts. Impress them on your children. Talk about them when you sit at home and when you walk along the road, when you lie

down and when you get up. Tie them as symbols on your hands and bind them on your foreheads. Write them on the door frames of your houses and on your gates (Deuteronomy 6:6–9, NIV).

This, however, brings up another key responsibility of the government: to protect people so that they can fulfill their responsibilities. The government should protect families so that they can nurture and educate children. This would include protecting them from crime, foreign invaders, or groups and people who would seek to steal parental rights. Similarly, governments should protect churches so that they are free to minister to the needy, proclaim the Gospel, and grow disciples.

Government: A Reflection of Man's Nature

Lord Acton, an English historian who died in 1902, developed an interesting phrase to describe the intersection between man's nature and government's power. He said, "Power tends to corrupt and absolute power corrupts absolutely."[1] Because Christians understand that humans have a sinful nature that is easily corrupted by unrestrained power, they believe that the power granted to the state should be dispersed. When power is concentrated in one man or a small group, abuse of that power seems inevitable. We know this for two reasons. First, history provides multiple examples of people who have abused their power. And second, the biblical view of human nature tells us that there is a greater likelihood that fallen people will abuse the power they have over others for selfish reasons.

The root of the problem is when those in authority begin to think and act as if they are the law, rather than realizing that they are under the law. Even though in the Old Testament, God allowed Israel to have a king (see Judges 8:22; 9:6; 2 Kings 14:21), the king was to be under God's law (Deuteronomy 17:14–20).

Christianity does not single out any particular form of government as the only acceptable one. Rather, it expects any type of government to conform to biblical principles, suggesting that this is more likely to occur when power is in the hands of many rather than in the hands of a few. But even with fewer people in power, there is a need for plenty of accountability, or "checks and balances."

That is why many Christians are persuaded that constitutional democracy (otherwise known as a representative republic) best preserves human dignity and liberty. As Charles Colson notes, "Democracy is not prescribed in the Bible, and Christians can and do live under other political systems. But Christians can hardly fail to love democracy, because of all systems it best assures human dignity, the essence of our creation in God's image."[2]

Nevertheless, God is sovereign over all governments and is even able to work through oppressive ones. Many examples can be found throughout the Bible including the Egyptian government in Genesis and Exodus, and the Babylonian and Persian governments in the book of Daniel.

Constitutional Democracy

A constitutional democracy is different than a pure democracy. In a **pure democracy**, the majority vote holds power, regardless of the needs of the minorities. Alexis de Tocqueville, a nineteenth century French author, pointedly called this the "tyranny of the majority."[3] His insights stir up a probing question: "If the majority rules absolutely, what happens when the majority is wrong?" Where is justice? But in a **constitutional democracy**, there are laws which protect minorities from the majority, or "mob rule," as some put it.

Pure Democracy: A system of government where the majority vote holds power, regardless of the needs of the minorities.

Although never explicitly stated, elements of constitutional democracy can be seen in the Scriptures. For instance, in Deuteronomy 1:9–18 Moses commands the people of Israel, "Choose some wise, understanding and respected men from each of your tribes, and I will set them over you" (v. 13). After the people did what Moses commanded, he recalled, "So I took the heads of your tribes, wise and knowledgeable men, and made them heads over you, leaders of thousands, leaders of hundreds, leaders of fifties, leaders of tens, and officers for your tribes" (v. 15).

And I charged your judges at that time: Hear the disputes between your brothers and judge fairly, whether the case is between brother Israelites or between one of them and an alien. Do not show partiality in judging; hear both small and great alike. Do not be afraid of any man, for judgment belongs to God. Bring me any case too hard for you, and I will hear it (Deuteronomy 1:16–18, NIV).

This kind of distribution of power, as well as a means of appeal (v. 17), exhibits a wise structure for ruling that not only distributes power, but also allows for mutual accountability among rulers. These rulers were to be chosen by the people from among the people. And Moses even supplies some qualifications and characteristics expected of those who rule. Because it promotes accountability, this political practice fully appreciates both the dignity and sinfulness of every person. But most importantly, it establishes that ultimate accountability is due to God.

> **Constitutional Democracy:**
> A system of government where laws exist that protect minorities from the majority, or "mob rule."

The Founding of the United States

The founders of the United States understood the dynamics of a biblical worldview, that the ideas from one area have implications in other areas. For example, our first president, George Washington, connected religion, morality, and government when he wrote, "Of all the dispositions and habits which lead to political prosperity, religion and morality are indispensable supports."[4]

John Adams, one of the signers of the *Declaration of Independence* and second president of the United States, also said, "[I]t is religion and morality alone which can establish the principles upon which freedom can securely stand. The only foundation of a free constitution is pure virtue."[5] Also look at John Quincy Adams, the son of John Adams. At age fourteen he was appointed by Congress as ambassador to Russia, and later served as a U.S. Senator, U.S. Minister to France and Britain, Secretary of State for President James Monroe, and finally as the sixth president of the United States. John Quincy Adams understood the relationship between the moral and civil aspects of the Ten Commandments:

> The law given from Sinai [the Ten Commandments] was a civil and municipal as well as a moral and religious code; it contained many statutes...of universal application—laws essential to the existence of men in society, and most of which have been enacted by every nation which ever professed any code of laws.[6]

We must admit that there are many problems with the United States today.[7] We also admit that the Constitution of the United States is an imperfect document, something even the founding fathers recognized when they provided for amendments to be added. Nevertheless, there are some notably good features of the structure of the United States government.

Although the founding fathers were not all professing Christians, they generally recognized not only the importance of acknowledging God, but also the importance of taking the sinfulness of human beings into account. Recognizing the natural tendency for power to corrupt, James Madison wrote the following,

> But what is government itself, but the greatest of all reflections on human nature? If men were angels, no government would be necessary. If angels were to govern men, neither external nor internal controls on government would be necessary. In framing a government, which is to be administered by men over men, the great difficulty lies in this: You must first enable the government to control the governed; and in the next place, oblige it to control itself.[8]

Because of man's fallen nature, Madison and the other founders knew that in order to build a government that would serve the people, the power of their leaders must be dispersed. This is why they designed our government with three separate branches: the executive, the legislative, and the judicial.

Other governments of the day did not install such checks and balances, probably because they did not fully understand the corruption of fallen humanity. The major secular movement of the day, known as the Enlightenment, carried the assumption that humans were essentially good. As author Tim LaHaye notes,

Unit Eight

If our Founding Fathers had been smitten with the idealism of the Enlightenment, the check and balance system would never have been written into our Constitution, and we would have established the same unstable form of government experienced by France, which has endured seven different governmental systems during the two hundred years that America has enjoyed only one.[9]

In 1789, the French Revolution dethroned God and enshrined human "reason" as the highest authority. This led to a blood-bath, with over 40,000 French citizens going to the guillotine, many simply on suspicion of not supporting the new regime. In addition to killing off political dissidents, the new French government sought to "dechristianize" the country by taking over the churches and killing priests who did not sign the new state constitution.

If ruling authorities do not acknowledge God and the fact that He has created us and granted us rights, then disaster results. "If God be God," writes Rushdoony, "then man has no rights apart from God, who is the only true source of all right and of all authority. Destroy the authority of God in human society, and the only right which remains is the right of power, the assertion of sheer force, so that might makes right."[10]

Christian Duty Toward Government

It is not uncommon in our current culture to find Christians who feel that their faith has little or nothing to do with politics. Even more generally, many people do not care for politics or politicians. There is an increasing distrust of our political systems, as well as those who run them. But rather than simply giving up on politics, Christians are called to understand the Christian view of politics and to be involved.

Those in positions of authority over others will have much expected of them. However, there is also much expected of Christians with regard to their rulers. "Submit yourselves to every ordinance of man for the Lord's sake," says the Apostle Peter, "whether to the king as supreme, or to governors, as to those who are sent by him for the punishment of evildoers and for the praise of those who do good" (1 Peter 2:13–14, NKJV). Let's look at several of these expectations, beginning with our duty to obey civil authorities.

DUTY #1: OBEDIENCE TO GOVERNMENT

Let's say you are living in Germany during the 1940s. The government has ordered all Jews to be taken away from the city and sent to death camps. Your best friend, who is Jewish, comes to your door one night and tells you that her family was picked up by the secret police that afternoon while she was away from the house. She doesn't know what to do, where to go, whom to trust. Before continuing, read Romans 13:5 and Acts 4:19.

> Therefore, it is necessary to submit to the authorities, not only because of possible punishment but also because of conscience (Romans 13:5, NIV).

> But Peter and John replied [to the high priest], "Judge for yourselves whether it is right in God's sight to obey you rather than God" (Acts 4:19, NIV).

Now, what would you do?
1. Help her by hiding her in your basement.
2. Tell her to go somewhere else.
3. Call the secret police to report her.

Did you struggle with the two passages from the Bible? There seems to be a conflict. Do you obey the government, according to Romans 13:5, or do you disobey the authorities, as Acts 4:19 suggests? How do you know which command applies best to this situation? Now read Matthew 22:37–39 for a possible solution to this dilemma.

He [Jesus] said to him, "Love the Lord your God with all your heart, with all your soul, and with all your mind. This is the greatest and most important commandment. The second is like it: Love your neighbor as yourself" (Matthew 22:37–39, HCSB).

Here Jesus said that the *first* command is to love God and the *second* is to love your neighbor. This suggests that some commands take priority over others. Because of this, some biblical scholars suggest that Jesus established the principle of the *greater command*. In other words, when there is a conflict between two commands in Scripture, you should obey the "greater" one.

In the following examples, determine which is the greater command to obey.

EXAMPLE 1: Two nations are at war. A woman living in a town controlled by the corrupt government is hiding some enemy spies. Military officers come to her door and ask if she knows where the spies are hiding. What should she do?

EXAMPLE 2: The government passes a law to control population growth. Nurses are ordered to kill certain newborn babies and allow others to live. What should the nurses do?

You can see from these two biblical examples that the greater principle is to save life, even if it means disobeying civil authorities. With this in mind, would you change how you decided to handle our initial situation with your Jewish friend? Why or why not?

These examples demonstrate how a consistent worldview helps you to understand how to handle life's situations. Here we combined Ethics (how we determine the moral thing to do) with Politics (how we relate to government) and arrived at a practical answer as to how to act.

Biblical revelation leaves no uncertainty in regard to the Christian's duty to obey civil authorities. Paul makes this clear in Romans 13. Christians are called to obey governmental authorities. If we are oppressed because we believe in God, that is an honor; but if we are punished for doing evil, then that is to our shame. The Apostle Peter wrote that there could be a blessing if we suffer for doing the right thing.

Everyone must submit himself to the governing authorities, for there is no authority except that which God has established. The authorities that exist have been established by God. Consequently, he who rebels against the authority is rebelling against what God has instituted, and those who do so will bring judgment on themselves. For rulers hold no terror for those who do right, but for those who do wrong. Do you want to be free from fear of the one in authority? Then do what is right and he will commend you. For he is God's servant to do you good. But if you do wrong, be afraid, for he does not bear the sword for nothing. He is God's servant, an agent of wrath to bring punishment on the wrongdoer. Therefore, it is necessary to submit to the authorities, not only because of possible punishment but also because of conscience. This is also why you pay taxes, for the authorities are God's servants, who give their full time to governing. Give everyone what you owe him: If you owe taxes, pay taxes; if revenue, then revenue; if respect, then respect; if honor, then honor (Romans 13:1–7, NIV).

Who is going to harm you if you are eager to do good? But even if you should suffer for what is right, you are blessed. 'Do not fear what they fear; do not be frightened.' [Isaiah 8:12]. But in your hearts set apart Christ as Lord. Always be prepared to give an answer to everyone who asks you to give the reason for the hope that you have. But do this with gentleness and respect, keeping a clear conscience, so that those who speak maliciously against your good behavior in Christ may be ashamed of their slander. It is better, if it is God's will, to suffer for doing good than for doing evil (1 Peter 3:13–17, NIV).

DUTY #2: PRAYER

The Christian's call to obey government authorities is not accomplished by simply obeying the laws of the land. Rather, in obedience to God, Christians are to pray for those in authority, asking God to bless them with righteous hearts and minds so they may live at peace with each other (1 Timothy 2:1–4; 1 Peter 2:13–14).

George Grant adds important depth to the Christian duty to obey authorities in this quote:

> Because God ordains civil government, the magistrates have real authority. But at the same time, because God ordains civil government, the magistrates are under authority. Caesar represents God's rule and so he must be obeyed. But precisely because he represents God, he must abide by the constraints that God has placed on him. He is a 'servant' (Romans 13:6) or a 'minister' (Romans 13:4) of God. He is thus bound to obedience just as the people are bound to obedience.[11]

DUTY #3: PROPER APPEAL

Christians are to use the proper means of appeal in the face of injustice. The Apostle Paul provides us with an example of a proper appeal to your rights as a citizen of a particular government. See how the situation develops in Acts 22.

> The commander ordered Paul to be taken into the barracks. He directed that he be flogged and questioned in order to find out why the people were shouting at him like this. As they stretched him out to flog him, Paul said to the centurion standing there, "Is it legal for you to flog a Roman citizen who hasn't even been found guilty?"
>
> When the centurion heard this, he went to the commander and reported it. "What are you going to do?" he asked. "This man is a Roman citizen."
>
> The commander went to Paul and asked, "Tell me, are you a Roman citizen?"
>
> "Yes, I am," he answered.
>
> Then the commander said, "I had to pay a big price for my citizenship."
>
> "But I was born a citizen," Paul replied.
>
> Those who were about to question him withdrew immediately. The commander himself was alarmed when he realized that he had put Paul, a Roman citizen, in chains (Acts 22:24–29, NIV).

Instead of arrogantly demanding the treatment due a Roman citizen, Paul asked a simple question based on the law: "Is it legal for you to flog a Roman citizen who hasn't even been found guilty?" By appealing to the law, rather than to his rights or even to the personal mercy of the centurion, Paul demonstrated how a Christian could make a proper appeal in any situation.

DUTY #4: CIVIL DISOBEDIENCE

God commands all humans to obey governing authorities, but not when the state requires them to disobey God. "All authority, whether in the home, school, state, church, or any other sphere, is subordinate authority and is under God and subject to his word," writes Rushdoony. "This means, first, that all obedience is subject to the prior obedience to God and His word, for 'We ought to obey God rather than men' (Acts 5:29; cf. 4:19)."[12]

Since governing authorities are fallen human beings, they sometimes overstep their God-given authority. Berkeley Michelson notes, "Jesus pointed out two spheres: the things that belong to the state and the things that belong to God (Matthew 22:15–22; Mark 12:13–17; Luke 20:20–26). Men must function in both spheres."[13]

> Then the Pharisees went out and laid plans to trap him in his words. They sent their disciples to him along with the Herodians.
>
> "Teacher," they said, "we know you are a man of integrity and that you teach the way of God in accordance with the truth. You aren't swayed by men, because you pay no attention to who they are. Tell us then, what is your opinion? Is it right to pay taxes to Caesar or not?"

But Jesus, knowing their evil intent, said, "You hypocrites, why are you trying to trap me? Show me the coin used for paying the tax." They brought him a denarius, and he asked them, "Whose portrait is this? And whose inscription?"

"Caesar's," they replied.

Then he said to them, "Give to Caesar what is Caesar's, and to God what is God's."

When they heard this, they were amazed. So they left him and went away (Matthew 22:15–22, NIV).

It is the Christian's responsibility to work for political reform through proper political channels. However, if the system remains unjust, it may become necessary for the Christian to engage in acts of civil disobedience. "On the one hand Scripture commands civil obedience—that individuals respect and live in subjection to governing authorities and pray for those in authority," writes Colson. "On the other [hand] it commands that Christians maintain their ultimate allegiance to the Kingdom of God. If there is a conflict, they are to obey God, not man. That may mean holding the state to moral account through civil disobedience. This dual citizenship requires a delicate balance. As Francis Schaeffer notes, 'The bottom line is that at a certain point there is not only the right, but the duty, to disobey the state.'"[14]

DUTY #5: POLITICAL INVOLVEMENT

For the Christian, involvement in the political realm is just as necessary as involvement in any other God-ordained institution, such as the family and the church. If "righteousness exalts a nation" (Proverbs 14:34), then it follows that the righteous must be involved in the workings of their nation. It is through the godly influence of righteous citizens that a city prospers (Proverbs 11:11).

Every Christian should cherish the opportunity to participate in government. This should at least involve studying the issues and casting a careful vote every year. Some Christians may also be called to run for political office, while others may serve in non-elected offices. Such involvement may affect public policies and help establish justice. Charles Colson says, "The real issue for Christians is not whether they should be involved in politics or contend for laws that affect moral behavior. The question is how."[15]

Shining God's Light in Society

Obeying God may mean serving in political office, and if it does, the Christian must act courageously, realizing that God honors those who are faithful to Him. This fact is amply demonstrated in the stories of such great men and women of God as Joseph (Genesis 39–40), David (2 Samuel), Daniel (Daniel 1–12), and Esther (Esther 2–8). However, what was true during Old Testament times can also be said for many Christians over the past 2,000 years.

God has granted some Christians the opportunity to serve in the highest governmental offices, some of whom have championed very difficult causes. William Wilberforce is an example. During the early 1800s, Wilberforce served in the British parliament and was instrumental in organizing the movement to end slavery in that country. What is so interesting about William Wilberforce is that after becoming a Christian, he thought about leaving politics. But his friend William Pitt, who later served as Prime Minister, encouraged him to stay in Parliament and serve God that way. Wilberforce spent the next forty-four years working tirelessly against great opposition before slavery was outlawed throughout Great Britain. Colson summarizes, "Wilberforce's dogged campaign to rid the British empire of the slave trade shows what can happen when a citizen of the Kingdom of God challenges corrupt structures within the kingdoms of man."[16]

Likewise in the U.S., the move to abolish slavery was led primarily by Christians. As early as 1700, Boston judge Samuel Sewall, a Presbyterian, wrote an anti-slavery pamphlet entitled *The Selling of Joseph.* At their annual meeting in 1758, Quakers banned from church membership anyone involved in the slave trade. In 1774, Benjamin Rush founded America's first antislavery society. Rush, a signer of the *Declaration of Independence,* commented, "Domestic slavery is repugnant to the principles of Christianity...."[17]

During the following years, Congregationalists, Presbyterians, Methodists, and Baptists began to take up the cause of the enslaved. By 1838, the American Anti-Slavery Society had 1,346 auxiliaries with close to 100,000 members. And it was primarily through the rallying of anti-slavery Protestant voters that Abraham Lincoln was reelected president in 1864.

While it took a bloody civil war to finally end slavery in America, Paul Johnson maintains that this war "can be described as the most characteristic religious episode in the whole of American history, since its roots and causes were not economic or political but religious and moral."[18]

Richard Land summarizes the influence of Christians on human rights issues this way:

> If you look at the Civil Rights Movement, if you look at the abolitionist movement, if you look at the labor reform movement, if you look at the child-labor reform movement, every major successful reform movement in our history has been significantly led, peopled, and supported by people of religious faith and, certainly, ministers being a significant portion of that number...[19]

Conclusion

The starting point for every political system is its religious foundation—specifically, in its answer to the question of God (*theology*). The purpose of the state is to bring order to society and to administer justice, which assumes certain *ethical* standards. *Psychology* reveals that man's sinful tendencies require a balance of power in government. Biblical *sociology* determines that the state has a limited role and should not interfere with the family and the church. And lastly, natural law and the Bible are the basis for making the *laws* of the land. It all forms a consistent and total picture—a biblical worldview of politics.

According to a biblical worldview, human governments are instituted by God to protect the innocent and punish the guilty. In doing these two things, government's purpose is to preserve the rights of all people against man's sinful tendencies to destroy those rights.

Christians recognize that in a fallen world power tends to corrupt. That is why we see the best form of government as one that disperses power among several authorities or departments of the government. But this power is not simply generated by human will; rather, it is delegated by God. Thus, human authorities are accountable to God for how they rule. Men are only intermediate rulers—God is our ultimate Ruler.

Christians cannot abandon the area of politics, assuming that someone else will influence it for good. Each of us, no matter our age, can participate to some degree in the political process. While Christians tend to follow one political party or another, the Biblical Christian worldview encourages us to seek to bring God's purposes and principles into the political arena regardless of the political party. Benjamin Rush, one of the founding fathers of our nation, put it this way, "I have alternatively been called an Aristocrat and a Democrat. I am neither. I am a Christocrat."[20] We should seek to follow Christ whatever we do, whether in school, in the home, or in the voting booth.

Endnotes

[1] http://www.bartleby.com/59/13/powertendsto.html.

[2] Charles Colson, *God and Government* (Grand Rapids, MI: Zondervan, 2007), 365.

[3] See Democracy in America, Volume I, Chapter XV.

[4] Quoted in David Barton, *Original Intent* (Aledo, TX: WallBuilder Press, 1996), 164.

[5] John Adams, *The Works of John Adams, Second President of the United States*, Charles Francis Adams, editor (Boston, MA: Little, Brown, 1854), Vol. IX, 401.

[6] John Quincy Adams, *Letters of John Quincy Adams, to His Son, on the Bible and Its Teachings* (Auburn, NY: James M. Alden, 1850), 61.

[7] For example, consider the current legality of abortion and sodomy.

[8] James Madison, *The Federalist Papers* (New York, NY: Pocket Books, 1964), no. 51, 122–123.

[9] Tim LaHaye, *Faith of our Founding Fathers* (Brentwood, TN: Wolgemuth and Hyatt, 1987), 71.

[10] Rousas J. Rushdoony, *The Politics of Guilt and Pity* (Fairfax, VA: Thoburn Press, 1978), 322.

[11] George Grant, *The Changing of the Guard: Biblical Principles for Political Action* (Ft. Worth, TX: Dominion Press, 1987), 18.

[12] Rousas J. Rushdoony, *The Institutes of Biblical Law* (Nutley, NJ: Craig Press, 1973), 214.

[13] A. Berkeley Mickelson, "State," in *Baker's Dictionary of Christian Ethics*, ed. Carl F.H. Henry (Grand Rapids, MI: Baker Books, 1973), 647.

[14] Colson, *God and Government*, 279.

[15] Charles Colson, *Kingdoms in Conflict* (Grand Rapids, MI: Zondervan, 1987), 280.

[16] Ibid.

[17] Quoted in David Barton, "The Race Card," *The Wallbuilder Report* (Fall 1995).

[18] Paul Johnson, *Christianity on Trial*, 50–51. (Note: While the causes of the Civil War certainly include political and economic factors, the underlying reason for much, if not most, of the abolitionist movement was religious and moral sentiments. Had it not been for the abolitionists, the conflict over slavery would not have been at issue, and there would have been little need for the South to secede from the Union.)

[19] http://richardlandanswers.com/

[20] Quote taken from http://www.faithofourfathers.org/biographies/rush.html.

A World of Ideas
Reading Discussion Questions

1. What is politics? What key question does politics seek to answer? What are the key ideas of Christian politics?

2. In what ways does government reflect the nature of God?

3. According to Christianity, what are the limits of government?

4. What are two reasons that Christians believe the abuse of power is inevitable when it is concentrated in the hands of one individual or a small group?

5. What is the primary difference between a constitutional democracy and a pure democracy?

6. Where in the Bible do we see an early example of a representative government?

7. What are two reasons why representative government is a wise form of government?

8. What is the principle of a "greater command?" Where do find examples of this in Scripture?

9. Christians are called to do what five things in relation to the state and those in authority?

10. When is it proper for Christians to engage in civil disobedience?

11. What three ways can Christians be involved in politics?

Politics Paragraph
Assignment

As you continue your study, write your own paragraph titled **My Christian Worldview of Politics**. *You will be able to correct it, add to it, put it into your Lightbearers Journal, and memorize it. Below is a checklist to help you with this assignment.*

- ☐ The paragraph defines politics from a Christian view and mentions that government is ordained by God and requires our obedience.
- ☐ It discusses that two key beliefs about man influenced the formation of the United States political system.
- ☐ It includes ways a Christian can carry out convictions in the political area.

Unit Eight

Politics
Video Outline

I. **Biblical Christian Politics:** _____

"Everyone must submit himself to the governing authorities, for there is no authority except that which God has established." — Romans 13:1

    A. America's founders understood _____ human nature. They also understood that humans were created in God's image.

    Because of man's fallen nature, there is a need for checks and balances among the powers of the state. Thus the founders designed American government so that each branch of the government has specific powers, yet these powers are counter-balanced by the other branches.

    B. The State

        1. Many governments elevate the state at the expense of the individual, causing their citizens to suffer.

        2. According to the Biblical Christian worldview, human government was instituted by God to protect people's unalienable rights. This simply means promoting justice.

The American Republic: Can We Keep It?

This article by Cal Thomas touches on several things Christians should keep in mind when thinking about politics. Read the article carefully and answer the questions as a class.

Ten score years ago, our forefathers ratified a Constitution for the newly independent United States of America. In 1787, freedom not only had a purpose and a meaning, it also had a price.

The freedom our founders sought was not a means for pursuing self-indulgence but a tool that could, as stated in the Preamble to the Constitution, "insure domestic Tranquility, promote the general Welfare, and secure the Blessings of Liberty to ourselves and our Posterity."

Often, it has been a visitor from a foreign land who has reminded us of the fragile privileges we enjoy and how tenuously we cling to them. De Tocqueville was one. Solzhenitsyn is another. Now comes Pope John Paul II.

In Columbia, South Carolina, the Pope warned against the continued breakdown of the family. He blamed the breakdown on "a false notion of individual freedom" and warned Americans to use their freedom wisely.

"It could be a great tragedy for the entire human family," said the Pope, "if the United States, which prides itself on its consecration to freedom, were to lose sight of the true meaning of that noble word. America, you cannot insist on the right to choose, without also insisting on the right to choose well, the duty to choose the truth." The Pope also said the breakdown had occurred because "fundamental values, essential to the well-being of individuals, families, and the entire nation, are being emptied of their real content."

He is right. Freedom, emptied of its real content, more closely fits the meaning of *license*: "freedom that allows or is used with irresponsibility; disregard for rules of personal conduct; licentiousness."

The late Bishop Fulton J. Sheen spoke of freedom's limits in 1979: "Rights are related to personal dignity and identity... But how do we know the identity of anything? By its limits. How do I know my identity? By my duties, my responsibilities—and they are principally to God, to neighbor, to my country..."

Our founders recognized such duties, which must be assumed with a deep sense of responsibility. Fifty-six of them signed the Declaration of Independence, but not all survived to see the Constitution's ratification. All paid a price for their commitment to obtain freedom for the common good. Nine died in the Revolutionary War. Five were captured by the British and died under torture. Twelve had their homes ransacked and burned to the ground. Dr. John Witherspoon's home and college library were burned. Thomas Keen was forced to move five times in as many months to escape capture. He settled at last in a log cabin on the Susquehanna. Thomas Nelson, Jr., when his home was occupied by British General Charles Cornwallis, urged General George Washington to open fire and destroy his house. He died in poverty.

The fifty-six had pledged their lives, their honor, and their liberty. Seventeen of the signers lost everything they had. Many lost their lives, all of them lost their liberty for a time, but none lost his honor. It was because they knew the meaning and purpose of freedom.

Today, "freedom" seems to mean the right to abort one's child or to censor certain lofty ideas from the public schools while tolerating the filthiest of pornography as First Amendment-protected speech and press. Conviction in political leaders is seen as "extremism." It is thought better to consult the polls to arrive at a bottom-line consensus than to posit firm standards of right and wrong and challenge the nation to follow. Had the founders behaved similarly, the Queen of England would be pictured on our money.

The United States was founded and the Constitution written on the basis of certain universally held presuppositions. Because those presuppositions are under attack and words like "freedom" have been, in the Pope's words, emptied of their real content, the future is less certain than perhaps at any time since our beginning.

We would do well to recall Benjamin Franklin's response to the woman who asked him what kind of government the founders had produced. "A republic, madam, if you can keep it." Keeping it, so far, has been our greatest achievement. Keeping it for our posterity will be our most formidable challenge.*

1. **What sacrifices were made by the signers of the Declaration of Independence?**

2. **What did the signers of the Declaration of Independence think freedom was?**

3. **What do many people today think freedom is?**

4. **What is the danger of having the wrong view of freedom?**

* Excerpted with permission from Cal Thomas, *Uncommon Sense*, (Brentwood, TN: Wolgemuth & Hyatt Publishers, 1990). Copyright Los Angeles Times Syndicate.

Letter to the Editor
Presentation Assignment

Letters exist to provide a forum for public comment or debate. A letter to the editor is meant to express your opinion and to educate people in your community about important issues. Many people who read the newspaper read these letters. Scan the newspaper and find an article or another letter to the editor you would like to respond to. You will present these letters in class. The following are some guidelines for writing a good letter.

Be Timely: Write your letter within a day of the article's date.

Include Contact Information: Include your full name, city, state, phone number (many news organizations will call you to verify you really wrote the letter—most will not print anonymous letters).

Be Clear: Make one main point.

Be Concise: 1–3 paragraphs, 3–8 sentences, 40–100 words. Short letters show confidence in your position.

Be Accurate: Letters that are factually inaccurate are not printed. Do not exaggerate. Your credibility will be put to the test. Anyone can respond to or criticize your comments.

Be Interesting: Editors are always looking for short and interesting headlines. Get your reader's attention and keep it to the end of your letter. Open with an interesting fact or strong statement and keep your points as interesting as possible.

Avoid Personal Attacks: Show respect for the opposite opinion. Being rude may cause people to disagree with you on principle.

Proofread: Re-read your letter. Check for grammar and spelling mistakes. If possible, ask another person to read your letter for accuracy and clarity.

Don't Worry if Your Letter is not Printed: Even if well-written, it might not be printed if it addresses the same issue as letters that have already been printed.

In your email, use the following format:

HEADING
  To the Editor: (If writing directly to the writer, substitute Dear Mr./Ms. ___)
  Re: "headline," Date of article

BODY
 1–3 paragraphs

CLOSING
  Your full name
  City, State
  Your phone number (only if requested by news organization)

Make Mine Freedom
Video Discussion Questions

1. Notice the name of the gentleman selling "ism" in a bottle—Dr. Utopia. What is a utopia?

2. Are utopias possible? Why or why not?

3. What is an "ism"?

4. List a few "isms" below. Think about what these words mean. Are they positive or negative. Why? (You don't have to write the reasons. This is only to provoke thought and to make you aware of the plethora of "isms" in the world today.)

5. Dr. Utopia asks everyone to sign away his or her freedom in order to get this wonderful new product called "ism". What would giving up this freedom mean to these individuals?

6. How does government involvement in business curb your freedom? Is this always bad?

7. What are some strategic ways Christians can fight against the loss of freedom?

8. Physical provision of food, clothing, and fellowship are primarily the responsibility of the _____.

9. Someone supporting a _____ view believes that only a single societal institution has importance.

10. _____ is the theory that God created many institutions within which man operates to create a society.

Political Charge
Exercise

As a follower of Christ, you cannot discount politics as your own personal concern. Rooted in Christian law, Christian ethics, and Christian history, politics is one avenue of action for the follower of Christ. These facets of your worldview are based on the character of God, and when you bring godly values into the political arena, you bring honor to God and dignity to the individual. Remember, government is a God-ordained institution that requires the use of godly principles. Government is necessary because human beings do not always operate within the will of God. Christian politics is nothing more than insisting with moral persuasion, personal example, and Christian participation, that government conform to a model of responsible leadership.

Look up, read, and discuss the following verses:

Administration of justice: Jeremiah 23:5; Amos 5:15
Protection of the weak and the poor: Isaiah 3:13–14; Amos 2:6, 5:12
Protection of the innocent: Romans 13:3
Promotion of equality under the law: Acts 10:34; Exodus 23:6
Restraint of evil and protection from hostile invasion: 2 Chronicles 26:9–15

You must look carefully at what is presented to you in this discipline. For some of you, this may be a call to serve. For all, it is a call to action. None of us can do everything, but each one can do something. You will grow to cherish the opportunity as a citizen, to participate in government. The price of withdrawing from this participation is to be ruled by nonbelievers who do not fear God. Walk carefully through this information, and think about what you can do.

Discuss the following questions as a class:

1. **What happens when Christians withdraw from politics?**

2. **What is moral persuasion?**

Dear Uncle
Video Discussion Questions

1. The federal and state income tax is one of the most easily identifiable taxes collected by the government, but there are many more "hidden" taxes. List some of these taxes.

2. Since the government has trillions of dollars at its disposal, isn't it fine to give out the many benefits and subsidies it currently distributes?

3. During Uncle Sam's dream, he mentions the many people who come to him for money, one of them being a lobbyist. What is a lobbyist? Are they good or bad for our country?

4. When Uncle Sam says, "to keep the torch of liberty burning brightly, all of us must do without some of the things we want; only in that way can we preserve our strength and remain free," what does he mean?

Chapter 11: How to Be Your Own Selfish Pig

1. What are some of the lies that our culture tells us?

2. Why does this kind of lifestyle ultimately lead to unhappiness?

3. What are we made for, specifically?

4. What danger is inherent in what the world offers, as far as values are concerned?

5. What are some ways you can stand against the world's values and live according to God's design?

6. What is wrong with the morning routine presented at the bottom of pages 106 and 107? What should we train ourselves to look like and act like instead?

7. According to C.S. Lewis, when will your real "new self" appear?

8. What does the little story "Marriage? Not All Roses . . ." teach?

9. **Reflection Question:** Can you sense what your purpose in life should be? How do you think God is leading you to have an impact on your family, community, and culture?

10. **Reflection Question:** Have you treated those with whom you have come in contact today the same way you would want to be treated? What is one area in your life where you have been acting like "your own selfish pig," and how can you change that?

LIGHTBEARERS

Unit Nine

A Summit Ministries Curriculum

Day	UNIT 09: syllabus & outline	SW	✓
1	Read *A World of Ideas* Reading...	215	
2	Read *A World of Ideas* Reading...	Ditto	
3	Review *A World of Ideas* Reading Discussion Questions............................	224	
4	Review *A World of Ideas* Reading Discussion Questions............................	Ditto	
	Assign **Economics Paragraph** [Rough Draft Due on Day 8].........................	225	
5	Watch **"Biblical Christian Worldview: Economics"** Video Outline................	226	
	Complete **Private Property** Exercise..	227	
	Complete **Sphere of Labor** Exercise..	228	
6	Assign **What Do You Value?** [Assignment Due on Day 11 or 12]...............	229	
	Watch **Fresh Laid Plans** Video...	---	
	Review **Fresh Laid Plans** Video Discussion Questions............................	230	
7	Read *What is Economics?* Reading..	231	
	Review *What is Economics?* Reading Discussion Questions........................	234	
8	Research **What Do You Value?** Presentation Assignment...........................	---	
	Turn in **Economics Paragraph** Rough Draft [Assignment Due on Day 13].......	---	
9	Watch **Inside Cackle Corner** Video...	---	
	Review **Inside Cackle Corner** Video Discussion Questions.......................	235	
10	Complete **What's Your Motivation** Exercise...	236	
11	Turn in & Share **What Do You Value?** Presentation Assignment.................	---	
12	Turn in & Share **What Do You Value?** Presentation Assignment.................	---	
13	Turn in **Economics Paragraph** Assignment...	---	
	Take **Learn to Discern** Quiz..	---	
	Prepare **Unit 09** Test...	---	
14	Take **Unit 09** Test...	---	
15			

A World of Ideas:
How Should We Use Our Resources?

Objects on this page are no smaller than they appear.

If you can read this, you are too close to your workbook.

KEYS TO UNDERSTANDING

Key Question: How should we use our resources?

Key Idea: Private ownership provides incentives for better stewardship and leads to economic advancement.

Key Terms: economics, free exchange, socialism, capitalism, interventionism, stewardship, incentive, social welfare

Key Verse: Colossians 1:16

"All things were created through Him and for Him" (Colossians 1:16, NKJV).

Molly's Question

You could always count on Molly to make the Tuesday Morning Bible Club interesting, and today was no exception. Deep in our study of the book of Acts, Molly suddenly blurted, "Okay, I've got a question! Acts says that Jesus' disciples living in Jerusalem shared everything they had, right? So why don't Christians do that today? If we're really serious about following the Lord, why don't we form a commune and share everything in common?"

What do you think about Molly's question? Should Christians refuse to own anything privately and instead share it all, like one big family? As it turns out, Molly is not alone. There are some Christians who go so far as to call for a *socialistic* system of government, where everyone shares equally in the economic "pie." They believe that the government should regulate the way people work and do business in order to distribute wealth more evenly among all citizens. After all, everyone sharing equally in a nation's wealth is only fair...or is it?

Almost every discussion of economics includes some elements of politics. That's why you learned about politics first. In fact, it is so natural to link economic ideas with political ideas that you can't really separate the two. So our question is now between two options:

Should the government be in control of the way people make and use their resources, property, or money (a system called socialism)?

OR

Should the government protect economic freedom to allow people to peacefully exchange goods and services with a minimum of government interference (called a free market economy)?

These kind of questions are all part of the topic of economics. Don't let that term fool you. It may sound a bit stuffy, but it deals with an area that is very important to you. Very simply, **economics** has to do with how you get what you want and keep what you get! More specifically, it deals with how we should exchange goods and services with other people so that everyone gets what he or she wants and needs. Ultimately, it comes down to how to best manage our resources.

If you would like to find an answer to Molly's question, read on! Being a Lightbearer also means understanding economic issues. This chapter introduces you to:

. . . The difference between socialism and a free market society
. . . Why ownership is a good thing
. . . Other practical tips on God's view of money and godly living

Economics: The study of how to best manage our resources.

Making Money by the Bible

Have you ever thought about how the economy in the United States works and how it is different from other nations of the world? In the U.S., people enjoy a standard of living that is one of the highest in the world. Just look at all the stuff we have that the majority of people living today do not. And it's not just because America has more natural resources. Other countries have similar resources, but their people can barely survive. Think of China, for example. Why do the majority of people in China live in poverty, while in the U.S. there is such a high standard of living?

The main reason is because the founders of this nation used biblical principles to establish how people could make and use money. Our earlier discussion of law revealed that God designed the universe to work according to certain laws or principles—in the natural world (physical laws), according to our consciences (moral laws), and even together with other people in our society (civil laws).

But there are also economic laws that determine the best way to get what you need. Based on the nature of God (holy and just) and the nature of mankind (made in God's image, yet sinful), a picture of these basic economic principles begins to emerge. But there is more. The kind of economic system a culture or nation chooses is closely tied to its political system.

Russell Kirk was a well-known American conservative political theorist who died in 1994. He explained it this way. "The economic problem blends into the political problem, and the political problem into the ethical problem, and the ethical problem into the religious problem."[1]

The main principle of biblical economics is **free exchange**. In this type of system, people should be free to produce goods and services (legally, of course) and sell them as they choose. History has proven that free and peaceful exchange (also called a free market), more than any other system of economics, allows the greatest standard of living and well being for the greatest number of people.

Free Exchange: An economic system that allows people to freely produce and sell goods and services as they choose.

A Biblical View of Work

Think about it: when was the idea of work first introduced to mankind? Some people associate work with God's punishment for Adam after he sinned, but the Bible actually paints a different picture. Look at Genesis 2:15 and Genesis 3:17–19. The interesting fact is that work was not part of the curse. God placed Adam in the garden to "work it and take care of it" *before* he and Eve sinned. Work was a part of God's original plan—His "good" plan for Adam before his fall. God designed life so that we are involved in His care and rule over creation. A theologian once said that when someone milks a cow, he or she is participating in God's creation.[2] So work is not a curse, but a part of God's blessing and design for humanity. When we work, we experience the dignity, responsibility, and fulfillment God created us to enjoy. Only after the fall did this blessing become a hardship.

> The Lord God took the man and put him in the Garden of Eden to work it and take care of it (Genesis 2:15, NIV).

> To Adam he said, "Because you listened to your wife and ate from the tree about which I commanded you, 'You must not eat of it,' cursed is the ground because of you; through painful toil you will eat of it all the days of your life. It will produce thorns and thistles for you, and you will eat the plants of the field. By the sweat of your brow you will eat your food until you return to the ground since from it you were taken; for dust you are and to dust you will return" (Genesis 3:17–19, NIV).

Work Has Its Rewards

After casting the man and the woman out of Eden, God decreed that men must face a life of toil (Genesis 3:17–19). But God, in His mercy, allowed those who work wisely and diligently to be rewarded with private property. Proverbs 10:4 states, "Lazy hands make a man poor, but diligent hands bring wealth"

(NIV). God has designed a world in which being able to own property encourages human beings to be fruitful and enjoy the work of their hands.

Does this mean that everyone who works hard will become wealthy? No. The Bible does not promise lots of material riches, but it does convey the idea that we should be able to utilize what we earn as a faithful manager of God's resources.

There are some Christians, though, who disagree on the issue of economics. While many believe the Bible teaches an economic system of private property and individual responsibility, others support socialism. **Socialism** is where the government controls the means to produce and distribute goods. Communist countries like China, Cuba, and North Korea operate under a socialist system of economics. In a purely socialistic state, the government owns everything and is in charge of all the factories, farms, and businesses, dictating where people work and how much they are paid.

In fact, some Christians even say that the Bible teaches a form of economic socialism, where the government should own the means of producing goods and services, or redistribute money from the wealthy to eliminate poverty. These people sometimes call themselves "Liberation Theologians." Often they expect that some form of socialism will help bring in the kingdom of God.

However appealing this may sound at first, there is a trap here that Christians should avoid. No economic system—whether capitalist, socialist, or any combination—is capable of *saving humankind.* No economic system is perfect, and no system will ever be perfect since we live in a fallen world. However, this does not mean that all economic systems are equal. The Christian's goal is to discern between economic systems to see which one is the most consistent with a biblical worldview.

> **Socialism**: An economic system that allows government control of property and the redistribution of personal wealth.

The Bible and Private Property

Think back to Molly's question at the beginning of this chapter: *Shouldn't Christians today share everything they have, like the early church did?* This would be a kind of socialism, where nobody owns anything and everyone shares what he or she has with the rest. But there's a problem with this application—it confuses what people did in the Bible in a specific situation with what God commands us to do as a normal way of life.

Molly's question came out of a passage in Acts 2. Here, context is key!. The Christians in Acts *voluntarily* shared *some* of their resources because of a unique situation. There were a large number of pilgrims who had come to Jerusalem for the festival of First Fruits, one of three annual festivals that all Jewish men were required to attend. After hearing Peter speak and becoming Christians, some stayed on longer. Since close to three thousand people accepted Jesus in one day alone, there were many who needed food and shelter. So with everyone contributing something, the early church was able to feed and care for the whole group for the time they were all in Jerusalem. But this was how the early Christians handled a unique situation. It does not automatically mean that a socialistic system should be normal practice for Christians in all times and situations.

The Bible actually teaches that people have the right to own property for themselves. For example, the commandment against stealing assumes that a person owns something of value that can be stolen. We find examples of this assumption of private property throughout Scripture. In 1 Kings 4:25, we read of people having their own vineyards and fig trees. And in Jeremiah 32 and Acts 5 we come across people owning great wealth and property.

So it seems clear that the Bible supports the idea of owning property. And this principle of private property is the foundation for a system of economics called **capitalism**, where everyone is allowed to keep what he or she earns and own private property. Here are a few verses that speak to this issue.

> **Capitalism**: An economic system that allows private ownership of property and the right to keep one's wealth.

All the believers were together and had everything in common. Selling their possessions and goods, they gave to anyone as he had need. Every day they continued to meet together in the temple courts. They broke bread in their homes and ate together with glad and sincere hearts… (Acts 2:44–46, NIV).

During Solomon's lifetime Judah and Israel, from Dan to Beersheba, lived in safety, each man under his own vine and fig tree (1 Kings 4:25, NIV).

Fields will be bought for silver, and deeds will be signed, sealed and witnessed in the territory of Benjamin, in the villages around Jerusalem, in the towns of Judah and in the towns of the hill country, of the western foothills and of the Negev, because I will restore their fortunes, declares the Lord (Jeremiah 32:44, NIV).

Now a man named Ananias, together with his wife Sapphira, also sold a piece of property. With his wife's full knowledge he kept back part of the money for himself, but brought the rest and put it at the apostles' feet. Then Peter said, "Ananias, how is it that Satan has so filled your heart that you have lied to the Holy Spirit and have kept for yourself some of the money you received for the land? Didn't it belong to you before it was sold? And after it was sold, wasn't the money at your disposal? What made you think of doing such a thing? You have not lied to men but to God" (Acts 5:1–4, NIV).

Socialism or Capitalism?

There are two opposing ways to think about who owns a nation's natural resources and how they should be used. As already mentioned, these two systems are called *socialism* and *capitalism*. The simplest differences between socialism and capitalism are outlined by Ronald H. Nash:

One dominant feature of capitalism is economic freedom, the right of people to exchange things voluntarily, free from force, fraud, and theft…Socialism, on the other hand, seeks to replace freedom of the market with a group of central planners who exercise control over essential market functions.[3]

These "essential market functions" controlled by the few include factories and industries as well as the price for goods. Essentially, socialism controls what, when, and how people buy and sell, both as it concerns products (like yo-yos) and services (like haircuts). Some people believe that only some industries should be owned and run by the government (e.g., fuels, postal services, education, emergency services), while others should be privately owned (e.g., restaurants, construction, media).

In our world, neither socialism nor the free market exist in a perfect form. All capitalist systems contain certain elements of socialism, and even socialistic systems have certain elements of capitalism built in. When government gets involved in the economy (beyond keeping an eye on force, theft, and fraud), then the system is called **interventionism**. Interventionism is a political term for significant activity undertaken by a state to influence the economy.

Interventionism: Significant activity undertaken by a state to influence the economy.

Economic Freedom Leads to Political Freedom

As we discovered during our journey into politics, it's in the nature of government to control people. That's why some governments have sought to reduce the state's potential for taking away liberty by creating separate branches of government. But there are two other ways government is kept in check.

The first is economic freedom. Economic freedom allows the development of private institutions, such as businesses, universities, and civic associations, which are important because they help disperse the ability of a powerful state to control people.

Second, private property is crucial to hold the state in check. Think about it: if you can buy a printing press or television station or sell newspapers, you have the opportunity to tell other citizens about what government officials are doing. If elected officials become corrupt or try to take too much power, then a "free press" can report this, and the offending politicians can be voted out of office.

But what would happen if there was no private property—such as independently held printing presses and television stations—and the government controlled what news was distributed? This is exactly what happened in Nazi Germany during World War II. The people of Germany, and the rest of the world, did not know that Hitler was sending Jews to death camps until toward the end of the war. That is because there was no free press—Hitler completely controlled the news media in his country. Also, Hitler (and Stalin in Russia) dictated that schools should only teach what would spread socialism and promote allegiance to their ideology.

The same is true today in socialist nations such as China, Cuba, and North Korea. But many Islamic nations also limit the freedom of their citizens. In their annual *Freedom in the World* report, Freedom House lists forty-five nations that received a rating of "Not Free." Of these, twenty-five have primarily Islamic populations. And of the top eight worst rated countries, five are Islamic (Libya, Somalia, Sudan, Turkmenistan, and Uzbekistan).[4]

Freedom, Justice, Order

Because a worldview that values human life and private property has such positive social results, many Christians believe that the best economic system should also contain checks and balances that guarantee the protection of human freedoms from mankind's sinful tendencies. While no economic system is flawless (since we live in a fallen world), many Christians have recognized that capitalism (or the free market system) is most in accord with biblical principles. Capitalism is the only system that not only provides for personal responsibility of resources, but also retains the freedom of all people.

However, the Christian approach to economics is less concerned with money and how to get rich than it is with freedom, justice, and order—*freedom* for people to use their resources within the bounds of *justice*, thus retaining and promoting *order* in society.

Ownership and Stewardship

Another important feature in economic discussions is the question of stewardship. **Stewardship** includes our use of and care for resources. A vital element of stewardship has to do with incentives. An **incentive** is something that would encourage or motivate someone to act. Consider the following economic opportunities.

Public places can be wonderful. Public parks in the midst of high-rise office buildings can supply people with the opportunity to retreat into a beautiful and relaxing environment. But have you ever been in a public restroom at a national park or even a local city park? Public restrooms tend to be some of the dirtiest places.

Now consider the bathroom at home. Does it normally smell like a sewer? Does it have nasty words and phone numbers scrawled on the walls? Probably not. So why do public bathrooms get so dirty and yucky, while home bathrooms tend to be quite clean and nice-smelling?

The basic difference is *ownership*. Some people say that we all own public places like parks and bathrooms. If that were really the case, then we should all expect to take our turn at cleaning them. Thankfully, most people will never face that horrible experience!

The reality is that public parks and restrooms are *not* owned by all of us—the city, state, or federal government owns them. That is why people are hired to take care of them. And that is also why the state tries to get money from taxes to pay for the park rangers, cleaning staff, construction workers, etc., who are needed to keep these public places clean and functional.

One thing that many public parks have done is institute fees for the use of camping areas or even for driving through the park. This helps raise the money needed to keep these places in working condition. Many who visit the parks complain when they have to pay fees to use them. But the fact is someone has to pay. Either it will be people using the public places (through fees) or everyone (through taxes), whether they used them or not.

Stewardship: Our use of and care for resources.

In considering public and private bathrooms, one more thing should be observed. *Ownership provides incentives for better stewardship*. When we own things, we tend to take better care of them. If you have to use your bathroom everyday, you are going to be more likely to clean it, or take turns cleaning it with the other people who use it. But public restrooms are just one example.

Incentive: Something that motivates someone to act.

Unit Nine

Welfare

At next week's Tuesday Morning Bible Club, armed with the information you studied during the week, you lay out an answer to Molly's question about Acts 2. But she still isn't satisfied. She says, "But the Bible says that we should love and care for one another, especially the poor. Look at all those millionaires and wealthy corporations that make so much money. It's just not fair. Wouldn't it be better to tax the rich so the government can help the poor?"

What do you say now? In a way, Molly has a point. What could be more noble than helping the poor? Shouldn't Christians strive for "economic equality" among all people? This idea raises the issue of how much involvement the state should assume in helping the poor. But before we tackle that question, we need a little background.

The idea of welfare, or well being, is related to the idea of incentives. For example, as we grow up, our parents take less and less care of our welfare so we will develop the incentive to take care of our welfare on our own. If they didn't hand over any of this responsibility, then we would never be motivated to take care of ourselves. For instance, what if your parents continued increasing your weekly allowance so that by the time you graduated from college they were giving you $250,000 a year? And not only that, they promise to keep giving you that much for the rest of your life. Would you be motivated to get a job? Probably not, unless you decided that wasn't enough to live on. On the other hand, if your parents did not give you an allowance at all, then you would have to go earn any spending money you needed.

So who should provide for the welfare of whom? Should the state create welfare programs to care for the poor? Should the Church be responsible for helping the needy? And what role should the family play?

From a biblical perspective, the family is the center of well being in society. During Old Testament times, each son received an inheritance from his father (unless there were no sons, in which case the daughters would receive the inheritance; see Numbers 27:1–11). But the firstborn son received a double inheritance (Deuteronomy 21:17). While this may seem unfair to us today, it was because the firstborn also had the primary responsibility for taking care of his parents in their old age, as well as any sisters who didn't marry. Daughters did not often receive an inheritance because their husbands would have the responsibility to provide for them out of their inheritance.

These expectations regarding relatives caring for other family members are seldom seen in our day. But even if this particular facet of Old Testament law is no longer operating, the principles of parents caring for their children, and vice versa, remains relevant today. Not only are parents to provide for their children (Proverbs 13:22; 2 Corinthians 12:14b), children are to "honor [their] parents" (Exodus 20:12; Ephesians 6:1–3), including taking care of them as needed. 1 Timothy 5 states, "But if anyone does not provide for his own, and especially for those of his household, he has denied the faith and is worse than an unbeliever" (1 Timothy 5:8, NKJV).

A good man leaves an inheritance for his children's children, but a sinner's wealth is stored up for the righteous (Proverbs 13:22, NIV).

Honor your father and your mother, so that you may live long in the land the Lord your God is giving you (Exodus 20:12, NIV).

While the family is the primary avenue for welfare in society, it is not the only one. Another avenue for welfare is the Church. In the Old Testament, the Israelites were to contribute a tenth of their goods to help the needy in the community, including aliens, the fatherless, and widows (Deuteronomy 14:29; 26:12).

When you have finished setting aside a tenth of all your produce in the third year, the year of the tithe, you shall give it to the Levite, the alien, the fatherless and the widow, so that they may eat in your towns and be satisfied (Deuteronomy 26:12, NIV).

In New Testament times, this kind of community welfare seems to have taken place by means of offerings and collections. When people in the congregation were in need, others were expected to give of their plenty to take care of the needy (as shown in the book of Acts). Other examples of this would be taking care of widows (Acts 6:1–7; 1 Timothy 5:3–16) and taking up collections to help other Christian congregations (2 Corinthians 8; Romans 15:25–27).

Modern Welfare Systems

The unfortunate fact is that modern government welfare systems (**social welfare**) have taken over the responsibilities of the family and the church in caring for the community. By installing high inheritance taxes, the government takes a large percentage of

> **Social Welfare:** A financial assistance program, run by the government and funded by tax payers, which seeks to help the poor.

people's inheritance and redistributes it to others. Even beyond that, current tax rates are fairly high partly because the government is attempting to take some of the money from wealthier people to support government programs for helping the poor.

Is this a good thing? First, consider that it is morally wrong to take something that belongs to someone else—this is called stealing. While it is one thing for the government to tax everyone equally and provide common benefits, such as roads and national defense, it is different when the government takes money from some people and only gives it to certain others. Seen in this light, it is immoral for the government to take the property of one person and give it to someone else, no matter how good the intentions.

Not only that, but government programs for the poor tend to place them in what might be called a "poverty trap." When the government removes incentives for work, then it is natural for people to avoid it. It is true that the poor and needy require help in the form of money and food, at least in the short term. However, government aid programs tend to create a dangerous climate of expectant help, or even a feeling of entitlement, where people say they deserve a certain amount of money or goods regardless of whether they are physically able to work.

Causes of Wealth and Poverty

Christianity affirms that God is sovereign over both wealth and poverty. Many who are wealthy fail to thank God and recognize that He is the source of all wealth. This was one of the great dangers that threatened the Israelites as they prepared to enter the Promised Land.

> Beware that you do not forget the LORD your God by not keeping His commandments...which I command you today, lest—when you have eaten and are full, and have built beautiful houses and dwell in them...and all that you have is multiplied; when your heart is lifted up, and you forget the LORD your God who brought you out of the land of Egypt...who led you through that great and terrible wilderness, in which were fiery serpents and scorpions and thirsty land where there was no water...who fed you in the wilderness with manna, which your fathers did not know, that He might humble you and that He might test you, to do you good in the end—then you say in your heart, 'My power and the might of my hand have gained me this wealth.' And you shall remember the LORD your God, for it is He who gives you power to get wealth, that He may establish His covenant which He swore to your fathers... (Deuteronomy 8:11–18, NKJV).

Honoring God with our possessions may lead to a blessing of even greater prosperity:

> Honor the LORD with your possessions, and with the firstfruits of all your increase; so your barns will be filled with plenty, and your vats will overflow with new wine (Proverbs 3:9–10, NKJV).

The Bible teaches that wealth follows work:

> He who tills his land will be satisfied with bread, but he who follows frivolity is devoid of understanding (Proverbs 12:11, NKJV).

In all labor there is profit, but idle chatter leads only to poverty (Proverbs 14:23, NKJV).

The Bible teaches that working with diligence can create prosperity:

The plans of the diligent lead surely to plenty, but those of everyone who is hasty, surely to poverty (Proverbs 21:5, NKJV).

But it also teaches that poverty can be the result of laziness:

Go to the ant, you sluggard! Consider her ways and be wise, which, having no captain, overseer or ruler, provides her supplies in the summer, and gathers her food in the harvest. How long will you slumber, O sluggard? When will you rise from your sleep? A little sleep, a little slumber, a little folding of the hands to sleep—so shall your poverty come on you like a prowler, and your need like an armed man (Proverbs 6:6–11, NKJV; see also Proverbs 20:13).

Poverty can also be the result of some natural disaster (Luke 13:4), a fact demonstrated by 2004 tsunami that killed over 200,000 people.

Virtuous and Vicious Wealth

The Christian appreciation for capitalism must not be separated from a *virtuous use* of our resources. Christians realize that to horde wealth for personal greed and power is vicious and self-destructive: "For the *love* of money is a root of all kinds of evil" (1 Timothy 6:10, NKJV). There are more important things to pursue in life than wealth alone (Proverbs 23:4–5). The Bible regularly teaches that one of the greatest temptations leading people away from God is the temptation of wealth. It may lead people to pursue dishonest gain (Ezekiel 22:29; Micah 2:2; Amos 5:11–12), use dishonest measures (Ezekiel 45:10–12; Hosea 12:7), or defraud workers of their wages (Malachi 3:5).

None of this means that wealth is inherently evil or that wealthy people are evil. Wealth can actually be a gift of God, a sign of blessing, and it can be used for good, such as helping the poor and the needy, supporting missionaries and ministry organizations, and paying for the education of others.

Helping the poor and needy with your wealth is a primary biblical virtue. "The righteous considers the cause of the poor, but the wicked does not understand such knowledge" (Proverbs 29:7, NKJV). Generosity to the poor leads to blessing (22:9; 28:27). The noble and virtuous wife of Proverbs 31:10–31 "extends her hand to the poor, yes, she reaches out her hands to the needy" (v. 20). We also find a strong warning in Proverbs 21:13: "Whoever shuts his ears to the cry of the poor will also cry himself and not be heard" (NKJV).

Conclusion

When it comes to economics, God has the best ideas. First, God has designed us to work. Even though work may be difficult because of Adam's sin, we can still enjoy being involved in whatever tasks God gives us to complete.

Second, through work we gain possessions that we can use to freely and peacefully exchange for other things that we need or desire. The Biblical Christian worldview teaches that a free market system allows the greatest personal freedom to make and spend money, and to improve our own economic situation.

Third, we should be willing to share our abundance. The Puritan work ethic summarizes the biblical understanding by saying, "Work as hard as you can, to make as much as you can, to give away as much as you can." When we have made this a normal part of our lives, we will naturally want to pass on that wisdom and experience to others who need to learn to help themselves. As the saying goes: Give someone a fish and he is fed for a day; teach him to fish and he is fed for a lifetime. Christians should be the first ones helping those in need and teaching them the skills they will need to prosper.

Endnotes

[1] Russell Kirk, *A Program for Conservatives*, 2nd rev. ed. (Chicago, IL: Henry Regnery, 1962), 5.

[2] This is a paraphrase of a quote attributed to Martin Luther.

[3] Ronald H. Nash, *Poverty and Wealth: The Christian Debate over Capitalism* (Westchester, IL: Crossway Books, 1987), 63.

[4] To view the *Map of Freedom 2007*, go to http://www.freedomhouse.org/template.cfm?page=363&year=2007

A World of Ideas
Reading Discussion Questions

1. What is economics? What key question does economics seek to answer? What are the key ideas of Christian economics?

2. What is the principle of free exchange? How does this work well with the Christian worldview?

3. Read Genesis 3:17–19 and answer the following questions.

    "To Adam he said, 'Because you listened to your wife and ate from the tree about which I commanded you, "You must not eat of it," cursed is the ground because of you; through painful toil you will eat of it all the days of your life. It will produce thorns and thistles for you, and you will eat the plants of the field. By the sweat of your brow you will eat your food until you return to the ground, since from it you were taken; for dust you are and to dust you will return'" (NIV).

    Question 1: What was the consequence of Adam's sin?
    Question 2: Because of God's curse on the ground, what would it now produce?
    Question 3: What words were used to describe Adam's labor?
    Question 4: Is work part of God's curse on mankind?

4. What are two ways to think about who owns a nation's natural resources and how they should be used? What is the term for the system that falls somewhere between?

5. When read and understood in context, what three conclusions can we surmise from the Acts passage often used to support socialism?

6. Besides the separation of powers, briefly explain two more ways government is kept in check.

7. What is stewardship and incentive? What simple principle does the example of public versus private bathrooms illustrate?

8. What happens when the government, through welfare and other aid programs, removes incentives for work?

9. Does the Bible view wealth and prosperity negatively? Support your answer with Scripture.

10. Reflection Question: How much of your resources (i.e. time, space, money, etc) do you give to those less fortunate?

Economics Paragraph
Assignment

*As you continue your study, write your own paragraph titled **My Christian Worldview of Economics**. You will be able to correct it, add to it, put it into your Lightbearers Journal, and memorize it. Below is a checklist to help you with this assignment.*

☐ The paragraph includes the Christian definition of economics.

☐ It includes statements about free enterprise, private property, economic competition, and justice as interpreted from a Christian perspective.

☐ It includes a statement concerning the relationship of freedom and economics.

Economics
Video Outline

I. **Biblical Christian Economics:** _____

    A. Private Property

        1. God has designed the social life of humans so that through the ownership of property people are motivated to greater _____.

        "The commandment, 'Thou shalt not steal' is the clearest declaration of the right to private property in the Old Testament." — Irving E. Howard

        2. The Bible clearly calls for ownership of property. This right to property stems from the duty to work. God has decreed that people work for their livelihood. He designed a world where adhering to this duty is rewarded. Thus, the existence of private property encourages people to be fruitful.

        3. Property is not intended to merely be hoarded or to simply be taken away. Rather, under the direction of God, humans are to work, be rewarded for their work, enjoy these rewards, and serve others as well.

    B. Work and Pay

    "For even when we were with you, we gave you this rule: 'If a man will not work, he shall not eat'" — 2 Thessalonians 3:10 (NIV)

        1. Justice requires that each person be rewarded according to his or her work.

        2. The biblical view of economics is the best way in which to create wealth and opportunity for the poor.

Private Property
Exercise

Some people in government believe that citizens shouldn't be allowed to own property. These individuals, known as **socialists**, *contend that private property should be abolished and that the government should own everything. To see if this is a biblical view, look up the following passages of Scripture and fill in the blanks:*

1. **1 Kings 4:25 says that each man lived under his own _____ and _____.**

2. **Jeremiah 32:44 indicates a future time when the nation of Israel will be free to _____ and _____.**

3. **In Acts 5:1–4, Peter was angry because Ananias _____ about what he had, not because he owned property.**

Some Christians believe that Christians shouldn't own property, taking this idea from a passage in Acts 2. To see if this is the biblical view taught in Acts, read the following passage carefully and select the option that best fills in the blanks:

"All the believers were together and had everything in common. Selling their possessions and goods, they gave to anyone as he had need. Every day they continued to meet together in the temple courts. They broke bread in their homes and ate together with glad and sincere hearts…" (Acts 2:44–46, NIV).

4. **The early believers _____ sold some of their property and pooled their resources (notice in Acts 2:46 that some still had houses).**
    a) voluntarily
    b) under compulsion

5. **There was _____ government agency forcing anyone to contribute.**
    a) no
    b) a big

6. **This was an illustration of Christian _____ rather than state welfare policy.**
    a) charity
    b) coercion

What is your conclusion about God's view of private property? Check the sentence that best describes your answer:

☐   God's design is for people to share all things in common.
☐   It's not clear from the Bible how we should best handle private ownership.
☐   The biblical view indicates that people have the right to own things privately and exchange them peacefully and freely.

Sphere of Labor
Exercise

Do you have to like *work? Well, probably not. But since it's a way of life, you might as well* enjoy *it. Look over the following verses to get God's perspective on work. Write your thoughts about each passage.*

Exodus 20:9–11

"Six days you shall labor and do all your work, but the seventh day is a Sabbath to the Lord your God. On it you shall not do any work, neither you, nor your son or daughter, nor your manservant or maidservant, nor your animals, nor the alien within your gates. For in six days the Lord made the heavens and the earth, the sea, and all that is in them, but he rested on the seventh day. Therefore the Lord blessed the Sabbath day and made it holy" (Exodus 20:9–11, NIV).

Deuteronomy 16:13–15

"Celebrate the Feast of Tabernacles for seven days after you have gathered the produce of your threshing floor and your winepress. Be joyful at your Feast—you, your sons and daughters, your menservants and maidservants, and the Levites, the aliens, the fatherless and the widows who live in your towns. For seven days celebrate the Feast to the Lord your God at the place the Lord will choose. For the Lord your God will bless you in all your harvest and in all the work of your hands, and your joy will be complete" (Deuteronomy 16:13–15, NIV).

Deuteronomy 24:19

"When you are harvesting in your field and you overlook a sheaf, do not go back to get it. Leave it for the alien, the fatherless and the widow, so that the Lord your God may bless you in all the work of your hands" (Deuteronomy 24:19, NIV).

Proverbs 12:14

"From the fruit of his lips a man is filled with good things as surely as the work of his hands rewards him" (Proverbs 12:14, NIV).

Proverbs 21:25

"The sluggard's craving will be the death of him, because his hands refuse to work" (Proverbs 21:25, NIV).

What Do You Value?
Presentation Assignment

How much money do you give to the poor? How much time do you devote to caring for those who are less fortunate? For this assignment you will need to look into a Christian organization that provides food, clothing, shelter, medicine, or aid to those in need. Find out information like when the organization was founded, its mission statement, its current projects, and any related statistics. Write up a report and be prepared to make a presentation of your findings to the rest of class.

Fresh Laid Plans
Video Discussion Question

Synopsis: Steady employment gives workers high purchasing power to keep the local businesses prosperous and the people happy.

Problem
The farmer had one-half his usual crop, so he had to raise his prices. The workers did not want (and some could not afford) the new prices.

Answer
Dr. Hoot's plan was to manipulate the law of supply and demand through three steps:
1. Fix prices
2. Provide a subsidy to the farmer
3. Tax businesses

Results
1. Higher taxes mean higher prices to consumer.
2. Higher prices to consumers mean fewer customers.
3. Fewer customers mean lower sales.
4. Lower sales requires lower payroll (lay-offs) or go bust.
5. Lay-offs mean less buying power.
6. Less buying power means less commerce to local businesses.

Answer
Dr. Hoot's plan was to fix all prices, wages, and profits in the community.
1. Roll back eggs to old price.
2. Cut production costs by reducing wages.
3. Ration all commodities (goods).
4. Government (Officer Rooster) grows in size.

Results
The emergence of a black market that encourages ordinary citizens to break the law. When citizens continually break the law, the result is anarchy.

1. **Thinking back to your reading and the definition of socialism, how does Officer Rooster symbolize the socialistic system of economics?**

2. **Discuss the chain reaction that occurs when Dr. Hoot puts his first plan of manipulating the law of supply and demand in to action.**

3. **What are the two foundational reasons why socialism can never work?**

What is Economics?
Reading

It is a mistake to think that economics deals only with the making, spending, saving, and investing of money or with the creation, development, and management of wealth. Economics, per se, covers a much larger territory. Economics studies the choices human beings make with regard to scarce resources. As we know, scarcity is an unavoidable feature of human existence. Since human wants and desires are always greater than available resources, we can never have everything we want. Therefore, human beings have to rank their alternatives and make choices among the available options. The human actions that are the subject of economics are conscious human choices with regard to individual goals.

Economic decisions often have nothing to do with money. Imagine a very busy person faced with many demands on his time. Suppose further that this person is given the opportunity to do several new things that he regards as more important than some of his other tasks. Since this person can only do so much in the time available to him, he begins to rank his options. He then uses his scarce time to pursue those goals that he has ranked highest. In this example, the person is engaged in a typically economic activity. Because of scarcity (in this case, scarcity of time), he has been forced to make conscious choices.

Sometimes choices between competing alternatives involve a trade-off between time and money. Suppose I want to buy tickets to an important baseball game that fifty thousand people want to attend. I have two choices: I can either spend hours in a long line waiting to buy the tickets myself for $15 each; or I could pay someone else to stand in line for me, in which case the tickets would cost $25 each. If I value my time more than the extra $10, I will select option two. If I value the $10 more than the time required to wait in line, I'll choose the first option.

The attainment of any scarce resource involves some cost. But it is a mistake to think of cost exclusively in terms of money. The cost of obtaining some scarce resource might include physical pain or a sacrifice of time and effort that might have brought me other goods. There is an important sense in which the cost I incur to obtain any scarce resource will include everything else that my money, time, and effort might have secured had I chosen a different alternative.

It is clear then that the two main ingredients in any economic study are scarcity and choice. The conscious pursuit of goals often leads humans to exchange things they desire less (such as time or money or some possession) for things they want more.

Microeconomics and Macroeconomics

Microeconomics is the branch of economics that focuses on smaller, individual units of economic activity. It studies the economic choices of single persons, households, and businesses. As one economist explains, "Microeconomics consists of looking at the economy through a microscope, as it were, to see how the millions of cells in the body economic—the individuals or households as consumers, and the individuals or firms as producers—play their part in the working of the whole organism."[1]

Macroeconomics looks at the larger picture. Instead of studying the economic activity of individual persons, families, and businesses, it examines the combined result or combination of the particular economic choices. Macroeconomics studies a nation's economy as a whole. In macroeconomics, the choices of individual persons and the activities of particular businesses are lumped together.

While economists are often interested in understanding the actions of groups such as unions, societies, organizations, and nations, the actions of these groups are explained best by concentrating on the actions of the individual human beings that make up the groups. The basic unit of economic analysis is the individual human being and the choices he or she makes.

Economics as a Way of Thinking

Some economists have pointed out the value of viewing economics not so much as a set of doctrines or conclusions, but as a distinctive way of thinking. The principles that underlie the economic way of thinking are not difficult to grasp; they are often matters of common sense. But anyone who is unaware of these principles will have difficulty understanding why some things are true in economics.

The Importance of Incentives

The economic way of thinking begins by recognizing the importance of incentives. The greater the benefits people expect to receive from an alternative, the more people are likely to choose that option. The greater the costs expected from an alternative, the fewer people are likely to select it.

If we understand what makes human beings tick, we can make general predictions as to how individuals or groups of individuals will respond to changes in their economic situation—in particular, how they will respond to new incentives. If a society establishes programs that provide unemployed people with cash and non-cash benefits that approximate or even exceed what they would earn working (after taxes), one can safely predict that many of these people will choose to remain unemployed. If a welfare program is set up in such a way that it provides incentives for unmarried women who become pregnant to remain unmarried, we should not be surprised when the rate of illegitimate births begins to increase. In economics, you get what you pay for. If you give people incentives to do A rather than B, the number of people who choose A—all other things being equal—will increase.

Everything Has a Price

Because human beings live in a world marked by scarcity, nothing is free. Every economic good has a price in the sense that before anyone can obtain it, something else must be sacrificed. It is impossible to get A (some economic good) without giving up B (some other economic good). The economic principle in view here is often expressed in such folk sayings as, "You can't have your cake and eat it too" and "There is no such thing as a free lunch." The unavoidable fact of scarcity forces us to make choices in which we sacrifice some things in order to obtain others.

Scarcity, Choice, and Personal Value

In a world of scarcity, choice and sacrifice are unavoidable. People's economic behavior is simply a reflection of their need to make choices and the relative value they place upon their options. In cases where it is impossible for someone to have both A and B, the choice that a person makes will reflect the relative value he places upon A and B. People's actions, then, are a reflection of their value scales. Their choices are made in order to help them secure alternatives that accord more closely with their values.

The value that different people place upon different economic goods varies from person to person. People's value scales are personal and different. It would be highly unusual to ever find two people who ranked every economic good in precisely the same way.

Economic Uncertainty

We seldom know enough about individual persons, even people especially close to us, to predict with total certainty what choices they will make among various economic goods. We may know that a particular friend ranks tickets to Chicago Cubs baseball games very high in his personal scale of values. But we may not know how smitten he has become with the young lady he met yesterday and how suddenly the prospect of a picnic at the beach with her has become more important than watching the Cubs play the Cardinals. Human value scales are more than intensely personal; they are always changing. Because people's economic choices reflect their ever-changing value scales, predictions about human economic choices will always be characterized by uncertainty.

The Importance of Long-Range Consequences

Economic theories are testable in terms of their success in predicting and explaining what takes place in the real world. One way of assessing any economic proposal is to ask what its long-range consequences will be. It is a mistake to notice only the short-term or immediate consequences of economic activity. Any proposal or policy can affect the way people view a situation and thus can alter their incentives in ways that change their choices. Such a change in incentives often produces other effects that become noticeable only in the long run.

Many economic policies have been enacted because in the short-term they appeared to produce desired consequences in the long run. This has often been true of policies designed to help the less fortunate. But measures that appeared beneficial when viewed in the short-term often look quite different after a few years. One reason this happens is because the policies produce incentives that lead people to modify their behavior in ways that turn the short-run success into a long-term disaster. Many recent proposals made in the name of Christian compassion or "Christian economics" are bad economics in the sense that they are counterproductive. A number of important studies document the claim that antipoverty programs in the United States have actually increased poverty.[2] According to economist James Gwartney:

> Seeking to promote the welfare of the poor, the disadvantaged, the unemployed, and the misfortunate, well-meaning citizens (including a good many evangelical Christians) have inadvertently supported forms of economic organization that have promoted the precise outcomes they sought to alleviate. For too long, socially concerned Christians have measured policies by the intentions of their advocates, rather than the predictable effectiveness of the programs. Put simply, in our haste to do something constructive, we have not thought very seriously about the impact, particularly in the long-run...on the well-being of the intended beneficiaries.[3]

Gwartney's quote is only one statement of many in which economists allege that America's welfare programs of the recent past contradict several basic principles of the economic way of thinking.

Many programs to help the poor are like heroin addiction. The unfortunate person who begins to experiment with the drug feels immediate satisfaction. A want he may not have known before is satisfied in ways he may not have thought possible. But while the newly-found want fosters the need for continuing satisfaction, the drug begins to take control. Soon the person cannot function without the drug; he has become an addict. In a similar way, various programs to help the poor may seem to provide some immediate relief. But as soon as people see what the new rules are, they change their behavior to reflect the new incentives or disincentives. When the unfortunate long-term effects of the policy finally become recognizable, it is often too late. Too many people are hooked. Any threat to the policies is viewed with the same dread the addict has when his supply of heroin is threatened. The possibility that a decrease in tax transfers might give people new incentives to become more self-reliant is often drowned in a sea of rhetoric about compassion.

Minimum wage legislation is another example of economic thinking in conflict with the economic way of thinking. Minimum wage laws are justified as action that will help low-skilled workers earn more money. However, such laws only force employers to lay more unskilled workers off. The law that was supposed to help unskilled workers earn more money has the long-range effect of making many unemployed.

Sound economic thinking, then, looks beyond the present and calculates the long-range consequences of recommended policies. The long-term harm generated by unsound economic policies will far exceed the limited, short-run benefits that may be received by some special interest group.

Conclusion

Sound economics will always accord with the guideposts of the economic way of thinking. When Christians begin to tout specific economic views or policies, they should be careful to examine them in the light of these principles.[4]

Endnotes

[1] A.P. Lerner, "Microeconomy Theory," *Perspectives in Economics*, ed. A.A. Brown, E. Neuberger, and M. Palmatier (New York: McGraw-Hill, 1968), 29.

[2] See James Gwartney and Thomas S. McCaleb, "Have Antipoverty Programs Increased Poverty?," *Cato Journal*, 4 (1985), 1–16.

[3] James Gwartney, "Social Progess, the Tax-Transfer Society and the Limits of Public Policy," unpublished paper (Department of Economics, Florida State University), 3.

[4] Excerpted from Ronald H. Nash, *Poverty and Wealth: Why Socialism Doesn't Work* (Westchester, IL: Crossway Books, 1986), 13–21. Used by permission.

What is Economics?
Reading Discussion Questions

1. What do most people think economics deals with? Why are they incorrect?

2. What two main elements are foundational to economics?

3. Define the following terms: microeconomics and macroeconomics.

4. Which of these two branches of economics is the best method for economic analysis? Why?

5. What do you have to know about economics in order to truly understand it?

6. What is an incentive? Do incentives work?

7. Since resources of all types are scarce (or limited), what does this mean for us practically?

8. Why is it difficult to predict with certainty the economic choices people will make?

9. What is the most reliable way of evaluating the merit of an economic policy?

10. Can economic incentives be misguided and hurt the people they are supposed to help? Why or why not?

Inside Cackle Corner
Video Discussion Questions

1. What enabled Mr. Redcomb to sell Mrs. Consumer a better product than Pop Webfoot could, but at the same price?

2. What did Pop Webfoot decide to spend his money on in order to make a better toaster?

3. "You've got to spend _____ to make _____, Boss."

4. How did Pop Webfoot raise capital?

5. Reflection Question: How does a business owner's ability to function independently benefit consumers?

What's Your Motivation?
Exercise

The purpose of this exercise is to put the power of incentive and competition into action. Your teacher will explain the details.

1. **During which stage did you try harder? Why?**

2. **How does this same principle of incentive play out in the area of economics?**

LIGHTBEARERS

Unit Ten

A Summit Ministries Curriculum

DAY	UNIT 10: syllabus & outline	SW	✓
1	Read *A World of Ideas* Reading..	239	
2	Read *A World of Ideas* Reading..	DITTO	
3	Review *A World of Ideas* Reading Discussion Questions.......................................	249	
4	Review *A World of Ideas* Reading Discussion Questions.......................................	DITTO	
	Assign **History Paragraph** [Rough Draft Due on Day 8]....................................	250	
5	Watch **"Biblical Christian Worldview: History"** Video....................................	251	
	Complete **Your Most Historical Moment** Exercise..	252	
6	Assign **Historical Figure** [Assignment Due on Day 11 or 12]........................	253	
	Watch **Who is This Jesus: Is He Risen?** Video Outline.................................	254	
7	Review **Who is This Jesus: Is He Risen?** Video Discussion Questions............	259	
8	Turn in **History Paragraph** [Assignment Due on Day 13].............................	---	
	Assign **Purpose and Plan** Exercise..	260	
9	Read *How to Be Your Own Selfish Pig* Reading (Ch. 7)...................................	---	
10	Review *How to Be Your Own Selfish Pig* Reading Discussion Questions (Ch. 7).......	261	
11	Turn in & Share **Historical Figure** Presentation Assignment...........................	---	
12	Turn in & Share **Historical Figure** Presentation Assignment...........................	---	
13	Turn in **History Paragraph** Assignment..	---	
	Prepare **Unit 10** Test..	---	
14	Take **Unit 10** Test...	---	
15			

A World of Ideas:
What is the Meaning of History?

Objects on this page are no smaller than they appear.

If you can read this, you are too close to your workbook.

KEYS TO UNDERSTANDING

Key Question: What is the meaning of history?

Key Ideas: God is sovereign over history. History has a purpose.

Key Terms: history, linear view of history, internal evidence, circular reasoning, external evidence, archaeology, historical resurrection

Key Verse: 1 Corinthians 15:14–15

"And if Christ has not been raised, our preaching is useless and so is your faith. More than that, we are then found to be false witnesses about God, for we have testified about God that he raised Christ from the dead. But he did not raise him if in fact the dead are not raised" (1 Corinthians 15:14–15, NIV).

Don't Know Much about History

The heading above is actually a line from a song popular in the 1960s, but it could also be the theme song for many students today. The reason **history** seems uninteresting to a lot of students is that the focus is usually on names, places, and dates. But these are only the dry bones of history. The real lifeblood of history is *ideas*. As we've said throughout this text, ideas rule the world.

Once you grasp the main ideas that have shaped the past, history becomes relevant to life today. Why? Because the big questions that people have about life don't change over time. The details change (who did what), the technology becomes more sophisticated (from gramophones to records to cassettes to CDs to MP3s, etc.), but the basic ideas remain the same.

For example, the idea of personal freedom—to live as you choose without interference—is one that has been expressed throughout the ages. This is the dominant idea that spurred the gladiator Spartacus in 71 BC to lead his fellow slaves in a series of battles against Rome. During the period of 1000 to 1200 AD, Christians from England and Western Europe marched into the Middle East to free fellow Christians who were languishing under Islamic domination. This series of battles, known as the Crusades, were an attempt to win back the territory that Muslim invaders had taken by force years earlier.[1]

Around 1300 AD, a peasant named William Wallace led an army of Scotsmen against King Edward of Britain in order to secure Scottish independence. As interpreted by the film *Braveheart,* Wallace's last word as he was being tortured to death for treason was the cry of "Freedom!"[2]

It was a desire for freedom that also led the Pilgrims to leave England and sail to the dangerous shores of America in 1620. This same spirit of freedom gave the founding fathers of the U.S. courage and determination to pen the *Declaration of Independence*, declaring freedom from English religious and political domination.

Freedom was on the minds of a group of slaves onboard the schooner *Amistad,* when, in 1839 at the height of the cross-Atlantic slave trade, they overpowered the captain and crew and sailed to the United States. During a trial to determine their fate, former U.S. president John Quincy Adams argued on their behalf. The resulting verdict declared them to be free men.[3]

All of these events from the past paint a picture of our common humanity—our desire to be free. We can learn important lessons from these past events. The Apostle Paul even writes that the events of the Old Testament "happened to them as examples, and they were written as a warning to us..." (1 Corinthians 10:11, HCSB). In fact, the Bible gives more space to historical events than it does to theological ideas. This means that we can learn valuable lessons from the experiences of those who lived before us, not only from the historical sections of the Bible, but also from other books about history.

History: The study of the past.

But more than learning isolated lessons from the past, a Christian worldview gives us the proper context for understanding the over-arching story of history. The Bible points to a definite progression of events. Its storyline begins "in the beginning," flows through time, and peaks at the resurrection of Jesus. Even our calendars show the importance of Christ—changing from BC (Before Christ) to AD (Anno Domini, meaning "In the year of our Lord"). The Bible also points to a future time when God will complete this earthly story and bring to account the lives and actions of all humans. At that time there will be a new heaven and a new earth, and mankind will enjoy harmony and peace.

One other point needs to be clarified. Just because history is last in our line-up doesn't mean it is less important than any of the other categories. Christians believe the basis for our entire worldview appeared in human history about two thousand years ago in the person of Jesus Christ. While "Christ died for our sins" is solid Christian theology, "Christ died" is history.

Think about it: "Christ died" is a statement concerning an event in history. The entire Christian worldview stands or falls on an understanding of this major episode from the past—specifically the life, death, and resurrection of Jesus Christ. If this historical event is false, then there is no Christianity. That's why it's so important to add the area of history to our total picture of the world. The study of history is not optional for the Christian—it is primary. Hopefully this chapter will help motivate you to dive into the ideas related to past events and discern their meaning for today.

> **The study of history is not optional for the Christian—it is primary.**

When you study history, you are looking at what happened to the people who lived before you. It is also the study of how the ideas people believed in the past affected their lives, so it gives you insights into how you should live your life.

Ideas have consequences. Remember this phrase? Reading about history is a great way to find out which ideas are successful and which ones don't work in real life. As you learn from the experience of others, you can avoid their mistakes and pattern your life on their successes.

Our discussion of history in this chapter will focus on what most Christians consider to be the main event in history: the resurrection of Jesus. This brings up several key questions that relate to a biblical worldview, like *What are the different views of history? Is the Bible, especially the four gospels, historically accurate? Was Jesus a real historical person? Did He rise from the dead?*

Think about it. These are important questions that need to be answered. You are basing your entire life—your whole future, even eternity—on what some book says about God and Jesus. In fact, your entire worldview, including all of the big questions covered in this text, depends on the ideas that come from the Bible. You had better be sure it is a reliable source.

In a moment we will focus on three vital things to determine when judging the historical trustworthiness of the Bible. But first, we need to briefly discuss the biblical view of history.

Christian History

Some worldviews, like Hinduism, see history as going in a circle. This means that events are repeated over and over again without ever reaching a final goal or end. In contrast to this view, the Christian understands that God is sovereign over the events of history and that history is progressing in a straight line toward a specific end or goal. This is called a **linear view of history**. Naturalists also have a linear view of history, however, for the atheist, history has no purpose.

In contrast, the Bible tells a cosmic story by starting at the beginning of the *creation* of the universe and life on this planet. The story then explains what went wrong with God's creation (the *fall* of Adam and Eve) and continues by outlining God's plan to bring people back into a relationship with Himself (*redemption*). It even includes how events will turn out in the future *consummation* of history. These are the main elements of the storyline: Creation, Fall, Redemption, and Consummation.

> **Linear View of History:** History is progressing in a straight line toward a specific end or goal.

Let's look at each major element of the story in a little more detail.

CREATION

The story begins with God creating all things (Genesis 1:1). As the pinnacle of His creation, God made man and woman (Genesis 1:26–27) and gave them authority over the world (Genesis 1:28; Psalm 115:16). At the same time, God set boundaries for the first human pair by prohibiting them from eating from one particular tree (Genesis 2:16–17).

FALL

Sometime after being created, Adam and Eve decided to turn from God's holy word and pursue their own path by eating from the tree of the knowledge of good and evil (Genesis 3:6). This not only brought a curse upon the earth (Genesis 3:17), but it also separated them from God (Genesis 3:8, 23). Another result was that all their descendents inherited this sinful nature (Genesis 6:5; Romans 3:23).

REDEMPTION

In spite of man's sin, God promised that mankind would ultimately triumph over sin (Genesis 3:15). God's plan included His promise to Abraham that all nations would be blessed through him and his descendants (Genesis 12:3). And finally, God promised a Messiah to bear the sins of His people (Isaiah 53:4–6).

At just the right time, God sent His son Jesus to redeem our sins (Romans 5:6; Galatians 4:4–7; Ephesians 1:9–10). Jesus' death on the cross not only released us from God's wrath to come (1 Thessalonians 1:9–10), but it also redeems us from bondage to sin even now (Romans 6:6, 17–18; Titus 2:11–14). It was Jesus' resurrection that proclaimed Him a victorious Savior (Romans 1:4). Through His death, which ratified the new covenant (Luke 22:20; Jeremiah 31:31), Jesus brought together Jews and Gentiles, creating a new unified entity: the Church (Galatians 3:28; Ephesians 2:11–18; Romans 15:7–13).

By the careful study of God's Word and the work of the Holy Spirit inside us, we continually strive to become more like Jesus in character and actions (Romans 8:29). In a sense, God is progressively restoring us to who He originally created us to be and do. God has also given us the privilege and responsibility of telling others about this amazing gift of redemption (Matthew 28:19–20).

CONSUMMATION

At an appointed time in the future (Acts 17:31), God will bring all humanity before Jesus either for reward, given to those who have believed, or punishment, given to those who have not believed (John 5:22, Romans 2:6–7). Those who have received Jesus Christ (John 3:16, John 5:24) will be set apart for eternal life, while everyone who has not received Jesus will be set aside for eternal destruction (John 3:36; Revelation 11:18). Full redemption takes place with the resurrection of our bodies (Philippians 3:20–21; Romans 8:22–23) and the renewal of the heavens and earth (Romans 8:21; Revelation 21:1–7), at which time there will be no more curse (Revelation 22:3).

The Historical Reliability of the Gospels

Those who are skeptical of the Bible often say that the Bible cannot be historically true. For example, the Bible mentions people, places, or events that are not recorded in other historical sources. Therefore, according to skeptics, these people or places must be made up. If this is true, then this would be evidence that the Bible is not from God.

Since a discussion of the historical accuracy of the entire Bible would take more time than we have here, let's limit our discussion to the New Testament books known as the Gospels (Matthew, Mark, Luke, and John) and what they say about Jesus. The following are four lines of evidence supporting the conclusion that the New Testament Gospels are historically true. The first three relate to factors inside the New Testament itself and are referred to as **internal evidence.**

Internal Evidence: Lines of evidence from the Scriptures that support the claims of the Bible.

Evidence #1: The Authors Were Interested in History

The first thing we need to notice is that the New Testament authors were interested in preserving history. They knew the difference between real history and fictional myths (1 Timothy 4:7; 2 Timothy 4:4; Titus 1:13–14). They also knew the value of eyewitness testimony. This can be seen in the fact that the apostles were required to be men who had actually seen Jesus (Acts 1:21–22; Hebrews 2:3). It can also be seen in the following words of Luke, Peter, and John:

> Many have undertaken to draw up an account of the things that have been fulfilled among us, just as they were handed down to us by those who from the first were eyewitnesses and servants of the word. Therefore, since I myself have carefully investigated everything from the beginning, it seemed good also to me to write an orderly account for you, most excellent Theophilus, so that you may know the certainty of the things you have been taught (Luke 1:1–4, NIV).

> We did not follow cleverly invented stories when we told you about the power and coming of our Lord Jesus Christ, but we were eyewitnesses of his majesty (2 Peter 1:16, NIV).

> The man who saw it has given testimony, and his testimony is true. He knows that he tells the truth, and he testifies so that you also may believe (John 19:35, NIV; see also 20:30–31; 21:24).

> That which was from the beginning, which we have heard, which we have seen with our eyes, which we have looked at and our hands have touched—this we proclaim concerning the Word of life. The life appeared; we have seen it and testify to it, and we proclaim to you the eternal life, which was with the Father and has appeared to us. We proclaim to you what we have seen and heard, so that you also may have fellowship with us. And our fellowship is with the Father and with his Son, Jesus Christ (1 John 1:1–3, NIV).

Not only did the early Christians value eyewitness testimony, but they also made some of their arguments by appealing to the eyewitness knowledge of unbelievers. Biblical scholar F.F. Bruce put it this way:

> [O]ne of the strong points in the original apostolic preaching is the confident appeal to the knowledge of the hearers; they not only said, "We are witnesses of these things," but also, "As you yourselves also know" (Acts 2:22). Had there been any tendency to depart from the facts in any material respect, the possible presence of hostile witnesses in the audience would have served as a further corrective.[4]

> For what I received I passed on to you as of first importance: that Christ died for our sins according to the Scriptures, that he was buried, that he was raised on the third day according to the Scriptures, and that he appeared to Peter, and then to the Twelve. After that, he appeared to more than five hundred of the brothers at the same time, most of whom are still living, though some have fallen asleep. Then he appeared to James, then to all the apostles, and last of all he appeared to me also, as to one abnormally born (1 Corinthians 15:3–8, NIV).

Evidence #2: The Authors Were Accustomed to Remembering Details

The second reason we can trust the Gospels is that they were written by men with a good memory for details. This is important to consider because some people claim that since the early Christians did not write anything down while Jesus was alive, their memories could be muddled or they could have just made stuff up. But, there are several problems with this objection.

First, the early Christians lived in a culture in which people had highly developed memories. Unlike our modern world, where we depend on being able to look things up, in the ancient world people tended to listen carefully to what they heard and work hard to remember details and stories told to them.

Second, most of Jesus' sayings are in a poetic form. Some were in brief statements like in the Sermon on the Mount (Matthew 5–7). At other times, Jesus taught in short stories, like the parable of the Good Samaritan. This style of teaching was intended to stick in the minds of those who heard it.

Third, in biblical times Jewish rabbis who were seen as especially wise had students who followed them around devotedly, living with them and learning everything the rabbis had to teach. Each rabbi expected his students to memorize and live by the key principles he taught from the Torah, or Jewish law (the Old Testament books we have today). This system of teaching went far beyond the classroom kind of learning we are accustomed to today and required extreme mental focus, logic, and memorization skills. We also know from certain ancient sources that these students sometimes did take notes. Some even developed a form of shorthand. So the claim that Jesus' disciples never wrote anything down while He was living cannot be proven.

Regardless of the probability that some things were written down at or near the time that Jesus spoke them, Christians also believe in the divine inspiration of the Bible. This means that since God never forgets what happens in history, He could help the writers of Scripture to accurately describe what happened, even if they were not there.

EVIDENCE #3: THE GOSPELS WERE WRITTEN WITHIN A GENERATION OF THE EVENTS

A third reason for trusting the Gospels is based on when they were written. Many critics of the Bible claim that the four Gospels were written late in the first century (or early in the second century). This would mean there was a lot of time for myths to develop around the stories of Jesus or for details to be forgotten, which would disqualify the Gospels as reliable historical accounts.

However, this kind of argument is usually based on a logical fallacy. Their thinking goes like this:

1. Miracles do not happen (a naturalistic worldview assumption)
2. The Gospels record Jesus prophesying about the fall of Jerusalem (which occurred in 70 AD, several generations after Jesus' death).
3. Therefore, since knowing the future ahead of time would be a miracle (and miracles do not happen, according to the starting assumption), the Gospels must have been written after 70 AD.

Do you see the problem with this line of thinking? It is called circular reasoning. **Circular reasoning** is a fallacy (or mistake in thinking) that occurs when someone tries to prove a point by restating it. In other words, you end with the same idea you began with. But this does not logically prove anything.

To understand why this is not logical, think about the following exchange:

Andy: "Jerry always tells the truth."
Betty: "How do you know that?"
Andy: "Because he told me that he always tells the truth."
Betty: "How do you know that he wasn't lying?"
Andy: "Well, because he *always* tells the truth."

In this example, Andy assumed that Jerry always told the truth, but also used that assumption as the proof of why it was true. In other words, like a dog chasing his own tail, Andy ended up in the same place he started.

This kind of circular approach takes place when critics of the New Testament begin by assuming that miracles cannot happen. They then use that assumption to conclude that a miracle they read in the Bible must not have actually happened but was simply a later addition to the text. Therefore, they say that we cannot trust the accuracy of the New Testament because it was written so long after the actual events. But, as we have just seen, this is a faulty way of thinking and not a good way to date when the Gospels were written.

Circular Reasoning: A fallacy that occurs when someone tries to prove a point by restating it.

A better approach for dating the Gospels can be presented this way:

- Both the Gospel of Luke and the book of Acts were written by Luke, a contemporary of Paul and the other apostles, and are clearly intended to be chronological volumes.
- The book of Acts focuses primarily on the ministries of the apostles Peter and Paul.
- In many places in the book of Acts, Peter and Paul discuss the persecution and death of Christians, especially Christian leaders. (For example, a description of the death of Jesus is in Acts 2:22–24, the death of Stephen is in Acts 7:54–8:1, and descriptions of plots against Paul are found in Acts 9:23–24 and 23:12–14.)
- However, the book of Acts ends while Paul is still in Rome, and never mentions Paul's death, which probably took place about 64 AD (and given Luke's attention to the persecution and deaths of other important church leaders, Paul's death would surely have been mentioned).
- Therefore, Acts must have been written before 64 AD.

These observations make a powerful case that the book of Acts was written before Paul's death in 64 AD. Now, considering that Acts is the second volume (compare Luke 1:1–4 with Acts 1:1–3), with the Gospel of Luke being the first volume, then the Gospel of Luke was written before Acts (therefore definitely before 64 AD). In addition, since Luke says that he consulted other accounts of Jesus' life (Luke 1:1–4), it is possible that Luke made use of Mark's gospel (a likely possibility, according to most scholars). And if so, then we can date Mark even earlier than Acts and Luke.

> Many have undertaken to draw up an account of the things that have been fulfilled among us, just as they were handed down to us by those who from the first were eyewitnesses and servants of the word. Therefore, since I myself have carefully investigated everything from the beginning, it seemed good also to me to write an orderly account for you, most excellent Theophilus, so that you may know the certainty of the things you have been taught (Luke 1:1–4, NIV).

> In my former book, Theophilus, I wrote about all that Jesus began to do and to teach until the day he was taken up to heaven, after giving instructions through the Holy Spirit to the apostles he had chosen. After his suffering, he showed himself to these men and gave many convincing proofs that he was alive. He appeared to them over a period of forty days and spoke about the kingdom of God (Acts 1:1–3, NIV).

How early does this take us? Well, that is difficult to say precisely. Maybe we should just stick with the fact that these books seem to have been written in the early 60s AD, and certainly prior to the death of Paul in 64 AD.

There are several other evidences supporting a pre-70 AD date for the gospels, though one is most significant: the fall of Jerusalem. Though Jerusalem was the most important city for Jews, and though its destruction in 70 AD was major news for Jews and Gentiles throughout the Mediterranean, the Gospel authors *never mention* it (nor do any other books in the New Testament). In comparison, you would have a difficult time retelling the history of the United States now without mentioning the September 11, 2001, terrorist attacks.

This seems strange, for Jesus prophesied that the temple would be destroyed (Matthew 24:1–2). Therefore, it would have added to the strength of their argument to have noted, either in the epistles or the gospels, something like, "Yes, Jesus is who He said He was. We know this because His prophecies were true. For example, He told us that the temple would be destroyed, and it was." However, the New Testament authors never mention the fall of Jerusalem or the destruction of the temple as a past event.

What can we conclude from all of this? In contrast to what the critics say, there is good historical evidence in the gospels themselves that they were written before 64 AD. This puts their writing within 30 years of the actual events, well within the lifespan of eyewitnesses, who could have corrected any exaggerations or mistakes. This lends more credibility that the gospels provide us with a reliable story of the events and sayings of Jesus.

Evidence from Archaeology

Following internal evidence, the second main area of our study of the historical reliability of the gospels will be evidence from outside the Bible, called **external evidence.** One of the most reliable sources of external evidence is archaeology. **Archaeology** has to do with the physical evidences of past societies recovered through excavation (for example, pottery, tools, inscriptions, etc.). Although it would take too long to survey all the archaeological discoveries that have been made in relation to the New Testament, here we will mention two examples.

Peter's house, mentioned in Mark 1:29 and Luke 7:44, has been discovered by archaeologists excavating a dig in ancient Capernaum:

> Considerable material has been brought to light at Capernaum, some of which bears on the location of Peter's house and his association with the mission among his fellow Jews. The house was built about the first century B.C. It became a center of religious activity, a house-church or meeting house, already in the second half of the first century A.D. *Minim* (as the Jewish Christians were later called) were numerous and lived continuously in Capernaum and kept alive this tradition; their graffiti on the plastered wall of the place of worship testify to their faith in Jesus, the Christ, the Lord, the Most High and Good, and to their veneration for Peter, the local saint.[5]

External Evidence: Evidence outside of the Bible that confirms the historical reliability of the Scriptures.

Also, in each of the Gospels we read about Pontius Pilate, the governor of Judea at the time of Jesus' death and resurrection (Matthew 27:2, 11–26; Mark 15:1–15; Luke 3:1; 23:1–25; John 18:28–19:16). For many years there was no external confirmation that Pilate was governor during the first century. However, in 1961 physical evidence was uncovered about Pilate's rule. Paul L. Maier describes the discovery:

> During the smoldering summer of 1961, some Italian archaeologists were excavating an ancient theater at Caesarea, the Mediterranean port that served as the Roman capital of Palestine, when they unearthed a two-by-three foot stone that bore some kind of inscription. Antonio Frova, who was in charge of the dig, cleaned out the lettering with a brush, and suddenly his eyes widened in disbelief while his face was cut by a vast grin. The left third of the inscription had been chipped away, but Frova reconstructed it in short order…"Pontius Pilate, Prefect of Judea, has presented the Tiberieum to the Caesareans."[6]

So whether you look at the evidence found within the gospels themselves or look outside the New Testament to the archeological record, there is abundant confirmation that the events that are recorded in the Bible are true to history. This, in turn, provides a foundation for accepting what is written about the central event in the story: the resurrection of Jesus.

Archaeology: The search for physical evidence of past societies and historical events.

The Resurrection of Jesus

Christian theologians agree that Christianity stands or falls on one thing—the resurrection of Jesus. The resurrection is a major issue for Christians, so major in fact that it sets Christianity apart from every other religion. Every other "good teacher" in history that critics compare Jesus to has left a body in his tomb. Jesus is special because His tomb is empty, proving that He is who He said He is.

Because of the centrality of Christ's resurrection, opponents of Christianity have tried to deny that Jesus actually rose from the dead. Walk onto most university campuses in the West today, and you will hear professors of religion say something like this: "Jesus was a great moral teacher, but he was not God. Jesus did not come back from the dead; it was just his teachings about loving others that 'came alive' in the hearts of his followers."

Unit Ten

How would you respond to comments like these? While some people deny that Jesus was resurrected, the evidence supporting this amazing event is very convincing. Here are a few of the historical events surrounding the resurrection of Jesus.

- Jesus' death was predicted (Matthew 12:40; Mark 8:31; John 2:19–21; 10:10–11; see also Psalm 22:16; Isaiah 53:5–10; Zechariah 12:10).
- He hung on the cross throughout the day (Mark 15:25, 33; the third hour = 9am, the sixth hour = noon, and the ninth hour = 3pm). Before that, He had been kept awake all night, beaten, and whipped (Mark 14:65; 15:15). When the Roman soldier pierced His side with a spear, blood and water flowed out (John 19:34), proving medically that Jesus had been dead for some time (John 19:30; Luke 23:46–49). Therefore, Jesus physically died upon the cross (Mark 15:37, 44–45).
- His body was sealed in a tomb (Matthew 27:57–61; Mark 15:42–47; Luke 23:50–56; John 19:38–42).
- His disciples were despairing and fearful because of the death of their leader (John 20:19).
- Over 36 hours later, when the tomb was visited, Jesus' body was no longer there (Matthew 28:1–8; Mark 16:1–8; Luke 24:1–10; John 20:1–8).
- The disciples and many other followers met with the resurrected Jesus. They saw Him, talked with Him, ate with Him, and even touched Him (John 20:16–18; Luke 24:13–49; Acts 1:3–4).
- The attitude of the disciples was transformed from cowardice and despair to great hope and boldness (Acts 2:42–47).

Even with all this eyewitness evidence, some people still insist that the resurrection could not have happened. They say that other explanations are more reasonable. Let's consider several of these arguments to see if they stand up to reason and the historical record.

Some claim that Jesus never really died, but that He passed out on the cross and was resuscitated in the tomb. This theory is unconvincing. First, the Roman governor, Pilate, made sure that Jesus was dead (Mark 15:42–45). Second, if Jesus did not really die on the cross, why would the disciples think that a battered, bruised, scabbed, dirty Jesus was the resurrected Lord of the universe? Rather than looking as though He has conquered death, He would have looked half-dead.

Another claim some critics have made is that the early Christians all went to the wrong tomb, that they simply forgot where it was. But this makes no sense. First, Joseph of Arimathea was a wealthy man, so his tomb would have been well marked. Second, the disciples initially spoke about the resurrection in Jerusalem, where people could easily disprove the resurrection by producing the body of Jesus. Those who opposed the disciples either could have produced the body of Jesus or could have argued that the disciples needed to show the empty tomb. But this did not happen.

Related to this was an early "conspiracy theory" promoted by the religious leaders—that the disciples stole the body (Matthew 28:11–15). However, history records that all of the disciples (except for the Apostle John, who died of old age in exile) died martyrs' deaths because they believed in a risen Christ. What is the probability that every one of the disciples would die for such a lie?

Even more importantly, though, this conspiracy idea assumes that the tomb was indeed empty. Why would Jesus' opponents have needed to "explain away" the disappearance unless Jesus' body was in fact gone? So both Jesus' friends and enemies agreed that the tomb was empty. This leaves the question *What happened to the body of Jesus?*

While the women were on their way, some of the guards went into the city and reported to the chief priests everything that had happened. When the chief priests had met with the elders and devised a plan, they gave the soldiers a large sum of money, telling them, "You are to say, 'His disciples came during the night and stole him away while we were asleep.' If this report gets to the governor, we will satisfy him and keep you out of trouble." So the soldiers took the money and did as they were instructed. And this story has been widely circulated among the Jews to this very day (Matthew 28:11–15, NIV).

The only reasonable explanation for the empty tomb is exactly what the disciples proclaimed: that Jesus was raised from the dead! The resurrection was, and is, the central point of the gospel message. And moreover, these followers of Jesus were willing to die rather than deny the resurrection. If it had been a story they all cooked up, why would they be willing to die martyrs' deaths just to keep up a charade?

In addition, only a true resurrection of Jesus could explain the dramatic conversion of one of early Christianity's greatest threats: the Apostle Paul. You can read about Paul's conversion experience in his own words in Acts 21:39–22:21. Also, Jesus' own brother, James, had a radical change of heart after the resurrection. Here is someone who actually grew up with Jesus and at one point even questioned Jesus' ministry (Mark 3:21). Yet James eventually became a leader in the Jerusalem church and was willing to die for his belief that Jesus was the risen Son of God.

> **Historical Resurrection**: The belief that the resurrection of Jesus was an actual event that happened in history.

Because of the importance of Jesus' resurrection, we have labeled the Christian worldview of history as "historical resurrection." **Historical resurrection** means that the resurrection of Jesus was an actual event that happened in history and is the hinge upon which history swings.

History with a Purpose

Have you ever asked the question, "What is my purpose in life?" That question, when asked on a personal level, actually implies a more far-reaching question: *is there any purpose to life in general?* In other words, does God have a plan and purpose for history?

A Biblical Christian worldview informs us that God does in fact have a plan. This plan for humanity is played out through the events that have happened in the past, through what is taking place today, and even includes what will happen in the future. His wonderful plan also involves *you*!

This belief about God's actions in history has vast ramifications for mankind. If the Christian philosophy of history is correct, then not only is the overall story of mankind invested with meaning, but every moment that each person lives is charged with purpose.

Let's get a biblical perspective on that last question about purpose in life. To do that, we have to step back and get a "Big Picture" view of God's purpose for His creation. From that vantage point, we can focus on His purpose for your life.

The Big Picture

First, read Acts 17:26–28: "From one man He has made every nation of men to live all over the earth and has determined their appointed times and the boundaries of where they live, so that they might seek God, and perhaps they might reach out and find Him, though He is not far from each one of us. For in Him we live and move and exist..." (HCSB).

From the Christian perspective, history is a beautiful unfolding of God's ultimate plan for mankind. Does this mean, however, that only the future holds any value for the Christian? In other words, does the Christian worldview destroy the role of the *present* in history? The answer is a resounding no. In the Christian view, God is active throughout history, so this perspective creates more meaning for every moment of time.

History is the progression of time, and you are currently living it. God is active right now, and the verses from Acts quoted above apply to you and everyone around you. But more than that, God also has a specific plan created just for you and your life. As Paul told the Ephesians, "For we are God's workmanship, created in Christ Jesus to do good works, which God prepared in advance for us to do" (Ephesians 2:10, NIV).

Because of His purpose and plan, there is great meaning for every moment of your life. By understanding a biblical worldview, you will gain a better understanding of how you fit into God's plan.

Conclusion

Christianity and history have always been allies. The Bible is rooted in the story of God's involvement with mankind throughout history. Without the historical resurrection of Jesus Christ, there would be no Christian worldview (1 Corinthians 15:14–15). The history recounted by the Bible is accurate, and the events described in it actually occurred.

> And if Christ has not been raised, our preaching is useless and so is your faith. More than that, we are then found to be false witnesses about God, for we have testified about God that he raised Christ from the dead. But he did not raise him if in fact the dead are not raised (1 Corinthians 15:14–15, NIV).

The Bible (the written Word) and Jesus Christ (the living Word) are the two cornerstones of the Christian worldview. If the Bible is not history, or if Jesus Christ is not "God with us" (Matthew 1:23) and the Savior of mankind (2 Timothy 1:10), Christianity crumbles. True history begins and ends with Jesus Christ, the "Alpha and Omega" (Revelation 1:8; 22:13).

The Christian view of history is purposeful, primarily because God is the Lord of history. Our view of history is hopeful because God has promised good things and His promises never fail (Titus 1:2; Hebrews 6:18). Our hope is grounded not in myths or mere belief, but in the truth of the resurrection of Jesus Christ, our living hope (1 Peter 1:3).

Endnotes

[1] A recent look at the Crusades is in *Kingdom of Heaven* (2005, directed by Sir Ridley Scott). One film critic wrote, "The £75 million film, which stars Orlando Bloom, Jeremy Irons and Liam Neeson, is described by the makers as being 'historically accurate' and designed to be 'a fascinating history lesson.' Academics, however—including Professor Jonathan Riley-Smith, Britain's leading authority on the Crusades—attacked the plot of *Kingdom of Heaven*, describing it as 'rubbish', 'ridiculous', 'complete fiction' and 'dangerous to Arab relations'…[adding] that Sir Ridley's efforts were misguided and pandered to Islamic fundamentalism. 'It's Osama bin Laden's version of history. It will fuel the Islamic fundamentalists.'" (http://www.telegraph.co.uk/news/main.jhtml?xml=/news/2004/01/18/wcrus18.xml&sSheet=/news/2004/01/18/ixworld.html)

[2] *Braveheart*, which won five Academy Awards in 1995, including Best Picture and Best Director, was a pseudo-historical drama depicting the life of William Wallace. The film was produced and directed by Mel Gibson, who also played the leading role.

[3] The film version of this event, *Amistad* (1997, directed by Steven Spielberg), retells the true story of fifty-three Africans who mutinied on a slave ship in 1839 and ended up on the shores of America to stand trial. Evangelical abolitionists had a major role in helping the slaves win their freedom, yet in the film these Christians are depicted as hypocrites and even indifferent toward the lives of the Africans. Brian Godawa writes, "The historically dominant force of liberation [for slaves], the Quakers, are relegated to the role of kooky protesters in the background chanting irrelevant slogans and remaining blatantly unconnected to their modern world." But in spite of the revisionist history, "*Amistad* contains one of the most thorough descriptions of the gospel from Genesis to John that has ever been shown in a movie." (Brian Godawa, *Hollywood Worldviews*, Downers Grove, IL: InterVarsity Press, 2002, 133–134.)

[4] F.F. Bruce, *The New Testament Documents: Are They Reliable?* (Downers Grove, IL: InterVarsity Press, 1960), 46.

[5] Gaalyah Cornfeld and David Noel Freedman, *Archaeology and the Bible: Book by Book* (New York: Harper and Row, 1976), 280.

[6] Paul L. Maier, *In the Fullness of Time* (San Francisco, CA: Harper Collins, 1991), 145.

A World of Ideas
Reading Discussion Questions

1. What is history? What key question does history seek to answer? What are the key ideas of Christian history?

2. On what does the entire Christian worldview stand or fall?

3. What is the Christian view of history? How does this compare with the transcendentalist and naturalist views of history.

4. The Christian story of history can be summed up in four parts. What are they?

5. What is internal evidence? What are three internal reasons for trusting the accuracy of the New Testament?

6. What is circular reasoning and how do some Bible critics commit this fallacy?

7. What is archeology? What are two pieces of archaeological evidence that supports the New Testament?

8. What are three arguments against the resurrection? What are some problems with these positions?

9. How do the lives of Paul an James lend evidence to the accuracy of Christianity?

10. Reflection Question: Paul clearly emphasizes the importance of the resurrection to Christianity in 1 Corinthians 15:14–15. Based on the internal and external evidence you have studied in this chapter, do you believe Jesus was raised from the dead?

History Paragraph
Assignment

As you continue your study, write your own paragraph titled ***My Christian Worldview of History***. Below is the checklist for your paragraph. Write the draft of your History paragraph here and hand it in to your teacher to look over. You will be able to correct it, add to it, put it into your Lightbearers Journal, and memorize it.

- ☐ The paragraph includes the Christian definition of history.
- ☐ It lists and defines the sources of evidence for the reliability of the Bible.
- ☐ It includes a statement about the historical importance of the resurrection.
- ☐ It explains why the Christian view of history gives the deepest meaning to life.

History
Video Outline

I. **Biblical Christian History:** _____

    A. The Christian religion is firmly grounded in _____.

    B. The Christian view of history is linear—there is a past, a present, and a future. History is progressing toward a certain end and God is the Lord of history.

    C. The Historical Reliability of the Bible

        1. The New Testament was largely written by _____, or by individuals who knew the eyewitnesses.

        2. The discovery of the _____ confirmed the textual accuracy of the Old Testament. These scrolls revealed that even though the Bible had been copied and recopied for thousands of years, its integrity has been retained.

        3. Further, _____ has consistently supported the records of historical events and geographical locations noted throughout the Bible.

        4. While many of today's liberal scholars try to deny that Jesus ever existed, the non-biblical references to Him provide ample reason to reject their denials.

"The early non-Christian testimonies concerning Jesus, though scanty, are sufficient to prove that he was a historical figure who lived in Palestine in the early years of the first century, that he gathered a group of followers about himself, and that he was condemned to death under Pontius Pilate. Today no competent scholar denies the historicity of Jesus." — Bruce Metzger

Your Most Important Historical Moment
Exercise

This assignment will not be graded, so take your time and be completely honest with yourself as you complete the following exercise.

Obviously, the most important historical moment in your life is the moment you begin to follow Jesus Christ, the momentous day you make the choice to devote the rest of your life to being obedient to God. Using the Bible as your source, your faith is historically solid. Your decision to follow Christ is not a hollow or meaningless decision. It is the most important decision of your life (or anyone's life).

Using the space provided in your Lightbearers Journal, write about the events surrounding the moment you gave your life to Christ. If it was recently, even through your studies in this book, share that time. If it was a long time ago, write what you remember or ask your parents to help you with the details. If you have grown up always trusting in Jesus, this would be a time to record your love for Him anew and praise God for showing His love for you throughout your life.

You may also want to use this time to re-commit your life to following Jesus. You have learned much about the Christian worldview over the last few months. Maybe you have been shown different areas of your life that need to be strengthened. Write those areas down and make a plan of action for how you can improve in those areas.

If you do not consider yourself a Christian, use this time to write down any objections to or questions about Christianity. Do not stop at just writing these things down. Use these thoughts as jumping off points for study or ask a mature believer to help you work through these issues.

Historical Figure
Presentation Assignment

Write a one page paper on a person in history who has had a significant impact on the Christian church. Ask questions such as: How did this person's background influence his or her role in history? Did the persom suffer persecution for their actions? What impact did the person's actions have upon the church or culture then and today?

Choose one of the names on the list below or write about someone of your own choosing (just make sure to ask your teacher if the person you have chosen is appropriate for this assignment).

- John Wycliffe
- John Huss
- William Tyndale
- Martin Luther
- John Calvin
- William Carey
- Augustine
- John Wesley
- Jonathan Edwards
- Cotton Mather
- William Wilberforce
- George Whitefield
- Polycarp
- John Newton
- John Cotton
- William Bradford
- Justin Martyr
- C.S. Lewis
- Timothy Dwight
- Thomas Shepherd
- William Booth
- Blaise Pascal
- Francis and Edith Schaeffer
- Phyllis Schlafly
- Mother Teresa

Who Is This Jesus: Is He Risen?
Video Outline

I. What are the Gospels?

    A. _____: biographical accounts of Jesus' life written by four different authors

        1. Matthew (former tax collector and apostle)

        2. Mark (student of Peter and Paul)

        3. Luke (physician and historian)

        4. John (apostle and author of other biblical works)

II. When were the Gospels written?

    A. Before or after 70 AD?

        1. Matthew, Mark, and Luke record Jesus predicting the destruction of Jerusalem within one generation

        2. Jerusalem and the temple were in fact destroyed by the Romans in 70 AD.

        3. If the Gospels were written before 70 AD, then Jesus miraculously predicted the future

        "Matthew delights in prophecy-fulfillment…[but] can you imagine that if Matthew had been written after the fall of Jerusalem, wild horses couldn't have prevent Matthew from saying, 'and Jesus' prediction was fulfilled when Jerusalem was destroyed.' He doesn't say that and that is very unlike Matthew." — Paul Maier

    B. If one assumes miracles are _____, then the accounts were written before 70 AD.

    C. If one assumes that miracles are _____, then the accounts must have been written after 70 AD.

III. Are the Gospels reliable?

    A. The Gospels record the disciples' foibles, mistakes, and failures

"The Disciples in the Gospels are a very mixed bunch. These people went on to be the leaders of the Church, and it would have been very easy for the early Church to write up the stories in such a way that you always have the Disciples exactly understanding everything…Instead you have them as a completely muddled bunch who have clearly their own agendas of what they thought Jesus was about…But actually that too is part of the historical reliability of the tradition."
— N.T. Wright

B. The Gospels don't appear to be myths

"If the Gospels are not eyewitness accounts, then they are a type of fantasy that has absolutely no parallel in all of literature. That some Galilean peasants—fishermen and tax collectors—invented not only the world's most gigantic hoax, but a totally unique form of literature, the realistic fantasy." — Peter Kreeft

C. The Gospel authors would have been challenged if they had lied

"The presence of hostile antagonistic witnesses actually became one of the most powerful forces for determining truth. They didn't dare fabricate. There were people there that hated what the Disciples stood for, hated what the Apostles stood for. And immediately they would have nailed them, they would have corrected them, saying 'Wait a minute, I was there; he didn't say that; he didn't go there.'" — D.A. Carson

D. The Gospel authors would not have likely risked their lives for a lie

"There is the simple question of the honesty of the men who wrote these texts. Why would they lie? What would they gain from it? Most of them it cost their lives to preach this."— Francis Martin

E. The Gospels are full of embarrassing stories

"If I am starting a world movement, I would hardly tell all of these embarrassing stories about myself: how I failed to believe Jesus, how I betrayed him, how I denied him. And the Gospels are full of these things." — Francis Martin

F. The Gospels have an aura of authenticity

"Women were not, in that day and age, looked upon very highly. All one has to do is read first-century Jewish documents and you realize they couldn't give testimony in a court of law, they couldn't report about what they had seen. So if someone is making up a story certainly they are not going to have the women being the ones to show up first." — Sam Lamerson

"In first-century Judaism the shepherds were one of the lowest of occupations. They were looked upon as dishonest; they also couldn't give testimony in a court of law. And yet the first appearance of Jesus, in the Gospel of Luke, is to the shepherds. " — Sam Lamerson

G. The Gospels give many historical details—multiple references to political figures, places, episodes (e.g., Luke relates the birth of Jesus to the time of Caesar Augustus)

IV. Is the Bible dependable?

A. Scribes copied what the believed to be the word of God very carefully

B. The early copies of the text are 96–97% in agreement

C. Over _____ early whole or partial copies of the Greek New Testament have been found and thousands more in other languages

V. Do other sources record the life of Jesus?

A. The life of Jesus was recorded in 20 non-biblical sources within 150 years of His death

B. The life of Jesus was also recorded in numerous writings of the early Church fathers

VI. Is Jesus the Christ (i.e., the Messiah)?

A. Jesus fulfilled Old Testament messianic prophecies

1. Psalm 22 (the crucifixion)

2. Judas's betrayal of Jesus for 30 pieces of silver

3. Jesus' abandonment by His disciples

4. The false testimony presented at His trial

"It would be mathematically impossible for anyone else ever to fulfill all these parameters of prophecy in the Old Testament better than Jesus did." — Paul Maier

VII. Did Jesus rise from the dead?

A. The New Testament records that over _____ eyewitnesses saw Jesus *after* He died

B. It is hard to account for the enormous and sudden growth of Christianity if Jesus wasn't raised

VIII. Theories against the Resurrection

A. _____: that Jesus' followers either lied, stole His body, or both

"To believe the Fraud Theory, you would have to accept that a small band of men, most of them fishermen, common people, fought off the Roman guard…broke the Roman seal…and then stole the body and spread abroad that Jesus had been raised from the dead." — D.A. Carson

B. _____: that Jesus didn't die, but merely fainted and then was revived

1. This theory defies what we know about crucifixion (death by asphyxiation)

2. If asphyxiation didn't kill Jesus, then the spear surely would have

3. If this theory were true, then Jesus would have had to escape the tomb and overtake His guards

C. _____: that Jesus' followers were hallucinating when they thought they saw the risen Jesus

1. This theory ignores that, generally, no two individuals (or 500) share the same hallucination

2. Hallucinations are not contagious

D. _____: that everyone involved failed to locate the correct burial chamber

1. This theory would mean that:

a. Jesus was laid at the wrong tomb

b. The guards stood before the wrong tomb

c. The women and the disciples ran to the wrong tomb

d. The burial clothes appeared in the wrong tomb

2. Even if those involved had the wrong tomb, Jesus appeared later to many others

E. _____: that Jesus rose from the dead spiritually and not bodily

    1. This theory ignores the claims of the Gospel writers, that they could see and touch Him.

    2. This theory fails to explain the rapid growth of the early Church. If the Romans had the body, they could have curbed the spread of Christianity.

    3. This theory goes against the Jewish beliefs of the disciples that the Messiah would *physically* conquer death.

F. Many critical scholars assume that miracles are impossible

    1. Does science disprove the existence of miracles?

    2. Science studies nature, yet miracles are supernatural events; we cannot prove or refute either category by using the other

IX. Evidence for the Resurrection

A. The 500 eyewitnesses (you only need one in a court of law)

B. The empty tomb

C. The doubts of the disciples

D. The transformation of the disciples (from fear to belief)

E. People do not die for a known lie (eleven Apostles were martyred)

X. The Growth of the Church

A. If Jesus' body was still in the tomb, then it is hard to understand why so many chose to follow Him

B. Jesus' resurrection is the best explanation for the growth of Christianity

Who Is This Jesus: Is He Risen?
Video Questions

1. When were Matthew, Mark, and Luke written? Why do critical scholars date Matthew, Mark, and Luke after 70 AD?

2. What reasons do we have for believing that the Gospels are reliable?

3. What reasons do we have for believing that the Gospels are dependable?

4. What reasons do we have for believing that Jesus rose from the dead?

5. What are some theories against the resurrection? What are the problems with these theories?

Purpose and Plan
Exercise

Do you realize that God has already revealed His purpose and plan for you? It involves all the principles and ideas found in the Bible. This study of a Biblical Christian worldview has introduced you to many of the plans God has in each area of life. Give some thought to the following questions and answer each one according to your newly formed Biblical Christian worldview. You will turn these in on day 13.

1. In Theology, you learned that God is relational. Given that, what is God's plan for you regarding your relationship to Him?

2. In Philosophy, you discovered that you can know what is true by studying both God's general revelation (His World) and special revelation (His Word). In light of this, what should be one of your goals in life?

3. The study of Biology demonstrated that you are a created being. Why does this give significance to your life?

4. Biblical Ethics revealed that God has established certain moral guidelines for living. How does that impact your life?

5. According to Christian Psychology, mankind is created in God's image, yet possesses a fallen sin nature after the fall. This idea relates to you in what two ways?

6. The family is a significant part of God's plan, according to biblical Sociology. What does that imply about God's work in your life? And which of the following best describes the biblical view of marriage?

   • Marriage can be defined any way I want it to be.
   • Living together without being officially married is okay as long as we love each other.
   • Being married and raising children are probably a part of God's plan for me, so I need to prepare myself for being a partner and a parent.

7. What is the main point of biblical Law, and how does that apply to you?

8. Knowing that God has a plan for Politics, how should you relate to our system of government?

9. In the area of Economics, God's will for your life includes how you earn and use money and other resources, like your time. How is this significant to you?

10. If God has revealed Himself and His ways throughout History, what does that imply about how you should apply yourself to understand the past?

How to Be Your Own Selfish Pig
Reading Discussion Questions

Chapter 7: A Bunch of Fairy Tales!

1. What primary belief of Eastern philosophies makes Susan reject them as truth?

2. What Scripture verse tells us the *purpose* of the Bible?

3. What proofs of the Bible's authenticity do we have that our grandfathers did not have?

4. What is another amazing aspect of the Bible?

5. What does Francis Schaeffer illustrate through the story of the cliff hanger?

6. What additional characteristic provides further evidence that the Bible is what it claims to be?

7. What are some specific aspects of the Christian faith that match up with reality?

8. What does all this evidence about the Bible give to the author and you?

9. The seven "other messages" outlined on pages 66–68 include Hinduism, Buddhism, Islam, Mormonism, Christian Science, Jehovah's Witness, and the Unification Church. Name a flaw in each message that contradicts the information we find in the Bible.

10. Reflection Question: Considering the historical reliability of the Bible (confirmed through various archaeological findings and numerous fulfilled prophecies), do you think it is reasonable to believe in what the Bible teaches, rather than other religious teachings? Why?

LIGHTBEARERS

Conclusion

A Summit Ministries Curriculum

DAY	CONCLUSION: syllabus & outline	SW	✓
1	Read *A World of Ideas* Reading...	265	
2	Read *A World of Ideas* Reading...	DITTO	
3	Take **Post-Test**...	273	
	Complete **Pre-Test/Post-Test** Analysis..	274	
	Complete **Your Strategy for Victory** Exercise...	275	
4	Complete **The Genesis Front** Exercise...	276	
	Complete **The Human Nature Front** Exercise..	277	
5	Complete **The Justice Front** Exercise..	278	
	Complete **The Kingdom Front** Exercise...	279	
6	Read *How to Be Your Own Selfish Pig* Reading (Ch. 12)............................	---	
7	Review *How to Be Your Own Selfish Pig* Reading Discussion Questions (Ch. 12)......	280	
8	Watch **Six Great Questions** Video Outline...	281	
9	Complete **Deadly Questions** Exercise...	283	
10	Complete **Prayer** Exercise...	285	
	Complete **Study** Exercise...	286	
11	Complete **Understand the Times** Exercise..	287	
12	Prepare **Comprehensive** Test..	---	
13	Take **Comprehensive** Test..	---	
14	Course Evaluation...	---	
15			

A World of Ideas:
Conclusion

Something to Get Excited About

It's been said that the heart cannot rejoice in what the mind rejects. So after studying all these different aspects of a Biblical Christian worldview, is your heart rejoicing? Are you excited about being a Christian? If not, maybe it's because your mind has been taken captive by hostile ideas concerning some aspect of Christianity.

Throughout this text, we explored important questions in life—questions related to God, reality, science, morality, politics, and you! We found that the Bible has satisfying answers to each of these questions. And we also discovered how these questions are the parts of a much bigger picture, a portrait of a total worldview.

But the goal in all of this was not just to give you more ideas to cram into your head, or for you to simply pass a test on the material and then forget it in a week. It is much more. Our desire is for you to understand how to think about the world and then be equipped to stand on these vital truths from God's Word and to pass them along to others.

As you know, this course is titled *Lightbearers*. Throughout this course, you've gotten information on what kinds of ideas a Lightbearer should have in order to live for Christ. In this final chapter you will be challenged to let these truths sink into your life, to actually *become* someone who can bear the light of Jesus. A Lightbearer is a person who not only knows the truth (the light), but also is ready to share that light with friends and neighbors who live in darkness. You should be able to know *what* you believe and tell others *why* you believe what you believe. Or, as the Apostle Peter puts it, to be able to "give the reason for the hope that you have" (1 Peter 3:15–16, NIV).

The Christian Worldview

First, let's review the journey we've taken so far. By this point, there is one thing you should know for sure: the Christian worldview is comprehensive and consistent. It's *comprehensive* because it provides answers to all of life's key questions. This is because it is a worldview that comes from God's revelation in the Bible and in His Son, Jesus Christ. "I am the way, the truth, and the life," Jesus declared (John 14:6). Elsewhere He revealed, "I say to you, he who hears My word and believes in Him who sent Me has everlasting life, and shall not come into judgment, but has passed from death into life" (John 5:24, NKJV).

A Biblical Christian worldview is also *consistent*. This means that all the parts fit together. Like the fruit on a tree develops naturally from the sap flowing from its roots, a worldview takes the ideas about God and produces related ideas in every other area of life.

The elements of a Biblical Christian worldview are summarized in the chart below:

AREA OF STUDY	KEY QUESTION	ANSWER
Theology	"What about God?"	Theism (Trinity)
Philosophy	"What is true and how do we know?"	Supernaturalism
Ethics	"How should we behave?"	Moral Absolutes
Biology	"What is the origin of life?"	God's Creation
Psychology	"What is human nature?"	Created in God's image/fallen
Sociology	"What makes a healthy society?"	Family, Church, State
Law	"What is the basis for law?"	Biblical/Natural Law
Politics	"What is the purpose of government?"	Justice, Freedom, Order
Economics	"How should we use our resources?"	Stewardship of resources
History	"What is the meaning of history?"	Historical Resurrection

The Fruit of a Christian Worldview

Although the history of Christianity is not without blemish, the overall results of Christianity since Jesus' resurrection are overwhelmingly positive.

As the Christian faith spread throughout the Roman Empire and beyond, there was a dramatic change in the way people lived their lives. As explained by famed historian Will Durant, "There is no greater drama in human record than the sight of a few Christians, scorned or oppressed by a succession of emperors, bearing all trial with fiery tenacity, multiplying quietly, building order while their enemies generated chaos, fighting the sword with the word, brutality with hope, and at last defeating the strongest state that history has ever known. Caesar and Christ had met in the arena, and Christ had won."[1]

The advance of Christianity did not stop with the Roman Empire. Jesus' commission to His followers was to make disciples of *all* the nations (Matthew 28:19–20). In their book *What If Jesus Had Never Been Born?*, D. James Kennedy and Jerry Newcombe provide a detailed discussion of the fruit of the Christian faith over the centuries. At the beginning of their book they supply this summary of the ways Christian belief impacted culture[2]:

- Hospitals, which essentially began in the Middle Ages.
- Universities, which also began during the Middle Ages. In addition, most of the world's greatest universities were started by Christians for Christian purposes.
- Literacy and education for the masses.
- Capitalism and free enterprise.
- Representative government, particularly as it was formulated in the United States of America.
- The separation of political powers.
- Civil liberties.
- The abolition of slavery, both in antiquity and in more recent times.
- Modern science.
- The discovery of the New World by Columbus.
- The elevation of the social status of women.

- Benevolence and charity (the "good Samaritan" ethic).
- Higher standards of justice.
- The elevation of the common man.
- The condemnation of adultery, homosexuality, and other sexual perversions. This has helped to preserve the human race, and it has spared many from heartache.
- High regard for human life.
- The civilization of many primitive cultures.
- The codification of many of the world's languages.
- Greater development of art and music (Christianity has always been the inspiration for the greatest works of art).
- The countless changed lives transformed from liabilities into assets to society because of the gospel.
- The eternal salvation of countless souls.

A tree is known by its fruit. As we discussed in the chapter on Law, atheistic worldviews inevitably lead their followers toward chaos and death. On the other hand, the Biblical Christian worldview promotes order, peace, and life.

Baloney Detectors

We all know that baloney is not "real" meat—it's just animal parts that are spiced up and mashed together. In other words, it's a cheap imitation of the real thing. In the same way, some ideas are *baloney*, cheap imitations of the truth. The Apostle Paul talked about detecting fake ideas when he wrote, "See to it that no one takes you captive through hollow and deceptive philosophy, which depends on human tradition and the basic principles of this world rather than on Christ" (Colossians 2:8, NIV). Hollow ideas. Deceptive philosophies. Cheap imitations of the truth.

Our world is a war-zone of ideas. Hostile worldviews are competing for your allegiance. As in any war, the choice is basic—either be captured, or take captives.

Taking Thoughts Captive

The next time you hear someone making a claim about an idea, turn on your baloney detector. You can do that by taking the idea "captive" and comparing it to the ideas that come from a biblical worldview. One way to do that is to dig a little deeper into the underlying assumptions the speaker has by asking the question, *"What do you mean by _____?"* and fill in the blank with the idea just expressed.

Okay, let's try this response on the following statement: "Christians just accept everything on faith." What baloney (imitation of the truth) do you detect in this statement? Did you notice there is a hidden idea that this person assumes to be true?

When someone challenges your faith in God in this way, the first thing you should do is to ask, "What do you mean by 'faith'?" The answer may surprise you. Most people today assume that a Christian's faith in God is what might be defined as "blind faith," that what we believe is based on...well, just "belief." In other words, the world thinks there is no evidence or logical reason behind our faith. It's more like a feeling or emotional conviction. No reasons, no evidence. It's because you just felt like "believing" today.

The idea that faith is "blind" is found throughout our culture. For example, in the film *Indiana Jones and the Last Crusade,* Harrison Ford plays the role of Indiana, who must retrieve the Holy Grail to save his father's life. He makes it through a series of obstacles only to find that he is standing at the edge of a deep chasm. He looks down to see nothing but empty space and a sheer cliff. His clue is to take a "step of faith." After much hesitation, Indy steps out "in faith" and finds he is actually walking on a camouflaged footbridge. This scene illustrates the secular idea that "faith" is believing something you can't see and don't have any proof exists. It was only after he "blindly" took that step that he felt and saw the solid bridge leading across the chasm.

Conclusion

So the question is: *Is it true that faith is blind?* Is this what the Bible describes as faith? As it turns out, the answer is no. The main verse defining true biblical faith is found in Hebrews 11:1, which reads "Now faith is being sure of what we hope for and certain of what we do not see" (NIV).

Some people reading this verse emphasize the phrases "hope for" and "not seen." But this can lead to a definition of faith that includes nothing more substantial than working up a sense of assurance when there is no real evidence or reason to support it. Like Indiana Jones, we step out in "blind" hope even when we don't see anything that will support our belief.

A better wording is this: "Now <u>faith</u> is the <u>substance</u> of things hoped for, the <u>evidence</u> of things not seen" (NKJV). Put this way, we find three key words in this verse that need to be defined. First, what is meant by the word *faith*? The original Greek word means "firm persuasion," or "a conviction based upon hearing."[3] This carries the meaning of *forensic proof.* For example, in Acts 17:31 Paul was speaking to the pagan leaders of the Greek city of Athens. He said, "For [God] has set a day when he will judge the world with justice by the man [Jesus] he has appointed. He has given *proof* of this to all men by raising him from the dead" (NIV). The kind of "proof" Paul was referring to was the same kind used in a court of law. He is saying that the evidence for Jesus' resurrection is the same sort of evidence presented during a trial to convince the judge or jury of the guilt or innocence of the defendant.

The second word we need to look at is *substance.* This word refers to something that is "set under" something else as a support. This means there is something substantial that supports your faith. It's not a "leap in the dark," it's a leap into the light! Trust is the logical result of understanding the evidence.

The third word is *evidence.* This refers to proof or a personal conviction based on facts. This is very similar to the idea of forensic proof as we noted under the definition of faith. Think of CSI and the kind of evidence necessary to prove a case in a court of law.

Therefore, the biblical definition of *faith* is totally different from what many people assume. It turns out that it is not "blind" belief, but a personal conviction based on solid evidence. Check out how this worked in the lives of the heroes of the faith listed in Hebrews 11.

But what kinds of facts support our faith? The New Testament provides numerous examples, many of which are related to the life, death, and especially the resurrection of Jesus.

One proof we can look at is when Jesus, after His crucifixion, appeared to His disciples in the Upper Room (John 14:8–14). While there, Philip asks Jesus for proof of His deity. Notice that Jesus does *not* respond to Philip, "Just believe." Instead, He said to believe in His divinity based on the evidence of the miracles He had performed. The miracles provided tangible proof of His deity.

> Philip said, "Lord, show us the Father and that will be enough for us." Jesus answered: "Don't you know me, Philip, even after I have been among you such a long time? Anyone who has seen me has seen the Father. How can you say, 'Show us the Father?' Don't you believe that I am in the Father, and that the Father is in me? The words I say to you are not just my own. Rather, it is the Father, living in me, who is doing his work. Believe me when I say that I am in the Father and the Father is in me; or at least believe on the evidence of the miracles themselves" (John 14:8–14, NIV).

Or consider how Thomas seriously doubted that Jesus had been raised from the dead. This is a legitimate doubt, since people don't normally come back from the dead! In John 20:24–29 Jesus does not say to Thomas, "Stop doubting and believe. Just believe." Jesus first provided physical evidence by offering His hands and side for Thomas's inspection. Thomas believed that Jesus was alive because he had seen and touched Jesus' body. He had evidence—physical proof—that convinced him Jesus had been raised from the dead and was therefore God Incarnate.

> "Now Thomas (called Didymus), one of the Twelve, was not with the disciples when Jesus came. So the other disciples told him, 'We have seen the Lord!' But he said to them, 'Unless I see the nail marks in his hands and put my finger where the nails were, and put my hand into his side, I will not believe it.' A week later his disciples were in the house again, and Thomas was with them. Though the doors were locked, Jesus came and stood among them and said, 'Peace be with

you!' Then he said to Thomas, 'Put your finger here; see my hands. Reach out your hand and put it into my side. Stop doubting and believe.' Thomas said to him, 'My Lord and my God!' Then Jesus told him, 'Because you have seen me, you have believed; blessed are those who have not seen and yet have believed' " (John 20:24–29, NIV).

Even though modern Christians do not have the same kind of opportunity that Thomas had to physically touch Jesus' scars, our conviction is based on the personal testimony of the disciples who *had* seen and touched Jesus. This kind of personal testimony is used every day in court to prove the guilt or innocence of a person. So even our faith today is not based on blind belief, but reliable eyewitness testimony.

The disciples were aware of the power of personal testimony, and used their experiences of seeing Jesus alive after the resurrection as they spoke to others. In fact, this was the central feature of their message. Luke writes in Acts 1:3, "After his suffering, he showed himself to these men and gave many convincing proofs that he was alive. He appeared to them over a period of forty days and spoke about the kingdom of God" (NIV).

Acts 2:1–36 describes the first recorded time the disciples spoke in public. Peter, as spokesman for the group, appealed first to the knowledge of those in the audience who had seen the miracles of Jesus, which he offered as evidence of His deity. "Jesus of Nazareth was a man accredited by God to you by miracles, wonders and signs, which God did among you through him, as you yourselves know" (vs. 22). Then Peter claimed to be an eyewitness of Jesus' resurrection, saying, "God has raised this Jesus to life, and we are all witnesses of the fact" (vs. 32). Based on these two facts, Peter concluded that everyone he spoke to, both those on that day and those reading his words thousands of years later, can be confident that Jesus is the Christ. "Therefore let all Israel be assured of this: God has made this Jesus, whom you crucified, both Lord and Christ" (vs. 36, NIV).

Later in his life, Peter wrote a letter to his fellow Christians to encourage them in their faith. In this letter he reminds them to continue to proclaim the message of salvation through Christ. In 1 Peter 3:15–16, he says that we should be able to give an answer to anyone who asks about our faith. The word for *answer* is the Greek term *apologia* (ap-ol-o-GEE-ah). It means "a plea," as in making a defense in a court of law. From this word we get our term **apologetics**, which means to defend the faith.

But Peter doesn't stop there. He goes on to write that we should give a "reason," or a systematic discourse. Can you give a well-organized defense of Christianity? That is what Peter is saying you should be able to do!

Always be prepared to give an answer to everyone who asks you to give the reason for the hope that you have. But do this with gentleness and respect… (1 Peter 3:15, NIV).

The foundation for an orderly, well-thought-out defense of your faith is "the hope that you have." But this doesn't mean that your faith is based on a "cross your fingers" kind of feeling. The word Peter used that is translated into English as "hope" actually means "confidence."[4] Your "hope" as relates to your faith is a confident attitude of trust, not just one of wishing for something. This feeling of confidence is based on what you know to be true. Again, this corroborates Peter's whole theme of believing on something that is based on certainty and proof.

Finally, Peter says that when we give our reasons for why we believe what we believe, we should do this in a gentle and respectful manner. In this way we demonstrate love to the person we are talking with. Since all people are made in God's image, we should always treat everyone with respect. Our motto should be: "Respect people, inspect ideas." This means that we are gentle with people but hard on any false ideas they may believe.

So, in summary, the Bible defines faith in positive ways. Faith is not a kind of wish fulfillment, a blind meaningless belief, or a wishy-washy feeling. True biblical faith refers to what we can know based on factual evidence.

Apologetics: to defend the faith.

A Message to Americans

Over one hundred and fifty years ago, a Frenchman named Alexis de Tocqueville visited America to study what made this fledgling nation so great. After spending months traveling across the nation, he wrote,

> There is no country in the whole world in which the Christian religion retains a greater influence over the souls of men than in America; and there can be no greater proof of its utility, and of its conformity to human nature, than that its influence is most powerfully felt over the most enlightened and free nation of the earth.[5]

Those were de Tocqueville's observations in the 1830s. Unfortunately, since that time America—and Western Civilization—has turned away from its Christian heritage. And the consequences are great indeed.

Who's to blame for this squandering of our Christian inheritance? (Check out Luke 15:11–32, especially verses 13–14.) Writing in 1981, the insightful Christian social analyst Francis Schaeffer placed the blame for the drift toward secularism and injustice at the doorstep of Christians. "The basic problem of the Christians in this country in the last eighty years or so, in regard to society and in regard to government, is that they have seen things in bits and pieces instead of totals." He laments that Christians have only gradually "become disturbed over permissiveness, pornography, the public schools, the breakdown of the family, and finally abortion. But they have not seen this as a totality—each thing being a part, a symptom of a much larger problem. They have failed to see that all of this has come about due to a shift in the worldview—that is, through a fundamental change in the overall way people think and view the world and life as a whole."[6]

Yet despite this downward trend, some Christians still believe their calling is to separate from the world because of its evil ways. In pursuing this course of inaction, they have allowed their Christian heritage to be plundered by anyone who holds a different worldview. Rather than being the salt and light of society, they have lost their saltiness and have become useless for Jesus Christ's kingdom (Matthew 5:13). George Grant offers these sobering words:

> The [Humanists] hold the seats of power: in government, in law, in education, in the media, in medicine, and in the judiciary. They care nothing for our morality. They abhor our "puritanical" values. They chafe against our piety. They despise our non-conformity. *But, they applaud our irrelevancy.* They appreciate our distraction from the things of this earth. They know that as long as *we* separate righteousness and justice, *they* will continue to have free reign. They will be able to continue to reshape life, liberty, and the pursuit of happiness in their own image. They will be able to perpetuate their slaughter of the unborn, their assault on the family, their defamation of all things holy, all things sacred, and all things pure. They will be able to transfer deity and rule from God Almighty to themselves, doing what is right in their own eyes (see Judges 21:25).[7]

We contend that instead of fleeing from the teachings of the Bible and the Christian worldview, what Americans need (in fact, what every nation needs) is to turn to Jesus Christ and His word in repentance and faith. Paul preached the gospel throughout the Mediterranean world with one primary purpose: that all nations might believe and obey Jesus (Romans 16:26).

A View for the World

While it is true that a Christian worldview gives us a true view *of* the world, enabling us to see the world as it really is, it is also true that a Christian worldview gives us a view *for* the world, inspiring us to engage the culture with the truth we know.[8] It gives us hope for a hurting world and direction for a world that has lost its way. Francis Schaeffer insisted that "as Christians we are not only to know the right world view, the world view that tells us the truth of what is, but consciously to act upon that world view so as to influence society in all its parts and facets across the whole spectrum of life…to the extent of our individual and collective ability."[9]

In 2 Corinthians 5, Paul describes Christians as "ambassadors." An ambassador is a person who lives in another country as the official spokesman for his country. As it turns out, everyone is an ambassador for something. It may be something good and worthwhile, or something bad and worthless. As a Lightbearer, you are called to be an ambassador for the most precious and worthwhile cause in the universe—the cause of Jesus Christ.

> Therefore, if anyone is in Christ, he is a new creation; old things have passed away; behold, all things have become new. Now all things are of God, who has reconciled us to Himself through Jesus Christ, and has given us the ministry of reconciliation, that is, that God was in Christ reconciling the world to Himself, not imputing their trespasses to them, and has committed to us the word of reconciliation. Now then, we are ambassadors for Christ… (2 Corinthians 5:17–20, NKJV).

As you consider all the problems our country faces, do you want to be part of the problem or part of the solution?

Concluding Remarks

Just a few final thoughts as we conclude. Be an authentic Lightbearer. Heed Paul's words: "Beware lest anyone cheat you through philosophy and empty deceit, according to the tradition of men, according to the basic principles of the world, and not according to Christ" (Colossians 2:8, NKJV)"

Now that you have been introduced to the "tradition[s] of men," and "the basic principles of the world," the Scriptures will hopefully take on a whole new meaning. You have a superior position in ten disciplines of life. You are equipped in a whole new way. The non-Christian worldviews have had their position shown to be irreconcilable with Christianity. The battle lines have been drawn. You are armed with understanding and truth from its very source, the Word of God.

> Jesus said to him, "I am the way, the truth, and the life. No one comes to the Father except through Me" (John 14:6, NKJV).

You are more than equipped to shatter the myths of opposing worldviews:

> The world is unprincipled. It's dog-eat-dog out there! The world doesn't fight fair. But we don't live or fight our battles that way—never have and never will. The tools of our trade aren't for marketing or manipulation, but they are for demolishing that entire massively corrupt culture. We use our powerful God-tools for smashing warped philosophies, tearing down barriers erected against the truth of God, fitting every loose thought and emotion and impulse into the structure of life shaped by Christ. (2 Corinthians 10:3–5, THE MESSAGE).

You have a responsibility to take part in the efforts to reclaim the ground that has been lost in nearly every arena of American life. Worldviews like Secular Humanism, Postmodernism, and Marxism currently have the loudest voice in colleges and universities, the media, the arts, music, law, business, medicine, psychology, sociology, public schools, and government. According to Dr. James C. Dobson, only two power centers in our society have not been claimed by humanism—the church and the family. But both are under tremendous pressure to surrender. Your light can help make the difference! Carry that light of Jesus Christ high. Keep it strong and bright!

> Let your light shine (Matthew 5:14–16).
> Pray (2 Chronicles 7:14; Colossians 1:9–14).
> Study (2 Timothy 2:15).
> Understand the times (1 Chronicles 12:32).
> Rebuild the foundations (Psalm 11:3).
> Spread God's truth with courage and conviction (Hebrews 11; 1 Peter 3:15–16).

Your challenge is to confront secular thinking wherever you find it. Taking such a stand will not be easy. In order to re-establish the influence of Christianity on our culture, it will take a rebirth of morality, a revival of spiritual interests, a renewal of intellectual honesty, and a recovery of courage. It will take strengthening the family and reawakening in our churches. Although these sound like daunting tasks, they can be done. We are ordered by our Commander to let our light shine, to stand up for truth, and to be morally responsible.

Truth is your greatest weapon, so know and wield it well! On your own, you might feel too small or weak to defend the faith and take back our culture, but by relying on Jesus Christ for your power and direction, you can accomplish amazing things for God in any area He calls you to make a difference.

We need dedicated Christians in every area of life. We need Christian artists, writers, actors, and musicians that can create the art, movies, and music that will feed the spirit and fuel the imagination of people to follow Jesus Christ, so that we can pull this nation out of the cultural sewer it is in. We need Christian scientists to show the world that faith and logic are not incompatible, that looking at the world through the lens of a Divine Creator actually explains reality best. We need Christian doctors, searching out the ways that God has created our human bodies to function best. We need Christian politicians, using the system our founding fathers developed to its best advantage in order to change the scope of law and living. And the list goes on.

Do you get the picture? Whatever talents God has given you should be used to glorify Him every day, to change our culture for the better.

We live in a world full of broken dreams, where truth is not always obvious. But the knowledge you have gained this year should help you unlock the truth, so that you can live differently and encourage others to live differently as well. You can make a difference in the world by using what you understand now about being a Lightbearer for Christ.

As you finish your school year, how are you going to put all this head knowledge into practice? Will you use your well-defined Christian worldview to answer Christ's call of "Follow me?" Will you stand firm on the truth of the Bible when those around you start to wobble and fall? Will you be the one to take God's light into a darkened world that needs His truth so desperately? We encourage you to pursue Jesus Christ with your entire heart, mind, soul, and body! Be the one, Lightbearer!

> ...so that you may become blameless and pure, children of God without fault in a crooked and depraved generation, in which you shine like stars in the universe as you hold out the word of life... (Philippians 2:15–16, NIV).

Endnotes

[1] Will Durant, *Caesar and Christ: A History of Roman Civilization and of Christianity from Their Beginnings to A.D. 325* (New York, NY: Simon and Schuster, 1944), 652.

[2] D. James Kennedy and Jerry Newcombe, *What If Jesus Had Never Been Born?* (Nashville, TN: Thomas Nelson, 1994), 3–4. See also Alvin Schmidt's *How Christianity Changed the World.*

[3] From *Vine's Expository Dictionary of Biblical Words.*

[4] Biblesoft's New Exhaustive Strong's Numbers and Concordance with Expanded Greek-Hebrew Dictionary.

[5] Alexis de Tocqueville, *Democracy in America*, 2 volumes (New Rochelle, NY: Arlington House, no date), 1:294.

[6] Francis A. Schaeffer, *A Christian Manifesto* (Westchester, IL: Crossway Books, 1981), 17.

[7] George Grant, *Trial and Error: The American Civil Liberties Union and Its Impact on Your Family* (Brentwood, TN: Wolgumeth & Hyatt, 1989), 133.

[8] Bill Brown, Gary Phillips, and John Stonestreet, *Making Sense of Your World,* 2nd ed. (Salem, WI: Sheffield Publishing Company, 2008), 8.

[9] Francis A. Schaeffer, *How Should We Then Live?* (Westchester, IL: Crossway Books, 1983), 87.

Pre-Test/Post-Test
Analysis

1. What was your favorite unit? Why?

2. How has your view of God broadened by taking this class?

3. How do you view yourself and others differently based on the information you have gained in this class?

4. What lifestyle changes have you made or will you make because of what you learned here?

5. How can you become more involved in your community?

6. How does your Christian worldview impact the career choices you will make?

7. What social implications does your Christian worldview have?

8. What insights did you gain about morality in this class?

9. What did you learn about where humans came from ? Why does that knowledge make a difference in the way you live?

10. What practical ways can you have an impact on the culture around you?

Your Strategy for Victory
Exercise

Now that you are armed with an understanding of the Biblical Christian worldview, it is important to understand the viewpoints of those who are in opposition to God's truth. By knowing the opposition, you can organize your own strategy on how to present and defend the truth. Notice this was Paul's strategy when he spoke to a pagan audience in Acts 17 (see Paul's defense of the faith to the leaders of Athens in Acts 17:16–34). As a Lightbearer and champion for the cause of Christ and the Christian worldview, you will need to understand the spiritual, intellectual, and moral front lines where the battle for hearts and minds is raging.

Since every idea being expressed in society depends on answering the question about God (theology), you can group the opponents of Christianity under the general heading of Humanism. Humanism assumes that God does not exist, and, therefore, man replaces God when it comes to determining the answers to life's key questions.

G.K. Chesterton warned long ago that if man will not believe in God, the danger is not that he will believe in nothing, but that he will believe in anything. In other words, by closing the door to the existence of God, humans have cut themselves off from any solid foundation for understanding life. Furthermore, people can be easily lured into trusting all kinds of untrue philosophies and religions.

Humanism, by its very definition, denies both God and Jesus Christ. This means that between Humanism and Christianity there is no middle ground. By pure logic, you cannot embrace both a God-centered view and a man-centered view, because they oppose each other. Draw the lines of discernment clearly, because these are your "front" lines of battle. In order to engage the battle you will need to develop a reasonable strategy for presenting and defending a Christian worldview.

On this battlefield you will spiritually, intellectually, and morally engage with humanism. Therefore, you need to explore and prepare your defense strategy on at least four fronts: *The Genesis Front*, *The Human Nature Front*, *The Justice Front*, and *The Kingdom Front*. On each front you will discover a way of thinking that will bring you victory. Let's look at each of these four fronts to learn how to engage the world of ideas.

The Genesis Front
Exercise

Two primary views stand head to head on this front: either mind came before matter, or matter came before mind. Either the mind of God is primary and the material universe is secondary, or matter is primary and mind is secondary.

You know already that the Bible declares God exists and is eternal. Your Christian worldview also states that He created the physical universe (John 1:1–3). In other words, mind came before matter—God created matter and out of it everything proceeded in a orderly way. Observable evidence in the world today shows that matter moves from order to disorder, which supports a "mind before matter" conclusion.

But humanism says, "There is no God; only matter exists, and that same matter evolved into mind." This side of *The Genesis Front* declares that the known universe evolved by chance into its present orderly state. It claims that life proceeds from disorder to order, so evolution could take place.

The Genesis Front also includes ideas about people. Naturalists say that matter finally evolved into us. It declares that in the beginning, life evolved from non-life. Though mankind is a long way from the animal world in manifest intelligence, Humanists tell us that we are only a step up from monkeys.

But can a mind that developed from an animal's mind be of any value? The atheistic worldview has no answers for the intricacies of the human mind and soul. However, the Christian worldview clearly states that man is made in the image and likeness of God (Genesis 1:26). You believe that a designed universe demands a Designer; the world and all of mankind are evidence of that truth.

Look at the evidence supporting the created universe, the human soul, and the truth of the Scriptures. Also consider how the humanist views are not reasonably supported. Can you state clearly the ideas that will make you victorious on *The Genesis Front*?

The Human Nature Front
Exercise

Christianity and Humanism clash once again on *The Human Nature Front*. Christianity declares that humans are fallen and in desperate need of personal salvation. Everywhere we look, past and present, we see the obvious evidence of mankind's sin nature. The Christian is not surprised when people treat each other badly and knows the only solution is a new life found through Jesus Christ.

On the other hand, Humanism declares that man is basically good and evolving into something better. In fact, humans are progressing toward perfection. They cannot deny, of course, that men behave immorally in the real world, but they blame society and its institutions. It is not some inner defect of sin that is the problem, but a person's environment that encourages the wrong kinds of actions. Thus, they believe it is urgent that we work together to usher in a new utopian society. In most cases, this means the answer to social ills is socialism (everyone having and sharing the same). However, socialism does not produce the ideal society. That's because history provides multiple examples of how socialism actually takes away man's incentive to better himself. The reason socialism does not work is because it tries to build a social framework on the wrong understanding of human nature.

Can you clearly state the realities that support your view on *The Human Nature Front*?

The Justice Front
Exercise

Because Humanism denies that God exists, it must find another authority to define law and justice. After all, if God does not exist, neither does God's law. Humanism must turn to man-made laws set up by the state. Thus, legal positivism (entrusting the state with authority for creating laws, rather than biblical/natural law) is based upon a materialistic view of man and government. This system of determining justice was used by Adolf Hitler, Stalin, and Mao Tse Tung as they sought to bring in their new world order. However, putting the state in charge leads to legal relativism, where law is ever-changing according to need or desire. When the state is the only basis for law, any law may be conceived and put into action.

The Christian worldview, on the other hand, relies solely on the character and attributes of God as the determiners of right and wrong, stating that there are moral absolutes (based on the unchanging nature of God) that must be followed at all times and for all people. This view of law is solid and unchanging, and has provided the foundation for the Magna Carta, the Declaration of Independence, and the Constitution of the United States, three landmark legal documents.

Look closely at the results of godly government in contrast to the rise and fall of communism. In reality, which was more productive and advantageous for mankind? Which system allows its people to thrive? Which system produces a higher standard of living?

"There is no country in the whole world," said Alexis de Tocqueville, "in which the Christian religion retains a greater influence over the souls of men than in America; and there can be no greater proof of its utility, and of its conformity to human nature, than that its influence is most powerfully felt over the most enlightened and free nation of the earth."

Contrast de Tocqueville's statement with Robert Jackson's observation concerning the results of Marxism in the first half of the twentieth century: "No half-century ever witnessed slaughter on such a scale, such cruelties and inhumanities, such wholesale deportations of people into slavery, such annihilations of minorities." Ideas have consequences, and the consequences of legal positivism are heartbreakingly tragic.

At its core, the debate here is about authority. According to a Christian worldview, humanity is accountable to God for its actions, both individually and collectively. Humanism, however, has rejected God as our authority and exalted mankind in His place. Without God to hold us accountable, people are "free" to act as they see fit. Without God, anything goes.

Therefore, the battle on *The Justice Front* is really between moral relativism and godly absolutes. Everything is not equally right before God. God is opposed to ethical systems that encourage evil men to destroy human value and dignity. The Christian worldview bases morality on the unchanging nature of God and understands that man's highest calling is to justice, honesty, and serving his fellowman. Can you state clearly how you will be victorious on *The Justice Front*?

Yet it shall not be so among you; but whoever desires to become great among you shall be your servant. And whoever of you desires to be first shall be slave of all. For even the Son of Man did not come to be served, but to serve, and to give His life a ransom for many (Mark 10:43–45, NKJV).

The Kingdom Front
Exercise

The battle on this final front concerns the view of history held by the two opposing sides. The Humanistic worldviews base their attitude toward history on the false premise that evolution is a fact. They promise their followers a continual, evolutionary ascent toward perfection. In essence, they promise an earthly "heaven" without the uncomfortable concept of a holy and just God. In this way, mankind does not need to be responsible for his actions.

Sadly, the vision of paradise humanists promise is inadequate. Although it appears to free mankind from all responsibility and governing authorities, it is not a supernatural kingdom, so death is the end of everything. There is no promise of life after death, so the short 80-100 years we live are all there is. In addition, there is no evidence that man is moving progressively toward perfection. In fact, the evidence is to the contrary. For all the years people have been trying to progress without God, there is nothing to show for their efforts except death and bloodshed. Such a hard and callous paradise could hardly be described as heaven on earth.

In contrast, consider the paradise God offers to His people. Because God promises eternal life, Christians can be assured that He will keep His promises. God has fully adopted us into His family with all rights to inheritance in the kingdom. We are now dwelling in relationship with Him, and when this life is over we will spend eternity in His magnificent presence. Instead of 100 years being the most we can hope for, we can actually count on 100 plus eternity. C.S. Lewis put it like this, "Aim at heaven and you'll get earth 'thrown in.' Aim at earth and you'll get neither."

Now, clearly state the reasons for claiming your victory on *The Kingdom Front*. Because Jesus holds the key to paradise in mankind's future, you may rehearse this victorious battle cry:

He has delivered us from the power of darkness and conveyed us into the kingdom of the Son of His love, in whom we have redemption through His blood, the forgiveness of sins. He is the image of the invisible God, the firstborn over all creation (Colossians 1:13–15, NKJV).

How to Be Your Own Selfish Pig
Reading Discussion Questions

Chapter 12: "You only go round once in life, so. . ."

1. What is a good question to ask people to find out what they believe life is all about?

2. How does believing whole-heartedly in the truth of the Bible change the way you act, according to Susan's talk with Kim?

3. What lesson did you learn from reading about Eric?

4. What was the "monster" that Susan battled in the story on pages 116 and 117? How did she overcome it?

5. The quote from C.S. Lewis on page 119 compares Christianity to the sun. What important truth does it teach?

6. **Reflection Question:** Are there questions you want to ask, like *Who am I? Where am I going? How will I get there?* and *How do I know?* How do you know God cares about answering your questions?

Six Great Questions
Video Outline

I.   What Do You Mean by That?

    A. What do you mean by "God?"

    B. What do you mean by "truth?"

    C. What do you mean by "choose?"

II.   How Do You Know That's _____?

    A. Third graders at the museum

    B. "This fossil is millions of years old."

III. Where Do You Get Your _____?

    A. "People are born gay."

    B. "10% of the population is gay."

        1. No study has verified this

        2. Test subjects for the Kinsey Study were prostitutes and prisoners

IV.   What Happens if You Are _____?

    A. "I don't think a loving God would send anyone to hell."

    B. **Note**: Be careful with this question because it can come back to you

V.   How Did You Come to That _____?

    A. "How did you become an atheist?"

        1. The Nazi holocaust

        2. But if Darwinism is true, did Hitler really do anything wrong?

VI. **Have You Ever Considered This?**

VII. **Some Helpful Rules, Goals, and Suggestions**

    A. Listen _____, answer _____

    B. Win the _____ and not the argument

    C. Argue but don't _____

    D. Realize that it might be a long-term investment

    E. Utilize your resources

        1. **Wrong Answer**: "I don't know"

        2. **Right Answer**: "I don't know, but let me find out and get back to you."

        3. Don't make up an answer!

Deadly Questions
Exercise

If you are well-studied and prepared, you are indeed Christ's champion. With your heart and mind filled and ready for some of the basic ideas that challenge your Christian worldview, you are called into the world to engage in a battle for Jesus (2 Corinthians 10:5).

Suppose you walk into a situation where someone is demonstrating that he or she believes in humanistic ideas. After all, you are trying to win over the person, not just crush them with your arguments (you could do that, but then you have thrown away your chance to change their hearts). Be aware, as you study and use these deadly questions, that people with ideas that are different from your own are not necessarily your enemy. Challenge the ideas, not the person. "But I say to you, love your enemies, bless those who curse you, do good to those who hate you, and pray for those who spitefully use you and persecute you…" (Matthew 5:44, NKJV).

So what can you do to combat false ideas and stand for the truth without losing the war by winning one battle? Your best tactic is to respectfully ask questions designed to get others thinking. These kinds of questions strike at the heart of your opponent's worldview. That is why we call them deadly questions, weapons for Christ's champions.

Weapon One: "What do you mean by _____?"
Always begin by asking your opponents to define their terms. For example, someone could say, "There is no such thing as a traditional family left in the United States today." You could reply by asking, "What do you mean by 'traditional family?'" Sometimes someone hasn't thought about exactly what he or she is including in a specific term. Plus, defining key words up front can come in handy later.

Weapon Two: "How do you know that to be true?"
You do not need to ask them whether or not they believe in truth. Just ask them to prove that what they are claiming to be true is in fact true. For example, if a teacher says, "Evolution is a fact," then ask, "How do you know that to be true?" This causes them to really look at the reasons behind their belief.

Weapon Three: "Where did you get your information?"
At least 30% of what is taught in classes is opinion, and is not based on fact. Just like you add footnotes to a research paper to support your written statements with facts, statistics, and other evidence, you should be ready to ask them to back up the truth of their statements with factual information.

Weapon Four: "What happens if you're wrong?"
Be careful with this one. They can very easily turn this one back on you. Use it when people are speaking more from emotion than from a reasoned question or comment.

Weapon Five: "How did you come to this conclusion?"
This question forces the speaker to move away from emotional and manipulative arguments, which are sometimes the easiest to use, and follow a path of logical reasoning. This is something most people are not prepared to do, and can again show them the problems with their worldview.

Weapon Six: "Have you ever considered _____?"
Here is where you can offer either a critique of their view, or an alternative view or explanation. But by using this non-threatening approach, you are still keeping the discussion on a friendly level. You aren't attacking their beliefs—just offering them an alternative they might not have considered before.

Weapon Seven: "Can you give me two sources who disagree with you, and explain why they do?"
With this question, you are asking your opponents to investigate views that oppose their own and to share that investigation with you. Asking this question can also reveal if they have weighed both sides or have simply made an uninformed decision without weighing all the possible information.

Weapon Eight: "Why do you believe you are right?"
Again, this has them look at the basis for their belief. Are they believing in something that actually has merit and can be proved, or simply because everyone else believes it too? Remember, you should be able to answer this important question yourself. You should always be able to state what you believe and why.

Weapon Nine: "Give me an alternate explanation for _____."
This is another question to move the discussion onto logical ground. It will often reveal that the issue you are debating is more complex than the presentation has shown thus far.

Weapon Ten: "If you are unwilling to defend the position, how do we know it is defensible?"
Use this one when a teacher is trying to appear objective by not taking sides on an issue, since it is a good question to help clarify his or her specific views on a subject.

This strategy of asking questions is a powerful one and must always be done without challenging the authority of the person you are questioning, especially a teacher. Let the questions be your weapons, rather than relying on an offensive attitude. You are better prepared than that! Be sure you are using these weapons to open the minds of those you question, not to pound them over the head. You are responsible not only to speak the truth, but also to speak it in love.

But, speaking the truth in love, may [we] grow up in all things into Him who is the head—Christ… (Ephesians 4:15, NKJV).

Prayer
Exercise

Use the Scripture passage below (Colossians 1:9–14) to develop an outline for intercessory prayer commitments by working through each of the ten disciplines. What personal prayer commitments are brought to mind by the basic concepts taught in theology, philosophy, ethics, and so forth? Think about how you will incorporate those concerns into petitions to God .

Do you have a group that meets each morning at the school where you can pray for classmates and teachers? Do you set aside some time each morning or evening to pray for yourself, your family, and your friends? What kinds of things do you generally pray for? Prayer should be an integral part of your everyday life. Use this time to make a game-plan for how you will strengthen your daily times of prayer. You may be asked to share your prayer ideas in class.

For this reason we also, since the day we heard it, do not cease to pray for you, and to ask that you may be filled with the knowledge of His will in all wisdom and spiritual understanding; that you may walk worthy of the Lord, fully pleasing Him, being fruitful in every good work and increasing in the knowledge of God; strengthened with all might, according to His glorious power, for all patience and longsuffering with joy; giving thanks to the Father who has qualified us to be partakers of the inheritance of the saints in the light. He has delivered us from the power of darkness and conveyed us into the kingdom of the Son of His love, in whom we have redemption through His blood, the forgiveness of sins. (Colossians 1:9–14, NKJV)

Study
Exercise

Here is an opportunity to develop a plan to make personal Bible study a regular part of your daily or weekly routine. During this time your class will discuss different ideas for how to become more consistent in your study of God's word. Be extremely practical about this activity. Be thinking about what you will study and when you will study. Developing a Christian worldview is a lifelong, ongoing process and developing good Bible study habits is a required first step in the process. You will be asked to share your ideas in class.

Be diligent to present yourself approved to God, a worker who does not need to be ashamed, rightly dividing the word of truth (2 Timothy 2:15, NKJV).

Understand the Times
Exercise

Keeping up with current events and issues that challenge our Christian worldview is a charge given to every Christian. Reading publications like World Magazine *or Focus on the Family's* Citizen Magazine, *watching Christian news websites, blogs, and emails, and listening to Christian talk radio are all ways to keep current on important issues. You will be discussing these and other ways that will help you be an informed Christian. It is only by thoroughly understanding our times that you will know what to do. You will be asked to share your ideas in class.*

Men of Issachar, who understood the times and knew what Israel should do… (1 Chronicles 12:32, NIV).

LIGHTBEARERS

Journal

A Summit Ministries Curriculum

Why Should I Keep a Journal?

Reason One

God asks us to **remember** his loving kindness toward us. Psalm 77:11 says, "I will remember the works of the LORD." Frankly, if you don't record how your prayers and decisions are blessed by God, you'll forget.

Reason Two

When you record your thoughts actions, successes and failures, and day-to-day growth in Christ, you have an opportunity to **evaluate** your growth in Christ. You can look back on things God has done in your life as significant points where God showed his faithfulness to you, reminding you of how he will continue to be faithful.

Reason Three

You are unique. Sometimes you will feel like just a number in a crowd, but do not let your feelings get in the way of the truth. God is not a mass-producer of human beings. He is a creator, or custom designer of human beings. He made you for a purpose—a purpose that is unique to you. Because he has done this, your **response** should be to honor him by spending time with him every day. Spending time in prayer and in God's Word helps to keep you focused on what *he* wants, not just what *you* want to do with your life.

Reason Four

Use of a journal can also add **understanding** to your life. Since God created the world, the best person to consult on trying to understand that world is God. You will encounter many people throughout your life who consider themselves the authority on understanding reality. Compared to the Scriptures, however, they do not know anything. By reading Scripture and praying and writing down your thoughts about everything you will gradually start to understand God's truth and how his Word makes the most sense out of everything around you (e.g. nature, human relationships, logic, etc.). As you practice viewing the world through the eyes of its Creator, you will gain important understanding.

What Do I Journal?

Write down your prayers, your thoughts and important events. Here are some possibilities:

- Prayers for friends, parents, relatives and your future spouse
- Guidance for life plans and school success
- Wisdom for your church, pastor and church leaders
- Salvation for unsaved friends
- Missions
- Insights while reading God's Word
- Thoughts about anything (no matter how silly it may seem)
- Your officials and leaders in government
- Dedication of all time, thoughts and resources for the day
- Include ways that you have applied (or need to apply) the Scriptures
- In other words, write down everything and anything that is important to you.

Throughout this journey, you will be asked to do certain exercises in this **Journal**. Keep it faithfully. You will definitely see the benefits.

Journal

Journal

Journal

Journal

Journal

Journal

Journal

Journal

Journal

Journal

Journal

Journal

Journal

Journal

Journal

Journal